Local People's Congresses in China

Young Nam Cho addresses two key questions in this comprehensive study of local people's congresses at both provincial and county levels. First, what kinds of roles did Chinese local legislatures actually perform in local politics, and to what degree? Second, how have Chinese local legislatures become political forces, and what kinds of development strategies have they employed, along with the Chinese Communist Party and local governments?

Dismissing the outdated conclusion that Chinese local legislatures are nothing but "rubber stamps," Cho's in-depth research in the Shanghai, Guangdong, and Tianjin areas proves that they have strengthened lawmaking and supervisory roles and thereby have become important political forces in local politics. Moreover, these legislatures have employed very sophisticated development strategies targeting different objectives: gaining the support of the party, cooperating with governments, and aggressively engaging courts.

Young Nam Cho is an associate professor of the Graduate School of International Studies at Seoul National University. He was a visiting Fellow of the Center for Contemporary Chinese Studies at Peking University (1997–98), visiting scholar in the Department of Political Science at Nankai University in Tianjin (2001–02), and visiting scholar at Harvard-Yenching Institute (2006–07). His research focuses on the Chinese legislative system, rule of law, state-society relations, and elite politics. He has published three books in Korean and has written articles for *China Quarterly, Asian Survey, Issues & Studies, Asian Perspective, Development and Society,* and *Korean Journal of Defense Analysis.* Dr. Cho graduated from the Department of East Asian History at Seoul National University in 1989. He received an M.A. and Ph.D. in political science from Seoul National University in 1996 and 1999, respectively.

T0384616

Local People's Congresses in China

Development and Transition

YOUNG NAM CHO

Seoul National University

CAMBRIDGE
UNIVERSITY PRESS

CAMBRIDGE UNIVERSITY PRESS
Cambridge, New York, Melbourne, Madrid, Cape Town, Singapore,
São Paulo, Delhi, Dubai, Tokyo, Mexico City

Cambridge University Press
32 Avenue of the Americas, New York, NY 10013-2473, USA

www.cambridge.org
Information on this title: www.cambridge.org/9780521182492

First published 2009
First paperback edition 2010

A catalog record for this publication is available from the British Library

Library of Congress Cataloging in Publication data
Cho, Young Nam.
Local people's congresses in China : development and transition/Young Nam Cho.
  p.   cm.
Includes bibliographical references and index.
ISBN 978-0-521-51562-7 (hardback)
1. Local government–China.   2. Political participation–China.   3. Legislative
bodies–China.   4. China–Politics and government–2002-   I. Title.
JS7357.A15C46 2009
328.51–dc22   2008031926

ISBN 978-0-521-51562-7 Hardback
ISBN 978-0-521-18249-2 Paperback

For my wife and son, Seongsook and Daegeon

Contents

List of Tables   *page* ix

Acknowledgments   xi

1   Introduction: Local Legislatures in
    Chinese Politics   1
2   The Politics of Lawmaking with
    Chinese Characteristics   18
3   Supervising Governments and Development
    Strategies   43
4   Supervising Courts and the Development
    of New State Organs   64
5   Role Fulfillment of Deputies to Local Legislatures   83
6   Symbiosis between Local Legislatures and
    Social Organizations   113
7   The Development of Local Legislatures and
    Political Leadership   143
8   Conclusion: The Development of Local
    Legislatures and Political Development in China   163

Selected References   173
Index   187

Tables

2.1. Number of local laws and administrative
regulations in Shanghai, 1980–2000   *page* 22
4.1. Court-related public letters and visits to people's
congresses: Heilongjiang Provincial People's
Congress, 1998   68
4.2. Appraisal of courts: People's congresses in
Henan Province, 1999   71
5.1. Number of people's congress deputies at various levels
(November 1, 1994)   86
5.2. Implementation of deputy proposals: Shanghai
Municipal People's Congress   94
5.3. People's congress deputy bills: Wuxi City People's
Congress, Jiangsu Province   99
5.4. Implementation of deputy bills: Wuxi City People's
Congress, Jiangsu Province   99
5.5. People's congress deputy composition: The NPC,
Tianjin Municipal and Nankai District People's
Congresses in Tianjin (1993–1997)   102
7.1. Legislative supervision over governments in
Tianjin in 2000   150

Acknowledgments

For more than a decade, I have devoted myself to investigating the Chinese legislative system. My interest in the topic began in 1996, when as a doctoral candidate I selected the Chinese national legislature (i.e., National People's Congress/NPC) for my dissertation theme. The NPC was then emerging as a new force in the Chinese political system; hence, analyzing the legislative development was of paramount importance in understanding China's political reform and democratic prospects. Based on my doctoral thesis, I published a book on the NPC in 2000 entitled *China's Political Reform and the National People's Congress*. Unfortunately, most China scholars were unaware of the existence of the book, as it was published in Korean! Nevertheless, I have continued my study of Chinese legislatures with the purpose of finishing a more complete work on the legislative system. This time my research focuses on local people's congresses in three coastal regions closely associated with China's rapid economic growth: Shanghai, Tianjin, and Guangdong. This book is the culmination of my decade-long research on the Chinese legislative system.

I am deeply indebted to many individuals and institutions for their generous support and contributions during the course of researching and writing this book. Most of all, I would like to sincerely thank all the interviewees from legislative bodies, executive branches, and social organizations across China. Some issues concerning legislatures, such as the relationship among the Party, governments, and legislatures, are still a politically sensitive topic, and I encountered many difficulties in collecting data and interviewing people. This book would never have been published without those who courageously accepted my request for an interview. Thus, I deeply regret that I cannot name these people here, for they must remain anonymous.

I have also benefited greatly from the help of many friends and colleagues in China during the extensive fieldwork conducted for this project. Professor Zhu Guanglei, my *lao pengyou* (old friend), invited me to stay at Nankai University of Tianjin as a visiting scholar during 2001 and 2002 and provided very important support for my research. Professor Yang Long of the same university also helped me further my studies. Professors Shen Guoming and Xu Mingqi at the Chinese Academy of Social Science in Shanghai and its staff members, Li Yihai and Zhao Nianguo, provided help with my research in the Shanghai area. Director Fu Lang and Coordinating Staff Zheng Hongmei from the Foreign Affairs Office of Guangdong Province Government provided support for my research in the Guangdong area. I would like to extend my sincere thanks to all of them.

Seoul National University, Korea Research Foundation, and Sungkok Foundation provided the financial support for this research. Without their generous grants, this research would have been much more difficult to complete. The Harvard-Yenching Institute provided a very comfortable year of writing during 2006 and 2007, and I thank its director (Professor Tu Weiming), staff members (Peter L. Kelley, Susan S. Alpert, Elaine Witham, Huang Wan-sheng, Ruohong Li, Nam Nguyen, and Edward J. Baker), and Professors Carter Eckert and Elizabeth Perry. During that period, as a visiting scholar, I was able to concentrate all my time and effort on writing this book while my wife and son cozily enjoyed their life in Boston with the Institute's kind and considerable support.

Jongho Jeong, Jae Cheol Kim, and Taeho Kim read parts of the manuscript and provided excellent comments and useful suggestions. I am sincerely indebted to my colleagues at the Graduate School of International Studies at Seoul National University, especially Jongho Jeong and Tae Gyun Park, for the support and encouragement I received from them. Thanks also go to Seoyoung Lee for her assistance in editing references and preparing the index. Special thanks are due to Professor David Hundt of Deakin University, who proofread the entire manuscript and made many valuable suggestions. In fact, he has proofread all my work in English since we were graduate students at Seoul National University.

I am grateful to the two anonymous reviewers from Cambridge University Press, who offered constructive comments on the entire manuscript. In particular, I owe an intellectual debt and special thanks to Professor Kevin O'Brien, who has influenced my studies on the topic of the Chinese legislative system since I first met him at Nankai University in 1998, when I was conducting the final fieldwork for my doctoral thesis on the NPC. I would like to thank Eric Crahan at Cambridge University Press for his enthusiastic support of the book. His kind remarks encouraged me to move ahead without hesitation when I was confused about how to improve my manuscript based on the reviewers' comments. Emily Spangler expertly guided the book through the production process, for which I am grateful.

Throughout the book, I draw upon previously published works. I would like to thank Cambridge University Press for permission to reprint my articles "From 'Rubber Stamps' to 'Iron Stamps': The Emergence of Chinese Local People's Congresses as Supervisory Powerhouse," *China Quarterly* 171 (September 2002): 724–40; "Symbiotic Neighbor or Extra-Court Judge? The Supervision over Courts by Chinese Local People's Congresses," *China Quarterly* 176 (December 2003): 1068–83; and "The Politics of Lawmaking in Chinese Local People's Congresses," *China Quarterly* 187 (September 2006): 592–609. I would also like to thank the Institute for Social Development and Policy Research at Seoul National University for permission to reprint my article "Public Supervisors and Reflectors: Role Fulfillment of Chinese People's Congresses in the Market Socialist Era," *Development and Society* 32, no. 2 (December 2003): 197–227.

Finally, I would like to thank my family, who have unequivocally offered absolute support for my research and endless encouragement to me. My wife, Seongsook Kim, and my son, Daegeon Cho, have been willing to spend weekends and most holidays without me during this research. They allowed me to conduct fieldwork alone for this project in China for the entire two years from 1997 to 1998 and from 2001 to 2002, and at least one month every year for the past decade. Without their understanding and support, I would not have completed this research. This book is dedicated to them.

I

Introduction: Local Legislatures in Chinese Politics

LEGISLATIVE DEVELOPMENT IN CHINA

In February 2001, the Shenyang Municipal People's Congress set off a small political earthquake when it vetoed the annual work report of the Intermediate People's Court. While the Gonghe County People's Congress in Qinghai Province had failed to approve a court annual work report in April 2000, the decision in Shenyang had far greater impact because it took place in the provincial capital of Liaoning rather than a county. Before and during the plenary session, the Chinese Communist Party (CCP) in Shenyang convened temporary meetings, which were attended by all members-cum-deputies (about 80 percent of all deputies). Notably, a resolution was passed at the meeting requiring all Party members to "select candidates whom the Party recommended and approve annual work reports of state organs which the Party considered in advance." Thus, the deputies' assertive rejection of the work report surprised the public as well as state leaders. After the veto, the Court, now under new leadership, implemented comprehensive reforms for six months to satisfy the deputies' demands. Finally, a new work report was submitted and passed at the legislature's temporary meeting, held in August 2001. Thus emerged the "Shenyang Incident" (*Shenyang sijian*), said to be "a first in Chinese constitutional history" and "a remarkable incident in Chinese democratic politics."[1]

[1] Shenyangshi renda changweihui (ed.), *Difangrenda daibiao gongzuo shijian yu tansuo* (*Practice and Exploration of Deputy Works in Local People's Congresses*) (Beijing: Zhongguo minzhu fazhi chubanshe, 2002), pp. 231–41.

Similarly, a series of unprecedented incidents involving local legislatures in Guangdong Province have taken place since early in this
decade, beginning with an interpellation bill introduced by deputies to
the Guangdong Provincial People's Congress in January 2000. Deputies
requested the Environmental Protection Bureau of the Provincial
Government to explain why it did not suspend work at factories that
had caused serious water pollution. Dissatisfied with the replies from the
Bureau's vice-director at hearings, the deputies were preparing to submit
a motion to discharge the vice-director and requested a meeting with
the vice-governor responsible for environmental affairs. Eventually, the
government accepted the deputies' request and later replaced the vice-
director in order to appease the deputies. A month later, the Standing
Committee of the Guangdong legislature refused to ratify two of ten
nominees for the directorship of government bureaus recommended by
the governor. The chairman was quoted as saying, "Nominees who did
not get a majority of votes in legislature could not be approved. It was
the result of legislative members' use of democratic power, and nothing
was more normal than this." The assertive activities of the legislatures
in Guangdong have continued for several years, and they have become
known as "Guangdong Phenomena" (*Guangdong xianxiang*).[2]

The Shenyang Incident and Guangdong Phenomena illustrate the
development of Chinese local people's congresses in the reform era as
meaningful forces in the Chinese political system, although they cannot
represent the ordinary operations of local legislatures across the country.
As previous studies indicate, Chinese legislatures, which were frequently
known as "rubber stamps" (*xiangpi tuzhang*) both in China and abroad,
are no longer appendages to the Party and governments. The National
People's Congress (NPC) now has an important influence on national
politics, especially on legislation.[3] Provincial people's congresses have

---

[2] Wu Xi, "Renda gongzuode Guangdong xianxiang" (Guangdong phenomena in works
of people's congresses), *Renmin yu quanli* (*People and Power*), No. 10 (2002), p. 39;
Yun Zhongqing (ed.), *Renda yanjiu wencui (Disijuan)* (*Best Selections of Studies
on People's Congresses: Book Four*) (Beijing: Zhongguo fazhi chubanshe, 2004),
pp. 613–20.

[3] Kevin O'Brien, *Reform without Liberalization: China's National People's Congress
and the Politics of Institutional Change* (New York: Cambridge University Press, 1990),
pp. 157–79; Murray Scot Tanner, *The Politics of Lawmaking in China: Institutions,
Processes, and Democratic Prospects* (New York: Oxford University Press, 1999),
pp. 231–52; Ming Xia, *The Dual Developmental State: Development Strategy and
Institutional Arrangements for China's Transition* (Aldershot: Ashgate, 2000),
pp. 100–35.

also grown in importance both as local lawmakers and as "information brokers" between the central and local levels by dint of their complex networks.[4] Some provincial legislatures have even turned down Party nominees for important leadership posts in an attempt to express local discontent over the center's personnel selections, or to remind the Party leadership not only to observe due legal procedures but also to respect legislatures' opinions concerning personnel affairs.[5] There are also claims in China that local legislatures' supervision of governments is more active and effective than that of the NPC.[6] These new trends demand more attention on the part of researchers in Chinese politics to local people's congresses.[7]

---

[4] Sen Lin, "A new pattern of democratization in China: The increase of provincial powers in economic legislation," *China Information*, Vol. 7, No. 3 (winter 1992–93), pp. 27–38; Chien-min Chao, "The procedure for local legislation in mainland China and legislation in national autonomous area," *Issues & Studies*, Vol. 30, No. 9 (September 1994), pp. 95–116; Xia, *The Dual Developmental State*, pp. 136–77; Ming Xia, "Political contestation and the emergence of the provincial People's Congresses as power in Chinese politics: A network explanation," *Journal of Contemporary China*, Vol. 9, No. 24 (2000), pp. 185–214; Roderick MacFarquhar, "Reports from the field: Provincial People's Congresses," *China Quarterly*, No. 155 (September 1998), pp. 656–67.

[5] A survey of 18 out of 30 provincial local people's congresses around 1988 found that they vetoed 49 of 712 party nominees (a rejection rate of 4 percent). Cai Dingjian, *Zhongguo renmin daibiao zhidu (People's Congress System in China)* (Revised edition) (Beijing: Falü chubanshe, 1998), pp. 359–60. On other cases, see An Chen, *Restructuring Political Power in China: Alliance and Opposition, 1978–98* (Boulder, CO, and London: Lynne Rienner Publishers, 1999), pp. 97–124; Xia, "Political contestation," pp. 206–09.

[6] Quanguorenda changweihui bangongting yanjiushi (ed.), *Zongjie tansuo zhanwang: 8jie quanguorenda gongzuo yanjiu baogao (Summary, Exploration, and Prospects: Investigation Report on the Works of the 8th NPC)* (Beijing: Zhongguo minzhu fazhi chubanshe, 1998), pp. 297–99; Dong Shouan (ed.), *Difang renda gongzuo xintan (New Exploration for the Works of Local People's Congresses)* (Beijing: Zhongguo minzhu fazhi chubanshe, 1998), pp. 283–84.

[7] On the organizational development of local people's congresses, see Kevin O'Brien, "Chinese People's Congresses and legislative embeddedness: Understanding early organizational development," *Comparative Political Studies*, Vol. 27, No. 1 (April 1994), pp. 80–109. On the representation roles of local people's congress deputies, see Kevin O'Brien, "Agents and remonstrators: Role accumulation by Chinese People's Congress deputies," *China Quarterly*, No. 138 (June 1994), pp. 359–79. On the vertical relationship between local people's congresses, see Kevin O'Brien and Laura M. Luehrmann, "Institutionalizing Chinese legislatures: Trade-offs between autonomy and capacity," *Legislative Studies Quarterly*, Vol. 23, No. 1 (February 1998), pp. 91–108. On the roles of county-level people's congresses, see Oscar Almén, "Authoritarianism Constrained: The Role of Local People's Congresses in China" (Ph.D. Dissertation: Göteborg University, 2005).

STUDYING CHINESE LOCAL LEGISLATURES

This book aims to analyze the role of Chinese local people's congresses in the political system and the developmental process that they have followed to become a meaningful political force in the reform era. It tackles the following two questions. First, what kinds of roles have Chinese local legislatures performed in local politics, and to what degree have they actually exerted influence on the polity, which is largely dominated by the CCP and governments? Second, if Chinese local legislatures, along with the CCP and governments, have become dominant political forces, how have they done so? What obstacles have the legislatures overcome, and what development strategies have they employed to cope with challenges in the process of development?

To this end, this book analyzes the following four subjects. First of all, it investigates two major functions of Chinese local people's congresses in detail: legislation and supervision. When discussing Chinese legislative development, the book's main priorities are to scrutinize the actual roles of local legislatures and the degree of their performance. Legislative development in China is meaningless unless Chinese legislatures carry out the functions that are delegated to them. Like their counterparts in other countries, Chinese legislatures perform four putative roles: legislation, supervision, representation, and regime-maintenance or support.[8] In the case of representation, the CCP, as the only authoritative actor in the Chinese party-state, claims a monopoly on important policies by representing the opinions and interests of an entire people. That is, the representation role of the legislatures is still marginal. However, if Chinese local legislatures exercise significant power in their other main functions (i.e., legislation and supervision), we can argue that the legislatures have strengthened their roles and thereby become meaningful political

---

[8] On the legislative functions, including socialist legislatures, see O'Brien, *Reform without Liberalization*, pp. 157–75; Robert A. Packenham, "Legislatures and political development," in Allen Kornberg and Lloyd D. Musolf (eds.), *Legislatures in Developmental Perspective* (Durham, NC: Duke University Press, 1970), pp. 521–82; David Close, "Introduction: Consolidating democracy in Latin America," in David Close (ed.), *Legislatures and the New Democracies in Latin America* (Boulder, CO: Lynne Rienner Publishers, 1995), pp. 1–15; Michael L. Mezey, "The functions of legislatures in the Third World," in Gerhard Loewenberg (ed.), *Handbook of Legislative Research* (Cambridge, MA: Harvard University Press, 1983), pp. 733–72; Daniel N. Nelson, "Editor's introduction: Communist legislatures and communist politics," *Legislative Studies Quarterly*, Vol. 5, No. 2 (May 1980), pp. 161–73; Peter Vanneman, *The Supreme Soviet* (Durham, NC: Duke University Press, 1977), pp. 151–75.

players. Thus, investigating Chinese local legislatures' lawmaking and supervisory roles is a core part of this research.

This book also examines the role fulfillment of deputies to Chinese people's congresses. Legislative members in all countries are required to represent their constituents in the arenas of policymaking, budget-allocation, and service-provision or errand-running. The deputies to the NPC and local legislatures, of which there were more than three million in the 1990s, are no exception. At least, as "people's deputies," they should try to champion some kind of public interest, even though they cannot accomplish policymaking and budget-allocation roles. In fact, the role fulfillment of Chinese legislative members has changed from "hand-raising machines" to "supervisors and reflectors" since the early 1990s. Also, the ordinary deputies have made a contribution to the development of local legislatures. For these reasons, this study examines the roles of deputies.

Furthermore, the book analyzes relations between Chinese local legislatures and social organizations. With the introduction of a market economy, interest differentiation and competition between social groups in China has intensified. As a consequence, social organizations that claim to represent the interests of specific social groups have increased, and their activities have gradually strengthened. This in turn has caused shifts in state-society relations. Relations between local legislatures and social organizations are part of these changes. As laws have become an important tool for both state and society in resolving conflicts and redistributing interests, social organizations have increasingly sought to participate in the lawmaking process of legislatures in order to protect their rights and interests. Local legislatures also have encouraged social organizations to engage in lawmaking in order to supplement their lack of personnel and organizational capabilities. As a result, relations between legislatures and social organizations have evolved in a manner that differs from ties between the Party/governments and social organizations. This new set of relations has increasingly affected legislative activities.

Finally, this book delves into the uneven development of Chinese local legislatures and the main factors that cause the differences. As previous studies on villagers' committees demonstrate, there are significant differences in the dissemination of villagers' democratic elections from region to region. Similarly, legislative activities indicate palpable disparities between local legislatures even within the same province, not to mention between legislatures in different provinces. For instance, in the Tianjin area, one district people's congress has actively carried out legislative oversight using strict new measures over the district government and court, while a neighboring district legislature has not shown any interest in effective supervision over state organs. This phenomenon is ubiquitous across the country, and we need to explore this matter in order to ascertain the process and characteristics of legislative development in China.

Based on these analyses, the book posits the following arguments: Most important of all, against conventional wisdom suggesting that Chinese local legislatures are nothing but "rubber stamps," Chinese local legislatures have strengthened lawmaking and supervisory roles and thereby become important political forces in the Chinese political system, along with the CCP and governments. Rather than democratic demands and pressure from below, the introduction of a market economy and legalization policy by the Party leadership on a national level have been the primary determinants of the enhanced status and intensified roles of Chinese legislatures. In addition, Chinese local legislatures have employed sophisticated development strategies targeting different objectives: getting the support of – rather than autonomy from – the Party, cooperation rather than confrontation with governments, and aggressive engagement in courts. They have also used a mobilization strategy to encourage social organizations and the public to participate in legislative activities. Chinese legislatures have had to utilize savvy development strategies chiefly due to their lower political status in the Chinese political system vis-à-vis governments, in addition to disadvantageous conditions such as their lack of legislative experience, poor material and personnel support, and defective legal and institutional assistance. Finally, local legislatures have developed unevenly, even within given administrative units. Political leadership of both the Party and legislatures, not the level of economic development, is the most important determinant of these differences.

METHODOLOGY

A REVIEW OF PREVIOUS STUDIES

Various analytical methods have been applied to the study of Third World legislatures. Functional and structural approaches (or the structural-functional approach) are most common. Studies on Chinese legislatures are no exception. When Kevin O'Brien analyzes the historical changes of the NPC and its major functions, he adopts an "integrated historical-structural approach," a variation of the structural approach.[9] The structural-functional approach is useful in exploring established legislative systems because of its focus on main functions, legislative structures, and interactions between legislatures and other state organs, especially the executive branch.

Similarly, this research adopts the structural-functional approach in order to investigate the actual functions and development processes of Chinese local legislatures. For instance, this book analyzes the main functions of Chinese local legislatures, such as legislation, supervision, and representation, as the functional approach prescribes. Furthermore, this study closely investigates the legislatures' relationships and interactions with other state organs of local governments and courts as well as the Party, based on the presumptions of the structural approach.

At the same time, however, the structural-functional approach has limitations when applied to studies on rapidly changing legislatures like Chinese people's congresses; that is, it cannot properly explain why certain legislative institutions develop in specific ways, and which factors are behind these developments. In particular, this approach likely fails to adequately elucidate informal political relations, which significantly influence the operation of legislatures but rarely surface in formal institutions. For these reasons, this study employs three complementary perspectives (i.e., marketization and legalization, actual power relations, and path dependence) to make up for the weak points of the structural-functional approach. This is discussed in more detail below.

Other scholars of Chinese legislatures have selected certain analytical approaches suitable for their research topics and purposes. For example, Murray S. Tanner investigates legislative politics in the NPC by employing a decision-making model approach, and proposes a garbage

---

[9] On the structural-functional approach and other methodologies in legislative studies, see O'Brien, *Reform without Liberalization*, pp. 8–11; Nelson W. Polsby, "Legislatures," in Fred I. Grenstein and Nelson W. Polsby (eds.), *Handbook of Political Science*, Vol. 5 (Reading, MA: Addison-Wesley, 1975), pp. 258–59; Mezey, "The functions of legislatures in the Third World," pp. 734–35; Leroy N. Rieselbach, *Congressional Politics: The Evolving Legislative System* (Boulder, CO: Westview Press, 1995), pp. 17–36; David M. Olson and Philip Norton, "Legislatures in democratic transition," in David M. Olson and Philip Norton (eds.), *The New Parliament of Central and Eastern Europe* (London: Frank Cass, 1996), p. 6, table 1; David M. Olson and Michael Mezey, "Parliament and public policy," in Olson and Mezey (eds.), *Legislatures in the Policy Process: The Dilemmas of Economic Policy* (Cambridge: Cambridge University Press, 1991), pp. 6–7; David M. Olson, *Democratic Legislative Institutions: A Comparative View* (Armonk, NY: M.E. Sharpe, 1994), pp. 132–43.

can model as the most appropriate one for Chinese legislative politics.[10] Tanner's approach may help us probe the politics of lawmaking in local legislatures, but we need more than this when analyzing the supervisory functions and overall developmental process of legislatures.

Meanwhile, Ming Xia examines the developmental process of provincial-level legislatures by using a network approach,[11] and An Chen similarly explores the development of county-level legislatures in terms of a checks-and-balances perspective.[12] Xia's approach provides insights insofar as it reveals the survival strategies of local legislatures, and Chen's perspective highlights the strategic thinking of the Party's top leadership about strengthening local legislatures in the 1980s. However, both these approaches have limitations. Xia's network approach pays much more attention to legislative leadership's strategic calculations than to the organizations' collective efforts to institutionalize lawmaking and supervisory mechanisms. Likewise, Chen's checks-and-balances view likely overestimates the strengthening of legislatures' roles in local politics. A system of checks and balances has yet to emerge in the Chinese party-state, where local legislatures cannot monitor local Party committees because the CCP dominates legislatures in terms of personnel, organization, and policy.

THREE PERSPECTIVES OF THIS RESEARCH

As mentioned previously, in addition to the structural-functional approach, this book adopts three perspectives when analyzing the roles of local legislatures in the Chinese political system and their developmental process: (1) marketization (*shichanghua*) and legalization (*fazhihua*), (2) actual power relations, and (3) path dependence. The first perspective is indispensable to understanding which specific roles of legislatures (such as legislation and supervision) have been strengthened and which others (like policymaking and representation) have not been so stringently reinforced. An actual power relations perspective provides a far better basis to examine the political circumstances of Chinese local legislatures and their development strategies. Finally, path dependence

---

[10] Tanner, *The Politics of Lawmaking in China*, pp. 12–40.
[11] Xia, *The Dual Developmental State*, pp. 144–72; Xia, "Political contestation," pp. 185–214; Ming Xia, "Informational efficiency, organizational development and the institutional linkages of the provincial people's congresses in China," *Journal of Legislative Studies*, Vol. 3, No. 3 (Autumn 1997), pp. 10–38.
[12] Chen, *Restructuring Political Power in China*, pp. 1–21.

is helpful in understanding the historical conditions and processes of legislative development in China. Although the three perspectives are closely interrelated, for the convenience of explanation, they are examined separately below.

The perspective of marketization and legalization helps us to understand the background of and processes by which the roles of Chinese local legislatures have been reinforced. Top Party leadership in the 1980s, for various reasons, began to take note of the legislative systems that had actually stopped operating for more than a decade. The drastic events of the Cultural Revolution (1966–76) brought home to reformist leaders like Deng Xiaoping the catastrophe of "rule by men" (*renzhi*). As a way to prevent the recurrence of those political disasters, Party leaders introduced "rule by law" (*fazhi*), which entailed the reconstruction of the Party/state institutions and the establishment of a functioning legal system. This led to the recovery of legislative systems in the 1980s. In addition, Party leadership had to strengthen both legislatures and elections in order to respond to widespread public doubt and criticism of socialism after the Cultural Revolution.[13] Besides, the most senior legislative leaders such as Peng Zhen and Wan Li have strived to buttress legislatures and thus consolidate their political power bases, pursuing their personal beliefs at the same time.[14]

The most important factors behind the move toward strengthening Chinese legislatures, however, were the introduction of a market economy and implementation of legalization policy. It is said in China that "the market economy is a rule of law economy." The introduction of a market economy urged China to establish a proper legal system to manage economic activities in the marketplace and to regulate new economic agents, including foreign companies and private entrepreneurs. Furthermore, only by establishing a legal system that could guarantee the interests of foreign investors and control their illegal activities could China attract larger inflows of foreign direct investment and protect Chinese economic interests.[15] Chiefly due to these considerations, the

---

[13] O'Brien, *Reform without Liberalization*, pp. 126–27; Cai, *People's Congress System in China*, pp. 76–77.

[14] Pitman B. Potter, "Curbing the party: Peng Zhen and Chinese legal culture," *Problems of Post-Communism*, Vol. 45, No. 3 (May/June 1998), pp. 17–28; Pitman B. Potter, *From Leninist Discipline to Socialist Legalism* (Stanford: Stanford University Press, 2003).

[15] Quanguorenda changweihui bangongting yanjiushi (ed.), *Renmin daibiao dahui chengli sishi zhounian jinian wenji* (*Papers on Commemorating the 40th Anniversary of People's Congresses*) (Beijing: Zhongguo minzhu fazhi chubanshe, 1995), p. 103;

lawmaking roles of the NPC and local legislatures have been markedly invigorated since the 1980s.

Meanwhile, since the early 1980s, the CCP has continued to implement the rationalization of governance (but not yet liberalization or democratization). Legalization policy (i.e., "rule by law" before the mid-1990s and "rule of law" since then) has been a key part of rationalization. Legalization refers to the establishment of a comprehensive system of enacting laws (*lifa*), enforcing laws (*zhifa*), and protecting laws (*shoufa*).[16] This policy necessitated the strengthening of the lawmaking and supervisory functions of Chinese legislatures, because a sound legal system cannot be established without a stronger lawmaking role of legislatures. Furthermore, the incomplete implementation of laws by governments and unfair application of laws by courts cannot be prevented without a stronger supervisory role of legislatures. In short, marketization and legalization have bolstered the lawmaking and supervisory roles of Chinese legislatures.

As previous research on Third World legislatures notes, examination of a legislature's structure and functions requires investigation not only into the legislature itself but also into interactions between the legislature and its political system. This is necessary because the specific functions that a legislature performs and the level of its performance tend to be determined less by the legislature itself than by the political system to which it belongs.[17] This is also the case in China, where the party-state has strongly influenced legislatures.

Legal or formal relations among the Party, legislatures, and governments come in conflict with actual power relations due to the peculiarity of the Chinese political system, one-party rule. Regarding Party-legislature relations, the Chinese Constitution describes the CCP as a "political party" that is required to act within the limits of the

Tao-tai Hsia and Wendy I. Zeldin, "Recent legal development in the People's Republic of China," *Harvard International Law Journal*, Vol. 28, No. 2 (Spring 1987), p. 256; Mary E. Gallagher, *Contagious Capitalism: Globalization and the Politics of Labor in China* (Princeton, NJ: Princeton University Press, 2005), pp. 98–132.

[16] Cai Dingjian, *Zhongguo xianfa jingjie (An Interpretation of Chinese Constitution)* (Beijing: Zhongguo minzhu fazhi chubanshe, 1996), p. 113.

[17] Jean Blondel, *Comparative Legislature* (Englewood Cliffs, NJ: Prentice-Hall, 1973), p. 26; Marvin G. Weinbaum, "Classification and change in legislative system: With particular application to Iran, Turkey, and Afghanistan," in G. R. Boynton and Chong Lim Kim (eds.), *Legislative Systems in Developing Countries* (Durham, NC: Duke University Press, 1975), p. 35; Martin C. Needler, "Conclusion: The legislature in a democratic Latin America," in Close, *Legislatures and the New Democracies in Latin America*, p. 158.

Constitution and other laws. And Chinese legislatures, as "state power organs," have the right to supervise all political parties, including the CCP. However, the CCP is also the "leadership core" (*lingdao hexin*) of the Chinese political system, directing all state organs, including legislatures. In reality, because actual power relations ("leadership core vs. state organ") always dominate over the legal/formal relations ("political party vs. state power organ"), Chinese legislatures are subordinated to the CCP: the Party leads and controls them in day-to-day activities.

Legislative-executive relations are more complicated. The Constitution states that governments, as "executive organs," are legally responsible to legislatures, and subject to legislative supervision. However, because legislatures and governments in the Chinese political system are state agencies that carry out Party policy, they should complement each other and cooperate on an equal footing. That is, legislative-executive relations are considered a division of labor, not a separation of powers. Furthermore, the political status of governments in the Party hierarchy has been generally higher than that of legislatures.[18] This means that in terms of actual power relations, governments hold a higher position than legislatures. As a consequence, Chinese legislatures have had difficulty exercising lawmaking and supervisory power due to the resistance of governments, even though the Constitution and pertinent laws allow legislatures such authority.

Consequently, Chinese legislatures have had to employ cautious development strategies to counter these disadvantageous political conditions. They have sought to secure clear jurisdiction from the intervention of the Party and governments, and to secure enough organizational capacities to carry out their roles. Both the lack of experience and poor institutional support of legislative activities have compelled legislative leaders to practice more sophisticated survival strategies. For these reasons, Chinese legislatures are said to have utilized a strategy of "embeddedness" in, rather than "autonomy" from, the CCP,[19] or a "competition-cum-cooperation strategy" in the process of legislative development.[20] In short, investigation of Chinese legislatures' roles requires that we pay attention to actual power relations rather than the legal/formal relations between the Party, legislatures, and governments.

[18] Cai, *People's Congress System in China*, pp. 37–38.
[19] O'Brien, "Chinese People's Congresses and legislative embeddedness," pp. 80–109; O'Brien and Luehrmann, "Institutionalizing Chinese legislatures," pp. 91–108.
[20] Xia, "Political contestation," pp. 185–214; Xia, "Informational efficiency," pp. 10–38.

Douglass North, who has studied the interrelations between economic development and institutions, proposes path dependence. According to him, "institutions are the humanly devised constraints that structure political, economic and social interaction," and they are composed of both "informal constraints" (such as sanctions, taboos, customs, traditions, and codes of conduct) and "formal rules" (constitutions, laws, and property rights).[21] North emphasizes two points through his theory of path dependence. First, extant institutions are based on past institutions, and they also constrain the selection of future institutions. So we cannot understand both present and future choices of institutions without considering the trajectory of past institutions. Second, although foreign occupation and revolution may cause discontinuous and abrupt institutional changes, once entrenched, institutions tend to evolve incrementally and cannot be easily cancelled or displaced with new institutions by considerations of economic efficiency.[22]

North's path dependence is useful in understanding the developmental process of Chinese legislatures. Most of all, legislative institutions and experiences formed during the socialist revolution and after the founding of the socialist state in 1949 have persistently influenced the Chinese legislative system. In explaining legislatures in China, it is noteworthy that the people's congress system (*renda zhidu*) is organized and operated in accordance with two principles: democratic centralism (*minzhu jizhong*) and legislative-executive integration (*yixing heyi*), a legacy of the revolutionary experiences of the Paris Commune in France and soviets in the Soviet Union. Democratic centralism suggests the following three propositions: first, people's congresses comprise deputies elected by the people, and they are responsible to the people and subject to the people's supervision; second, state organs are organized by people's congresses, and they are responsible to people's congresses and subject to people's congresses' supervision; third, in central-local relations, localities exercise proactive initiative under the center's unified leadership.[23]

---

[21] Douglass C. North, "Institutions," *Journal of Economic Perspectives*, Vol. 5, No. 1 (Winter 1991), p. 97.

[22] North, "Institutions," pp. 97–112; Douglass C. North, *Institutional Changes and Economic Performance* (Cambridge: Cambridge University Press, 1990), pp. 92–104.

[23] Cai, *People's Congress System in China*, pp. 87–88; Yuan Ruiliang, *Renmin daibiao dahui zhidu xingcheng fazhanshi* (*A History of Formation and Development of People's Congress Systems*) (Beijing: Renmin chubanshe, 1994), pp. 445–53.

In reality, however, democratic centralism was perceived and implemented not as an organizational principle of state organs but as a work style (*gongzuo zuofeng*) emphasizing that Party policy had to be carried out by all Party members after the policy had been decided by democratic discussions, or as a mass line (*qunzhong luxian*) stressing the combination of the spontaneity of the masses and the effectiveness of Party leadership.[24] As a consequence, democratic centralism was used as an excuse to legitimate the subordination of all state organs and social organizations – including legislatures – to the CCP. By a similar logic, the principle of legislative-executive integration denied the necessity of legislatures' independent operations, and this led to the subordination of legislatures to governments. Viewed this way, it is no accident that Chinese legislatures sharply decreased their activities during the Anti-Rightist Campaign (1957–58) and the Great Leap Forward (1958–59) and came to a standstill during the Cultural Revolution (1966–76). This can be seen as a cumulative outcome arising from the influence of early legislative institutions.[25]

When Chinese legislatures started to recover from their decade-long hibernation around 1979, they could not escape the straitjacket of the early legislative institutions because those were the direct experiences on which legislatures could draw. Accordingly, democratic centralism and legislative-executive integration were acknowledged again as the organizational and operational principles of the Chinese legislative system, and the Western-style legislative system was rejected except for the limited application of lawmaking techniques and experiences concerning economic-related legislation. Although China's socioeconomic structure has undergone great change with the expanded implementation of reform and opening-up policies in the 1990s and continues to pressure Chinese legislatures to transform, legislative institutions have retained much of their initial form.[26] It is thus no surprise that Kevin O'Brien

[24] Cai, *People's Congress System in China*, pp. 85–87.
[25] Ibid., pp. 12–73; Yuan Ruiliang, *A History of Formation and Development*, pp. 323–538; Yun Shihong and Zhu Kaiyang (eds.), *Renmin daibiao dahui zhidu fazhanshi* (*A History of Development of People's Congress Systems*) (Nanchang: Jiangxi renmin chubanshe, 2002), pp. 92–194; Liu Zheng and Cheng Xiangqing, *Renmin daibiao dahui zhidude lilun he shijian* (*Theory and Practice of People's Congress Systems*) (Beijing: Zhongguo minzhu fazhi chubanshe, 2003), pp. 1–27.
[26] Some Chinese researchers and legislative staff have recently argued that legislative-executive integration was not the organizational principle of socialist legislatures in the past. That is, legislatures (i.e., soviets) and governments in the Soviet Union were operated independently from the 1930s. Moreover, they criticize

characterizes the development of the NPC in the 1980s as "reform without liberalization."[27]

ANALYTIC LEVELS AND DATA

This book focuses on Chinese local people's congresses at both provincial-level (*shengji*: provinces, municipalities under the direct control of the central government, and autonomous regions) and county-level (*xianji*: counties, cities, and districts) administrative units. Provincial-level legislatures wield four types of authority granted by the Constitution: legislation, supervision, decision making on important matters, and personnel. In reality, they spend the most energy and time enacting local laws enforceable within their jurisdictions and occasionally supervising state organs at the same level. In terms of inter-legislative relations, as a headquarters-like organ for all local legislatures at various levels in their jurisdiction, provincial legislatures both support and supervise the activities of lower-level legislatures. Meanwhile, county-level legislatures exert three types of authority (supervision, decision making, and personnel) and tend to concentrate on supervision over state organs under the leadership of provincial legislatures. Provincial- and county-level legislatures, in contrast to township-level (*xiangji*: townships and towns) legislatures, are relatively well equipped with bureaucratic agencies and personnel necessary to accomplish ordinary tasks. Thus, focusing on provincial- and county-level legislatures is appropriate for this study.

This book selects three coastal regions for analysis: Shanghai and Tianjin Municipalities and Guangdong Province. It also refers to other provinces when necessary. They, as the most economically advanced regions in China, have led economic reforms and development. As a result, the lawmaking functions of legislatures in these regions have been strengthened from the early period of the reform era in order to establish a legal system equipped to carry out economic reforms and attract foreign investment. For instance, the Shanghai legislature initiated pioneering local laws urgently needed for further economic reforms in the region. It also set standards for other provinces to emulate, given that the NPC had not enacted pertinent laws. The Guangdong legislature

this principle because it objects to the functional differentiation between legislatures and governments and results in a serious impediment to further legislative development. Cai, *People's Congress System in China*, pp. 89–94; Liu and Cheng, *Theory and Practice of People's Congress Systems*, pp. 108–15.

[27] O'Brien, *Reform without Liberalization*.

has also been a leader in legislation and supervision. In particular, since Guangdong Province and Shenzhen Municipality were selected as experimental areas for the policy of "governance according to law" (*yifa zhiguo*) in the mid-1990s, the supervisory roles of the legislatures have greatly intensified. The Guangdong Phenomena, mentioned earlier, was one of the results.

A caveat is necessary here: local people's congresses in Shanghai and Guangdong have been very active compared to those in the other inland provinces; consequently, they cannot be regarded as representative cases of how local legislatures operate in China. Instead, their innovations in strengthening lawmaking and supervisory functions make them pioneers and possible models for other local legislatures. Therefore, we need to be careful about generalizing these cases all over the country. But as the Chinese history of reform and opening-up policy in the past three decades demonstrates, other local legislatures located in economically less-developed regions have already followed or have begun to follow in their footsteps. I provide more detailed evidence of this trend in later chapters.

Finally, this book relies on a wide range of source materials, including both literary and interview documents that I collected and transcribed in China for about ten years, from 1997 to 2006. Notably, I intensively interviewed senior leaders, officials, and staffers from local legislatures, governments, and social organizations in the regions from 2000 to 2006. For instance, I visited several county and district people's congresses in the Tianjin area for interviews for two weeks in July 2000. In addition, I stayed in Tianjin for one year from February 2001 to January 2002, conducting interviews and collecting literary materials. In the case of Shanghai, from August 2001 to January 2004, I conducted four rounds of interviews at the legislature, government, and social organizations. Finally, I interviewed senior leaders, officials, and staffers of state organs and social organizations in the Guangdong region three times from August 2004 to February 2006.

STRUCTURE OF THE BOOK

This book, along with the introductory and concluding chapters (1 and 8), includes six chapters arranged by research topics. Chapters 2 through 4 inquire into the main functions of local legislatures in the Chinese political system. Chapter 2 investigates the lawmaking role of local people's congresses by focusing on the Shanghai legislature. After gradually securing lawmaking authority from the Party and governments and institutionalizing lawmaking procedures since the 1990s, Chinese local legislatures have become key forces in lawmaking politics, in which they coordinate the conflicts of social interests and represent various groups' voices. As a consequence, the legislative politics has changed from a lop-sided bureaucratic decision-making process dominated by governments under Party leadership to a more consultative and sophisticated process in which diversified political actors participate.

Chapter 3 explores Chinese local legislatures' supervision over governments by focusing on supervisory measures, actual supervisory effectiveness, and survival strategies that they have employed to overcome the resistance of governments. Meanwhile, Chapter 4 examines the supervision over courts and courts' reactions to the legislative supervision, highlighting the characteristics of new state organs' development strategies and processes. Local legislatures have strived to supervise governments and courts effectively by pioneering new supervisory measures, among other methods. They thereby have begun to significantly influence local politics since the early 1990s. In the process, they have adopted the strategy of gaining the support of the CCP and cooperating with governments instead of confronting them. And, in the case of supervision over courts, Chinese legislatures have been more aggressive, to the extent that they sometimes intervene in fair adjudication processes. In this way, the legislatures have applied different supervisory strategies depending on the target organs.

Chapter 5 analyzes the representation role of legislative members and the degree of their role fulfillment. Chinese legislators played different roles in the 1990s from those of the 1980s. They try to represent constituents' interests as "public supervisors" and "opinion reflectors" more than as "regime agents" and "remonstrators." Moreover, deputies with different social backgrounds show different role orientations. In sum, Chinese legislators have become more representative than before. Chapter 6 deals with relations between local legislatures and social organizations. Previous studies have focused on state-society relations in China chiefly from a marketization perspective, drawing attention to relations between the Party/governments and social organizations. In contrast, this chapter emphasizes the necessity of adopting a legalization perspective in addition to one of marketization. It also argues that we must expand the meaning of the "state" to include legislatures and courts, rather than limiting the focus of analysis to the Party and governments. These perspectives provide a richer and more nuanced view of state-society relations than accounts that concentrate on the relations between the Party/governments and social organizations.

Chapter 7 delves into the uneven legislative development and the main factors causing this disparity, selecting eighteen county and district legislatures in the Tianjin area as a case study. Just as the patterns of democratic elections for villagers' committees vary markedly, there are palpable differences in legislative supervision between local legislatures in the same provincial unit. And the political leadership of the CCP and legislatures, not the level of economic development, is a vital factor causing the differences. Finally, Chapter 8 briefly summarizes the findings of this study and discusses the implications of legislative development in relation to overall political development in China. If we interpret political development as "democratization," the introduction of free elections is imperative, and prior legislative development is thus less relevant to political development in China. But if political development is taken to encompass political "institutionalization," previous experiences with legislative development can be seen to significantly contribute to China's political development.

2

The Politics of Lawmaking with Chinese Characteristics

With the advent of a market economy and the implementation of "governance according to law" (*yifa zhiguo*) policy in China, laws have grown in importance as both a tool of government to rule the country and a measure to safeguard the rights and interests of ordinary people. As a consequence, legislative politics, which takes place in the NPC and local people's congresses, has become a process of serious decision making. At the same time, China's lawmaking system, as Murray S. Tanner successfully illustrated, has shifted from a unitary, hierarchical system to "a multi-stage, multi-arena" system chiefly composed of the CCP, the State Council, and the NPC. Power in the lawmaking system is distributed among various individuals and organizations as well.[1] In fact, as Tanner, Ta-kuang Chang, and Cao Siyuan showed, the NPC played a decisive role in two examples of legislation even in the 1980s: the Enterprise Bankruptcy Law in 1986 and the State-owned Industrial Enterprise Law in 1988.[2]

---

[1] Murray Scot Tanner, *The Politics of Lawmaking in China: Institutions, Processes, and Democratic Prospects* (New York: Oxford University Press, 1999), pp. 34, 132, 234–35. On other studies on the NPC's lawmaking function and procedures, see Kevin O'Brien, *Reform without Liberalization: China's National People's Congress and the Politics of Institutional Change* (New York: Cambridge University Press, 1990), 130–41, 158–64; Murray Scot Tanner, "Organization and politics in China's post-Mao lawmaking system," in Putman B. Potter (ed.), *Domestic Law Reforms in Post-Mao China* (Armonk, NY: M.E. Sharpe, 1994), pp. 56–93; Ann Seidman, Robert B. Seidman, and Janice Payne (eds.), *Legislative Drafting for Market Reform: Some Lessons from China* (London: Macmillan, 1997).

[2] Tanner, *The Politics of Lawmaking*, pp. 135–205; Ta-kuang Chang, "The making of the Chinese bankruptcy law: A study in the Chinese legislative process," *Harvard International Law Journal*, Vol. 28, No. 2 (Spring 1987), pp. 370–71; Cao Siyuan,

Is there a pattern similar to the development of the NPC in the legislative politics of the provincial people's congresses? In this regard, local legislatures across the country have pioneered local laws to satisfy the urgent needs for economic reforms and development in their respective regions, given that the NPC did not enact pertinent laws.[3] And compared to legislative supervision, local legislative bodies can act more firmly and safely in the case of legislation, because they have been gradually recognized as the proper authority of lawmaking in the reform era.[4] Under these circumstances, local people's congresses can attempt to consolidate the lawmaking power given to them by institutionalizing the lawmaking process and broadening their organizational capacities, confronting governments, when necessary, instead of tamely conceding to or cooperating with them.

This chapter analyzes the politics of lawmaking in Chinese provincial people's congresses in order to reveal the changes in the political processes that occurred in the reform era. To this end, it will briefly examine the shifting relations between the CCP, governments, and legislatures, as well as lawmaking institutions themselves since the 1990s. It will then investigate the specific roles and activities of major forces, including government agencies, legislative committees, and social organizations, by analyzing a few cases of lawmaking. Finally, I selected the Shanghai People's Congresses for case studies of lawmaking politics.

When the introduction of a market economy and governance according to law policy compelled the CCP to open the political arena of lawmaking, the political process in China – although the country remained a party-state – became more consultative and sophisticated, while political actors became more diversified and competitive. In local legislative politics, the simple time of the Party's leadership and government's domination ended, as government agencies, legislative committees, and even various social organizations began to take part in open-ended contestation

Pochan fengyun (*A Stormy Situation of Bankruptcy*) (Beijing: Zhongyang bianyi chubanshe, 1996), pp. 1–169.

[3] Local legislatures have been able to do this chiefly because China has implemented a policy of decentralization of legislative powers since the early 1980s. See Sen Lin, "A new pattern of democratization in China: The increase of provincial powers in economic legislation," *China Information*, Vol. 7, No. 3 (Winter 1992–93), pp. 27–38.

[4] Kevin O'Brien, "Chinese People's Congresses and legislative embeddedness: Understanding early organizational development," *Comparative Political Studies*, Vol. 27, No. 1 (April 1994), pp. 80–109; An Chen, *Restructuring Political Power in China: Alliance and Opposition, 1978–98* (Boulder, CO and London: Lynne Rienner Publishers, 1999), pp. 183–227.

of persuasion, frequently clashing and cooperating with each other on a
case-by-case basis to augment their organizational interests. Provincial
people's congresses, after having secured their lawmaking authority since
the late 1990s, have played two distinct roles: that of coordinators of
conflicts of interest and representatives of various social groups' voices.
In addition, social organizations have been emerging as new forces in
lawmaking, supported by local legislatures in their attempt to improve
their stand against government dominance in lawmaking politics.

RELATIONS BETWEEN LEGISLATURES AND THE PARTY

In principle, Chinese legislatures should report to, and get prior approval
from, the CCP in all important matters of lawmaking.[5] But in practice,
the Party leadership has radically shifted its course from direct participation in the making of individual laws to an indirect and comprehensive
role that oversees the lawmaking processes as a whole.[6] In this sense,
legislative-Party relations are no longer a key issue in local lawmaking
politics, different from the relations between the NPC and the Party
Center. Locally, the relations between the legislative and the executive
are the crucial issue, as discussed in more detail later.

The Shanghai legislature until around the early 1990s had to report
almost all legal bills to the territorial Party in order to obtain approval
before a draft could be deliberated. However, since then the legislature
has been able to enact most local laws without the Party's prior review
except in a few cases. Now the legislature just compiles and reports
annual legislative plans (*jihua*) at the beginning of every year, and five-
year plans (*guihua*) generally at the beginning of new periods, on the
basis of proposals submitted by government agencies, legislative committees, and its members. For example, the legislature reported a five-year

---

[5] Chen Tiedi, "Chongfen fahui renda dangzude hexin baozhang zuoyong" (To guarantee
the secured core roles of Party groups in people's congresses), *Shanghai renda yuekan*
(*Monthly People's Congresses in Shanghai*), No. 11 (November 2000), pp. 5–7; Huang
Ju, "Nuli ba Shanghai de renda gongzuo zuode genghao" (To make efforts so that
people's congresses in Shanghai well play their roles), *Shanghai renda yuekan*, No. 6
(June 1998), pp. 3–6.

[6] On the changing relationship between the Party and the NPC and, in particular, on
the detailed contents and significance of Central Document Number 8, see Tanner,
The Politics of Lawmaking in China, pp. 48–49, 51–71; Peng Chong, *Minzhu fazhi
lunji* (*Collections on Democracy and Rule of Law*) (Beijing: Zhongguo minzhu fazhi
chubanshe, 1993), pp. 173–75; Cai Dingjian, *Zhongguo renda zhidu* (*People's Congress
System in China*) (Beijing: Shehui kexue wenxian chubanshe, 1993), pp. 253–54.

legislative plan to the Party for the first time in 1998, and reported the second five-year plan in 2003.[7] A directive from Huang Ju, the Shanghai Party secretary from 1994 to 2002, made this possible.[8]

The Shanghai legislature, of course, still referred some individual cases of lawmaking to the Party for consideration in the 1990s. But they were very few: of 153 local laws enacted from 1990 to 2000 in Shanghai, my documentation and interview data indicate that the legislature reported only five to the Party. And since 2000, a senior legislative leader attested, the legislature has not reported a single draft of a law to the Party.[9] In addition, the Party interfered in the aforementioned five cases mainly at the legislature's request.

The five cases of lawmaking that the Shanghai legislature reported to the Party can be divided into three categories. The first comprised important laws, such as the Trade Unions Regulation introduced in 1995.[10] The second was sensitive laws, such as the Religious Affairs Regulation enacted in 1995. This was considered to be very sensitive because the prestigious leaders of Catholic and Protestant churches in the country were concentrated in Shanghai, and Shanghai had more than one million people with religious affiliations. Besides, government agencies and religious organizations, when the law was discussed, had very different notions as to its purpose: the former stressed control and the latter emphasized protection of the right to religion.[11] The Conscription Work Regulation in 1994 and the Civil Defense Regulation in 1999 were considered sensitive cases as they were directly related to the military. The Party was therefore asked to get involved.[12] The third category was difficult laws, that is, those for which the legislature failed to resolve severe differences of opinion and asked the Party to make a final decision. The Firework Security Regulation in 1994 belongs in this category. When the legislature enacted the local law that

---

[7] Shanghai renda changweihui yanjiushi (ed.), *Shijian yu tansuo* (*Practice and Exploration*) (Vol. 4) (Shanghai: Fudan daxue chubanshe, 2003), pp. 130–31; Xiao Dong, "Zhonggong Shanghai shiwei pizhun benshi wunian lifa guihua" (The Shanghai Party Committee approved the five-year legislative plan of this period), *Shanghai renda yuekan*, No. 5 (May 1999), pp. 5–6.

[8] Interview with a senior leader of the Shanghai legislature: Shanghai, August 2003.

[9] Ibid.

[10] "Difang lifa bufa jiakuaide wunian" (Five years of speedy footsteps in local lawmaking), *Shanghai renda yuekan*, No. 9 (September 1997), pp. 6–8.

[11] Xu Zuxiong and Zhu Yanwen (eds.), *Minzhu fazhi yu renda zhidu* (*Democratic Legal System and People's Congress Institutions*) (Shanghai: Fudan daxue chubanshe, 1999), pp. 266–72.

[12] Chen, "To guarantee the secured core roles of Party groups," p. 6.

TABLE 2.1. *Number of local laws and administrative regulations in Shanghai, 1980–2000*

Years	Total Number	Local Laws*		Administrative Regulations*	
		Number	%	Number	%
1980–1989	451	50	11.08	401	88.92
1990–1996	408	84	20.58	324	79.42
1996–2000	183	69	37.71	114	62.29
Total	1,042	203	19.48	839	80.52

*: Local laws are enacted by the Shanghai People's Congress, and administrative regulations by the Shanghai Government.
Source: Ying Songnian and Yuan Shuhong (eds.), *Zouxiang yifa zhengfu* (*Towards Governments Based on Laws*) (Beijing: Falü chubanshe, 2001), p. 506.

strictly prohibited setting off fireworks in the city during holidays, it encountered substantial objections from citizens. The legislature sent the draft law to the Party and asked that it decide whether the legislation was to be promulgated.[13]

There are two possible causes for the CCP being less involved today in the making of new laws. Most important is the Party's limited capability. The number of laws produced by the Shanghai legislature has dramatically increased since the 1990s. As Table 2.1 notes, the legislature promulgated 153 local laws between 1990 and 2000, compared to only 50 in the decade from 1980 to 1989. As a result, it is actually beyond the Party's capability to review all individual legal bills. In addition, the majority of local laws that are related to economic policies do not need the Party's involvement in terms of political sensitivity. For instance, 59 (43 percent) of the 136 local laws the Shanghai legislature enacted from 1980 to 1998 belong to this category. A roughly similar relation can be found for provincial people's congresses in other regions: more than 50 percent of local laws are concerned with economic reforms.[14]

[13] Interview with a senior leader of the Shanghai legislature: Shanghai, August 2003.
[14] About 60 percent of local laws that legislatures in Heilongjiang, Hebei, and Gansu Provinces have promulgated in the past two decades are related to economic reform and development. See Li Linke, "Jiaqiang lifa gongzuo, baozhang jingji fazhan" (To strengthen lawmaking work and guarantee economic development), *Difang renda jianshe* (*Construction of Local People's Congresses*), No. 2 (February 1999), pp. 7–8; Ma Bin, "Difang lifa jige lilun wenti yu Gansu 20nian difang lifa shijian" (Several theoretical problems in local lawmaking and twenty-year's practice of local lawmaking

Resolving technical problems and coordinating different opinions among government agencies and social groups is a key task in enacting such local laws, and this requires thorough investigation and coordination by lawmaking bodies, not the political decisions of the Party.

RELATIONS BETWEEN LEGISLATURES AND LOCAL GOVERNMENTS

In the Chinese system of lawmaking, "department protectionism" (*bumenzhuyi*) is considered to be the most crucial and tricky issue in the whole reform era, and the Tenth NPC period (2003–07) was no exception.[15] It refers to the phenomenon whereby governments in general and their agencies in particular make efforts, by way of lawmaking, to expand organizational interests and evade corresponding responsibilities.[16]

The problems caused by "department protectionism" are as follows. First of all, the conflicts of interest among government agencies frequently retard the legislation of urgent laws. A case in point was the Law on Road Security passed by the NPC Standing Committee in 2003, ten years after the Ministry of Public Security of the State Council had started to draft it. The main issue was which agencies should have jurisdiction over vehicles for agricultural use: the agencies of agricultural mechanics and road transportation security struggled for a decade to secure that authority. Only after reaching a compromise, whereby the agency of road transportation security assumed jurisdiction over all vehicles (including those for agricultural use) while allowing the agency of agricultural mechanics to deal with the registration of farm tractors, was this law promulgated.[17]

---

in Gansu), *Renda yanjiu (Study of People's Congresses)*, No. 6 (June 1999) (available at www.rdyj.com.cn/rdqk-6-t.thml).

[15] Wu Bangguo, "Tigao lifa zhiliang shi benjie lifa gongzuode zhongdian" (To enhance lawmaking quality is the focal point of legislation work in this period of the NPC), *Zhongguo renda (China's People's Congresses)*, No. 21 (October 2003), pp. 2–6.

[16] Tanner, *The Politics of Lawmaking*, pp. 120–21. Chinese articles criticizing the problems of "department protectionism" are too numerous to cite. See Ji Liangru, "Lüelun difang lifa zhongde bumen zhuyi" (A brief discussion on department protectionism in local lawmaking), *Renda gongzuo tongxun (Bulletin of People's Congresses)*, No. 14 (July 1995), pp. 21–24; Liu Yunlong, "Difang lifazhong bumen liyi qingxiangde biaoxian, weihai, chengyin ji duice" (Appearances, harms, causes, and countermeasures of the tendency of departmental selfishness in local lawmaking), *Renda gongzuo tongxun*, No. 10 (May 1996), pp. 13–15, 35.

[17] Xu Yan, "Yiren weiben wei shengming zhizun: 'daolu anquanfa' tongguo suiji" (To put people first and supreme respect for life: a short story on the passage of the Road Security Law), *Zhongguo renda*, No. 21 (October 2003), pp. 20–22.

In addition, government agencies increase their powers and interests instead of addressing problems in some cases. For example, one regional firefighting agency drafted a fire control regulation which ensured that certain companies reportedly affiliated with the agency could monopolize the sale and installation of firefighting equipment; in a similar way, an urban construction agency advanced its interests by promulgating a regulation on construction market administration. Finally, local laws are sometimes not well enforced because of provisions that contradict each other. The two agencies of land regulation and urban construction of the same local government drafted separate local laws which contradicted each other by prescribing different permission and punishment for the same matter.[18]

"Department protectionism" has been widespread mainly because governments, as compared to legislatures, dominate the lawmaking processes, especially with regard to preparing legislative plans and drafting laws. This originates in their decisively more advantageous position in terms of capacity, including information, organizational, and personnel supports. Therefore, the most challenging task facing Chinese legislatures has been to cope with "department protectionism," and several measures have been proposed and adopted to overcome this problem.[19] These are discussed in some detail below.

The Shanghai government, not the legislature, overwhelmingly led the lawmaking processes in the 1980s. The legislature, in a strict sense, did not enact but just passed local laws that had been prepared, considered, and proclaimed by the government until the mid-1980s.[20] The government has also proposed and drafted most local laws since the 1990s. For instance, the total number of local laws that were compiled

[18] Ji Liangru, "A brief discussion on department protectionism in local lawmaking," p. 21; Cai Dingjian and Wang Chenguang (eds.), *Renmin daibiao dahui ershinian fazhan yu gaige (Twenty-Years' Development and Reform of People's Congresses)* (Beijing: Zhongguo jiancha chubanshe, 2001), p. 82.
[19] Wu Hong, "Kefu difang lifa zhong bumen liyi qingxiangde jidian sikao" (Several considerations to overcome departmental selfishness in local lawmaking), *Minzhu fazhi jianshe (Construction of Democracy and Rule by Law)*, No. 2 (February 2001), pp. 37–38; Liu Mianyi, "Cong chengxude jiaodu tan kefu lifa zhongde bumen liyi" (A discussion to overcome departmental selfishness in procedure's perspective), *Zhongguo renda*, No. 16 (August 2003), pp. 6, 12–13.
[20] Xu Xianghua (ed.), *Xin shiqi Zhongguo lifa fansi (A Reflection on Chinese Lawmaking in New Era)* (Shanghai: Xuelin chubanshe, 2004), p. 276. On detailed lawmaking cases in that period, see Cai Bingwen (ed.), *Shanghai renmin daibiao dahui zhi (Annals of Shanghai People's Congress)* (Shanghai: Shanghai shehui kexueyuan chubanshe, 1998), pp. 259–69.

in annual lawmaking plans by the Shanghai legislature from 2000 to 2002 was forty-one: of these, the government proposed thirty-five (85.4 percent).[21] And, of forty local laws enacted in Shanghai from 1998 to 2002, the government drafted thirty-four (85 percent).[22] This shows that the legislative-executive relations in Shanghai also fit in with the "90 percent rule," which applies to most legislative bodies in the world: the cabinet proposes at least 90 percent of the legislative agenda, and at least 90 percent of what it proposes is enacted.[23]

The Shanghai legislature, like legislative bodies in other countries, cannot and will not be able to dominate the lawmaking process in the contemporary administrative state, as the "90 percent rule" suggests. In particular, legislatures' roles are very limited in the case of economic policymaking.[24] So when we evaluate the roles of legislatures in the lawmaking process, we should focus on the degree to which the legislature, by rejecting or amending drafts proposed by the government, is able to constrain the executive branch and prevent it from making policy unilaterally.[25] The Shanghai People's Congress has surely moved in this direction since the late 1990s.

Most of all, the legal-political conditions for the Shanghai legislature have improved. That is, local laws have gained more weight relative to administrative regulations (*xingzheng guizhang*) promulgated by government, since governance according to law became more firmly rooted in the 1990s. As Table 2.1 shows, the percentage of local laws among all regulations increased from 11.08 percent during 1980 to 1989 to 37.71 percent during 1996 to 2000. This suggests that the administrative lawmaking power of the government has given way to some augmentation of the lawmaking authority of the legislature. This tendency has been intensified with China's entry into the World Trade Organization

---

[21] Fazhi gongzuo weiyuanhui, "Shanghaishi renda changweihui niandu shenyi fagui caoan jihua (2000, 2001, 2002)" (Annual legislative plans of the Shanghai People's Congress Standing Committee in 2000, 2001, and 2002) (available at www.spcsc.sh.cn).

[22] Gu Ping, "Guanyu gaijin fagui qicao gongzuode sikao" (A consideration on the reform of drafting work of local laws), *Shanghai renda yuekan*, No. 1 (January 2003) (available at www.spcsc.sh.cn).

[23] David M. Olson, *Democratic Legislative Institutions: A Comparative View* (Armonk, NY: M.E. Sharpe, 1994), p. 84.

[24] David M. Olson and Michael L. Mezey, "Parliaments and public policy," in Olson and Mezey (eds.), *Legislatures in the Policy Process* (Cambridge: Cambridge University Press, 1991), pp. 4–5.

[25] Michael L. Mezey, *Comparative Legislatures* (Durham, NC: Duke University Press, 1979), pp. 25–26.

(WTO) in 2001 and the implementation of the Administrative Licensing Law in 2004.[26]

In addition, the organizational capability of the Shanghai legislature has been strengthened. For example, of the sixty-five members of the Standing Committee of Shanghai People's Congress, about half are full-time members (*zhuanzhi weiyuan*), an increase of about 10 percent compared with the previous period (1998–2002). The increase in the ratio of full-time members is significant, because they are most responsible for the investigation and deliberation of drafted laws.[27] For reference, all six members of the Legislative Affairs Work Committee (*fazhi gongzuo weiuyuanhui/ fagongwei*) and six out of nine in the Legislative Committee (*fazhi weiyuanhui*) are full-timers. The number of legislative staff has also increased. Now, 160 staffers directly or indirectly perform lawmaking-related work: thirty of them specialize in lawmaking affairs, and most are law school graduates.[28]

Finally, the legislatures, in an effort to cope with "department protectionism," have also introduced several new institutions and thus increased their lawmaking authority. These include the changes of lawmaking guidelines from "experience-based legislation" (*jingyan lifa*) to "legislation in advance" (*chaoqian lifa*), the strengthening of legislature's initiative in lawmaking plans, more diversified drafters, the introduction of "opening-up legislation" (*kaimen lifa*), and stricter deliberation of legislative drafts.[29] The NPC, based on its own experience, has made efforts to disseminate improved lawmaking systems nationwide, and local people's congresses have been willing to accept the NPC's suggestions. The Legislation Law enacted in 2000 can be considered the sum of previous experiences, and its enactment became a watershed in the institutionalization of Chinese lawmaking systems. Now we discuss the measures in more detail.

---

[26] Dali L. Yang, *Remaking the Chinese Leviathan: Market Transition and the Politics of Governance in China* (Stanford: Stanford University Press, 2004), pp. 161–64; Yuan Xudon, "Xingzheng xukefa dui difang lifa yingxiangde jidian sikao" (Several considerations on the effect of the Administrative Licensing Law on local lawmaking), *Zhongguo renda*, No. 22 (November 2003), pp. 11–13.

[27] Cai and Wang, *Twenty-Years' Development and Reform*, p. 95.

[28] Interview with a senior leader of the Shanghai legislature: Shanghai, February 2004.

[29] On the lawmaking processes, see Tanner, *The Politics of Lawmaking*, pp. 209–30; Cai, *People's Congress System in China*, pp. 301–19. On Shanghai case, see Shanghai renda, *Practice and Exploration*, pp. 128–47; Xu, *A Reflection on Chinese Lawmaking*, pp. 245–311.

Changing Lawmaking Guidelines and the Diversification of Drafters

The government's initiative in setting the lawmaking agenda and its accompanying "department protectionism" were based on a specific legislation guideline in the 1980s. Chinese legislatures complied with the "experience-based lawmaking" theory which former NPC Standing Committee Chairman Peng Zhen and other senior leaders produced. This guideline states that Chinese legislatures should consider China's specific conditions and experiences, and that they can enact laws based on accumulated experiences only when the conditions for implementation are ripe. Hence, no laws can be enacted without the accumulation of enough experiences and appropriate conditions for implementation.[30] Because of this guideline, laws merely followed reforms, instead of leading them, and the legislation of urgent and necessary laws was sometimes indefinitely postponed with an excuse of inopportune conditions and lack of experience.

Furthermore, the guideline accentuated the lawmaking initiative of governments, not of legislatures: governments tended to promulgate administrative regulations instead of laws and they decided lawmaking schedules and the contents of laws based on their own judgment and experience. In contrast, legislatures were reduced to passive organs which had to wait until governments proposed legal bills. Finally, this guideline emphasized a legal instrumentalism already widespread in Chinese society. The notion that laws are a tool of the state to rule and control society overshadowed the idea that laws are a weapon of the people to safeguard their rights and interests against the encroachment of state power.[31]

In the early 1990s, however, a new concept of lawmaking, "lawmaking in advance," emerged, arguing that, when necessary, laws can be promulgated to lead and consolidate reforms without opportune conditions for implementation or experience. This new conception

---

[30] Peng Zhen, *Lun xinshiqide shehuizhuyi minzhu yu fazhi jianshe* (*A Discussion on Socialist Democracy and Construction of Rule of Law in the New Era*) (Beijing: Zhongyang wenxian chubanshe, 1989), pp. 244–50; Peng, *Collections on Democracy and Rule of Law*, p. 5.

[31] Cai and Wang, *Twenty-Years' Development and Reform*, pp. 57–74; Liu and Cheng, *Theory and Practice of People's Congress Institutions*, p. 286; Han Li, "Zhongguo lifa guocheng zhongde feizhengshi guize" (Informal rules in the Chinese lawmaking procedures), *Zhanlüe yu guanli* (*Strategy and Management*), No. 5 (May 2001), pp. 16–27.

provided legislatures with a chance to initiate legislative plans and manage the entire lawmaking process on the grounds of investigating social demands for laws. In fact, the NPC since the late 1980s and the provincial people's congresses since the mid-1990s have developed annual and five-year lawmaking plans. That is, Chinese legislatures have shifted from passive to active organs in the lawmaking process. With the new lawmaking concept, China also could begin to escape from its legal instrumentalism and introduce "legal protectionism." In fact, this new concept made it possible for the NPC to enact a series of pertinent laws, including the Administrative Litigation Law (1989), the Consumer Protection Law (1993), the State Compensation Law (1994), the Administrative Punishment Law (1996), the Criminal Procedure Law (1997), and the Administrative Review Law (1999), all of which were intended to regulate governments' behaviors and protect people's rights and interests.

Of course, the guideline of "experience-based lawmaking" is officially still in force. An authentic interpretation of the Legislation Law insists on the importance and validity of this concept.[32] Therefore, two guidelines coexist and the transition from the old to the new concept is taking place.

Chinese legislatures have also tried to diversify the drafters of local laws because "department protectionism" chiefly results from the monopoly of drafting rights by governments. First, local legislatures try to assume a greater role in drafting important local laws that could influence society. But obvious constraints exist in this endeavor because of the limited capability of legislatures. For instance, as previously noted, the Shanghai legislature drafted only 15 percent of local laws from 1998 to 2002. In addition, scholars and professionals are invited to take part in drawing up draft laws, even though one agency officially takes the initiative for drafting. For example, when the Construction Bureau of the Shanghai Government drafted the Regulation of Shanghai on Construction Market Administration in 1997, Shanghai Construction College, together with the Legislation Affairs Office (*fazhi bangongshi*) of the government, participated in the small drafting group (*qicao xiaozu*).[33] In other regions, legislatures sometimes empower academic institutes to

---

[32] Qiao Xiaoyang (ed.), *Lifafa jianghua* (*An Introduction to the Legislation Law*) (Beijing: Zhongguo minzhu fazhi chubanshe, 2000), pp. 22–23.

[33] Shen Honghua, "Guifan jianzhu shichangde yibu zhongyao fagui" (An important local law to regulate construction market), *Shanghai renda yuekan*, No. 12 (December 1999), pp. 7–8.

draft laws. The Regulation of Guangdong on Agent Administration and the Implementation Measure of Hubei on the Elderly People's Rights Protection Law belong to this category.[34]

MUCH STRICTER DELIBERATION OF DRAFT LAWS

The most effective way to cope with "department protectionism" is to conduct more thorough deliberations of drafted laws in accordance with regulations specified by legislatures themselves. This is because legislatures exercise their authority during the deliberation stage of lawmaking, while governments have better means for agenda-setting and drafting laws.

Two new systems in this regard are worth mentioning here. The first is the introduction of the two-step deliberation and three-reading (*liangshen sandu*) system.[35] Until the early 1990s, most local legislatures passed drafted laws after just a first deliberation. Consequently, laws proposed and drafted by governments were passed without substantive changes, and legislative deliberation tended to be considered a necessary formality. But since the Shanghai legislature introduced the system in 1998, all drafts of laws have to be deliberated at least twice and read three times in plenary sessions or standing committee meetings, except for trivial amendments to several words and phrases. Because the legislature convenes regular meetings of its standing committee once every two months, it can deliberate drafts for at least four months.[36]

The second new system is the introduction of a unified investigation and deliberation (*tongyi shenyi*) system. In common with most legislative

---

[34] Huang Liqun, "Lüelun gaijin difang lifade tichu jizhi he qicao jizhi" (A brief discussion on the improvement of proposal and drafting systems in local lawmaking), *Zhongguo renda*, No. 4 (February 2003), pp. 29–31.

[35] The NPC officially introduced a two-step deliberation system in 1987 and has practiced a three-step system since 1998 with the purpose of enhancing the "quality" of legislation. During the same period, several provincial people's congresses also introduced three-step systems, including Tianjin and Anhui. Of course, the stricter deliberation system cannot automatically guarantee Chinese legislatures' lawmaking authority. In fact, the NPC and local people's congresses still complain about the noncooperative attitude and sometimes obstruction of governments during deliberation of draft laws. See Cai and Wang, *Twenty-Years' Development and Reform*, pp. 427–40.

[36] Shanghai renda, *Practice and Exploration*, pp. 128–47; Wan Zongyan, "Guanyu difang lifa shenyi zhidude ruogan wenti" (On several problems of deliberation system in local lawmaking), *Shanghai renda yuekan*, No. 10 (October 2002) (available at www.spcsc.sh.cn); Interview with a senior leader of the Shanghai legislature: Shanghai, February 2004.

bodies in liberal democracies, the Shanghai legislature's special committees (*zhuanmen weiyuanhui*) used to take chief responsibility for deliberating legislative drafts. On the one hand, this system has the merit that relevant committees can exercise their special capabilities in the deliberation processes. On the other, it entails several problems. For example, legislatures will hardly be able to address "department protectionism" because of the close relationship between special committees responsible for deliberation and government agencies drafting laws. In addition, special committees are likely to pay more attention to the contents of drafted laws than to legal formality, so that local laws deliberated by special committees sometimes conflict with "parent laws" and other local laws.

To address these problems, the Shanghai People's Congress established the Legislative Affairs Work Committee in 1998, which conducted a unified deliberation of all drafted laws. According to the provisions of the Legislation Law, the Legislative Committee was established in 2001 for the same purpose, and the legislature changed the Work Committee into a staff office of the Legislative Committee. A division of labor between the Legislative Committee and other special committees was then put into effect. Special committees conduct the preliminary deliberation of drafted laws and present deliberating reports in written form for the first deliberation meeting. Also, special committee members, as nonvoting observers, can participate in the unified deliberation of the Legislative Committee. The Legislative Committee then takes over unified deliberation after the first deliberation and reports the deliberating opinions and proposals for revising the original draft laws in written form to the legislature when the second deliberation resumes.[37] The legislature generally respects the Committee's suggestions. In this way, the Legislative Committee, as a kind of "prestigious committee" in the lawmaking organ, exercises leadership in the process of deliberating legislative drafts and can help address part of the problem of department protectionism.[38]

"OPENING-UP LEGISLATION"

The last innovation employed to cope with department protectionism is "opening-up legislation" or "democratic legislation" (*minzhu lifa*).

---

[37] Shanghai renda, *Practice and Exploration*, pp. 50–67; Interview with a senior leader of the Shanghai legislature: Shanghai, August 2003.

[38] Xu, *A Reflection on Chinese Lawmaking*, pp. 100, 292–93, 299.

This refers to measures taken by the legislature, in an effort to make up for its weaker capability relative to government, to encourage social organizations and the public to actively participate in drafting and deliberating legal bills.[39] Two institutions are important: legislation hearings (*lifa tingzhenghui*) and the solicitation of public opinions by publicizing drafts.

China's first legislation hearing was convened in Guangdong in 1999, when the legislature enacted a regulation concerning construction project bidding.[40] The Legislation Law confirmed this procedure in 2000, and now most provincial legislatures employ legislative hearings when they promulgate important local laws. The NPC also convened legislative hearings when it revised the Marriage Law in 2001. The Shanghai legislature is no exception. It has held four legislative hearings since it introduced hearings for the first time in 2001 to 2004.[41] By employing legislative hearings, the legislature can redress parts of department protectionism in the name of public opinion: that is, legislative hearings provide the legislature with a base to fend off government agencies' requests.[42]

The system of soliciting public opinion has been widely employed across the country since the late 1990s. Recently, Chinese legislatures have often put drafts for laws in local newspapers and gathered public comments and suggestions when enacting local laws that seemed to seriously influence ordinary people's lives. For example, the Shanghai legislature solicited public suggestions on a total of ten draft laws from 1998 to 2004.[43] The legislature also sends almost all draft laws to lower-level people's congresses and social organizations and seeks their comments and suggestions. The legislature, it is argued, has recently paid much attention to public suggestions when deliberating, and in this sense

---

[39] Ibid., pp. 156–57.

[40] Ling Su, "Zhe shijishang ye shi benjie renda changweihui gongzuode jiben jingyan" (This is also substantively fundamental experiences of this period's people's congress), *Renmin zhi sheng* (*People's Voice*), No. 1 (January 2003), pp. 4–9.

[41] Shanghai renda, *Practice and Exploration*, p. 62; Gan Guanghua, "Shanghai: xiaoyuan shanghai shigu chuli youfa keyi" (Shanghai: provided local laws to deal with injury accidents at schools), *Zhongguo renda*, No. 19 (September 2001), pp. 9–11.

[42] On the significance of introducing legislative hearings, see Laura Paler, "China's Legislation Law and the making of a more orderly and representative legislative system," *China Quarterly* 182 (June 2005), pp. 301–18.

[43] Wen Qing, "Shanghai: difang lifa 24nian zhuduo chuangxin" (Shanghai: various innovations of local lawmaking for 24 years), *Renminwang* (*People's Net*), August 27, 2004 (available at www.people.com.cn).

public opinion has become significant in the lawmaking process since the late 1990s.[44]

In the following two cases, government agencies, legislature committees, and social organizations clashed and cooperated with each other in lawmaking based on their interests. And the Shanghai legislature played crucial roles in coordinating conflicting interests and representing the voices from various groups. Finally, the Party was not involved in the lawmaking process, and the roles of government agencies were more limited than anticipated.

THE LEGISLATION OF THE LABOR CONTRACT REGULATION

When the Shanghai People's Congress enacted the Labor Contract Regulation in 2001, there were severe conflicts among government agencies, legislative committees, and social organizations. This was because the local law was closely related to the interests of social groups: both labor and business could be seriously affected depending upon how the law was enacted. Therefore, trade unions and business organizations, such as the Federation of Industry and Commerce (*gongshanglian*) and trade associations (*hangye xiehui*), made the utmost effort to steer the lawmaking process toward their interests. In addition, both executive agencies (the Labor Bureau and the Economy Committee) and legislative special committees (the Financial & Economic Affairs Committee [*caijingwei*] and the Legislative Committee) were deeply involved in the lawmaking process as promoters of certain social groups' interests and coordinators of conflicting interests.

The NPC enacted the Labor Law in 1994, and the Shanghai government promulgated the Provision of Shanghai on Labor Contract in 1994. In the 1990s, the labor contract system expanded across the region, and about three million laborers worked under the contract system in 2000 (a contract rate of 98 percent). But the Contract Provision in Shanghai did not keep up with the rapidly changing reality. For instance, the Provision did not provide any guidance about labor contracts after an enterprise went bankrupt. Labor disputes dramatically increased as a result: 11,046 cases of labor mediation were submitted

[44] Interview with a senior leader of the Shanghai legislature: Shanghai, February 2004.

to the Shanghai Labor Arbitration Committee in 2000, 40.7 percent more than in the previous year. For this reason, the Shanghai legislature put the legislation of the labor contract regulation on the 2001 annual legislative schedule.[45]

A drafting group was composed of three executive agencies (the Labor Bureau, the Economy Committee, and the Legislative Affairs Office), two legislative committees (the Legislative Affairs Work Committee and the Financial & Economic Affairs Committee), and the Shanghai General Trade Union (SGTU). In the actual drafting process, according to a leader of the SGTU, the Labor Bureau and the Union played core roles, and other participating members just read and made comments on the draft. In the drafting stage, the SGTU tried to secure laborers' interests, while the Labor Bureau as a representative of government attempted to take care of the opinions of both labor and business. During this process, against conventional wisdom that suggested the Bureau and the SGTU would form an alliance against a coalition composed of business-related executive agencies and social organizations, the Bureau and the Union severely clashed because the former, a union leader insisted, took sides with business on key issues. As a result, the draft generally met the demands of business.[46]

There were three primary issues in the lawmaking process. The first was the aim of the legislation. The first article of the Labor Law enacted in 1994, a "mother law" of the Labor Contract Regulation in Shanghai, stipulates, "This Law was enacted to safeguard the lawful rights and interests of laborers, coordinate labor relations, and establish and maintain a labor contract system appropriate to the socialist market economy." On this basis, the SGTU argued that the Regulation also ought to "safeguard the lawful rights and interests of laborers" as its primary goal. In contrast, business organizations and economic-related government agencies argued that "to safeguard the lawful rights and interests of both parties of labor contract" should be the primary goal of legislation. It was reasonable, they argued, that the Regulation was meant to protect the interests of both business enterprises and laborers, because enterprises were a main contacting party in labor contracts.

---

[45] Shanghai renda changweihui fagongwei (ed.), '*Shanghaishi laodong hetong tiaoli' shiyi (An Interpretation on the Shanghai Labor Contract Regulation)* (Shanghai: Shanghai renmin chubanshe, 2002), pp. 101–10.

[46] Shanghai renda, *An Interpretation on the Shanghai Labor Contract Regulation*, pp. 104–09; Interview with senior leaders of the SGTU and the Federation of Industry and Commerce: Shanghai, February 2004.

The second issue in the lawmaking process was whether the Regulation should or should not maintain the "10+3 provision," and this was critical for the business circle. The former Shanghai Labor Provision introduced in 1994 contained an article stating that an enterprise could not cancel labor contracts or lay off workers who were within three years of retirement after having worked for the company for more than ten years. The SGTU insisted on maintaining the provision to protect elderly laborers' rights and interests, while the business coalition criticized the provision as a legacy of the planned economy, lagging far behind the times.

The most important issue was about granting trade unions the right to interfere with labor contracts, which was critical for the trade unions' status and roles in enterprises. Laborers, the Union argued, were such weak parties compared to enterprises in labor contracts that trade unions should have the right to be involved in labor agreements. Therefore, the provision that "an enterprise should listen to the opinions of a trade union when it would unilaterally cancel labor contracts, and the cancellation of contracts would be invalid and void without prior consultation with the trade union" should be inserted into the Regulation. Business organizations did not agree with this argument on the ground that trade unions were not a contracting party.[47]

With regard to these three issues, the legislative committees presented different opinion reports when they deliberated the draft. The Financial & Economic Affairs Committee sided firmly with the SGTU: In the report of deliberating opinions, the Committee defended the three arguments of the Union.[48] In contrast, the Legislative Committee had different ideas. First, the Committee did not accept the SGTU's argument in relation to the law's mission. As a result, the first Article of the Regulation states, "This Regulation was enacted to coordinate labor relations, and establish and maintain a labor contract system appropriate to the socialist market economy." Second, the Committee also rejected the "10+3 provision." This provision, the Committee argued, was a

---

[47] Interview with senior leaders of the SGTU and the Federation of Industry and Commerce: Shanghai, February 2004; Shanghai renda, *An Interpretation on the Shanghai Labor Contract Regulation*, pp. 104–09; Zheng Guangjun, "Xinxi renmin tancheng zhiyan: Shirenda changweihui shenyi laodong hetong tiaoli caoan" (Minded people, candidly spoke without reservation: the Municipal People's Congress deliberated the draft law of the labor contract regulation), *Shanghai renda yuekan*, No. 10 (October 2003) (available at www.spcsc.sh.cn).

[48] Shanghai renda, *An Interpretation on the Shanghai Labor Contract Regulation*, pp. 111–15.

kind of discrimination unfavorable to Chinese enterprises after China's accession to the WTO; elderly laborers themselves would be victims of this provision, because companies would avoid making contracts with elderly laborers under this condition. However, the Committee accepted the demand that trade unions should have the right to interfere with labor contracts.

Why did the two legislative committees suggest different deliberating opinions? The most important factor is that special committees have close relations with certain executive agencies and social organizations outside governments.[49] Certain legislative committees, executive agencies, and social organizations, belonging to "a similar system" (*xitong*), have maintained ongoing working relations, and personnel interchanges between them have occurred quite often. For example, the members of the Financial & Economic Affairs Committee are mostly recruited from among people in leading positions in relevant government agencies and social organizations, including trade unions. Other committees are similarly set up. For this reason, legislative committees tend to represent the voices of certain executive agencies and social organizations when they deliberate drafted laws.

In contrast, the Legislative Committee does not maintain such a cozy relationship with executive agencies and social organizations. Significantly, the Committee as an organ responsible for the unified deliberation of drafted laws has few reasons and motives to maintain ongoing working relations with them. Neither are certain constituents overrepresented among the members of the Legislative Committee. This is the main reason that the Committee can deliberate legal bills on the basis of legal rationality, and can coordinate conflicts of interest among major forces. In particular, the Committee tends to restrict other special committees when it thinks that they are inordinately favoring a certain government agency or social group.[50]

Meanwhile, some senior leaders of the SGTU believed that the Labor Contract Regulation reflected their opinions relatively faithfully.

---

[49] Tanner argued that the special committee members' behavior seemed to be far closer to the professional legislator model than the iron triangles model. Tanner, *The Politics of Lawmaking*, p. 108. In fact, there is not a consistent model that explains every case of lawmaking in Chinese legislatures. However, the author's interview data and literature materials about the provincial people's congresses in Tianjin, Shanghai, and Guangdong indicate that the iron triangles model rather than the professional legislator model can apply to the behaviors of the special committee members.

[50] Xu, *A Reflection on Chinese Lawmaking*, pp. 292–93; Interview with a senior leader of the Shanghai legislature: Shanghai, August 2003.

Concerning the mission of the local law, the Regulation did not correspond to the Union's preference, but it did not meet the business alliance's demands either. Originally, the SGTU had thought that the Regulation did not need to include the legislation's mission, because the Labor Law had already stated it in its first Article. But in the lawmaking process, the business coalition made an attempt to change the main focus of the local law, and the SGTU took a firm position against this. In order to block further attempts by the business coalition, the Union submitted a new proposal that the Regulation should not include both arguments, and, finally, the Regulation made no mention of it at all.[51]

The SGTU was not at all dissatisfied with the outcome of the conflict about the "10+3 provision" either. From the outset, the SGTU had not intended to argue too strongly for this provision's maintenance, because the leaders already knew that it was unreasonable and inappropriate in a market economy. Free labor contract systems were widespread in Shanghai, and this special article could not play a crucial role in protecting the rights and interests of most laborers. Some workers even thought that it was not bad for them to retire early and to find new jobs if they could get adequate compensation. Therefore, the SGTU sought to use the "10+3 provision" as a bargaining chip, and for this reason, it could agree to the cancellation of this provision. Instead, the SGTU strongly insisted on the inclusion of an article that gave trade unions the right to interfere with labor contracts, and in the end the Union was successful.[52]

In short, the final version of the Regulation was a result of compromises between confronting forces, in which the legislature played a vital role in coordinating conflicts of interest. The SGTU won a substantive point because the Regulation allowed trade unions to interfere in labor contracts as lawful agents, while business enterprises were able to repeal the "10+3 provision."

THE AMENDMENTS OF THE CONSUMERS' RIGHTS PROTECTION REGULATION

The revision of the Consumers' Rights Protection Regulation in 2002 caused as much conflict as the Labor Contract Regulation. The local law could have an enormous effect not only on the interests of ordinary

---

[51] Interview with a senior leader of the SGTU: Shanghai, February 2004.
[52] Ibid.

citizens and business enterprises but also on those of some executive agencies and social organizations.

Protecting consumer rights was a big social issue in Shanghai by the mid- to late 1980s, as the region became one of the most economically developed areas in China. The Shanghai legislature, in an attempt to address the problem, enacted the Regulation of Shanghai on Protection of Lawful Rights and Interests of Consumers in 1988. Thereafter, the NPC promulgated the Consumers' Rights Protection Law in 1993, and the Shanghai legislature amended the Regulation in 1994. However, even the revised Regulation did not keep up with the rapid changes in Chinese society. For instance, public complaints about such new commodities as "commercial" houses (*shangpinfang*), automobiles, medical treatment, and education had radically increased because of insufficient provisions. And the Regulation did not even mention new patterns of consumption, including door-to-door and Internet sales. Further, more thorough protection of consumers' rights was demanded with China's impending accession to the WTO. For these reasons, the Shanghai legislature compiled the revision of the Regulation in the 2001 annual legislative plan.[53]

Preparation for the draft revision started in late 2000. Officially, the Industrial & Commercial Administration Bureau of the Shanghai government and the Legislative Affairs Work Committee of the legislature took the drafting role. But in the actual drafting process, the Shanghai Consumer Association (SCA) led the drafting process, and the Legislative Affairs Work Committee supported it by reviewing the draft from a legal perspective. The lawmaking process brought about enormous debates, and the Legislation Affairs Office of the government convened legislation hearings and solicited opinions from government agencies, social organizations, and the public. Finally, the Shanghai legislature passed the revision of the Regulation in October 2002.[54]

Three issues were highlighted at the drafting stage, the first two of which were critical for the SCA to expand its organizational interests. The first issue was the limits of the SCA's mediation. The Association argued that three items about which consumers had raised serious complaints

---

[53] Shanghaishi renda changweihui fagongwei (ed.), '*Shanghaishi xiaofeizhe quanyi baohu tiaoli*' *shiyi* (*An Interpretation on the Shanghai Consumers' Rights Protection Regulation*) (Shanghai: Shanghai renmin chubanshe, 2003), pp. 151–53.

[54] Shanghaishi renda, *An Interpretation on the Shanghai Consumers' Rights Protection Regulation*, pp. 153–54, 171–75.

should be included in the remit of its mediation: "profit-making" education (*yinglixing peixun*), medical services, and "commercial" houses.
In contrast, the Education Committee and the Public Health Bureau of
the government and social organizations in the educational and medical
areas insisted that education and medical services were "public goods"
rather than general consumer goods, and thus they should not be subject
to mediation. In particular, because a specified regulation dealing with
medical disputes had already been enacted, it was not necessary for the
Regulation to duplicate it.

The second issue was the introduction of the "three systems" to
strengthen the SCA's authority. In order to safeguard consumers'
rights and interests, the Association and the Bureau argued, its supervisory authority over the production and sale of business enterprises
should be strengthened. In this capacity, the revised Regulation should
introduce the three systems: that is, the publication of consumer
information and consumer complaints and annual supervisory deliberation. But business organizations and economic agencies opposed
the introduction of any measures to intensify the Association's power
without provisions to check and punish the Association's potential
malfunctions.

The third issue was the introduction of a recall (*zhaohui*) system.
A recall system was indispensable, the Association strongly argued,
to address consumer complaints about products such as electric home
appliances and cars. Indeed, consumers in some countries were able
to get compensation for defective goods under pertinent laws, while
Chinese consumers could not because such laws did not exist. Business
organizations and related government agencies disagreed with this argument: even the "mother law" did not mention recall, and other regions
throughout the country had not yet introduced it.[55]

The Industrial & Commercial Bureau, as the official drafter of the
revision of the Regulation, accepted the Consumer Association's arguments relatively faithfully at the drafting stage. In fact, the Association
and the Bureau were "two members of one family": the Consumers'
Right Protection Section of the Bureau was the "supervising agency"
(*zhuguan bumen*) of the Association; most leading members (except for
the chairman) and staffers of the Association also transferred from the
Bureau. Therefore, it is understandable that the Bureau actively accepted

[55] Ibid., pp. 155–61; Interview with senior leaders of the SCA: Shanghai, February
2004.

the Association's demands.[56] Ultimately, the draft made "profit-making" education and "commercial" houses subject to mediation, but excluded medical services; also it included the three systems and a recall system. In the end, a kind of "department protectionism" appeared at the drafting stage: the Bureau and the Association cooperated to advance their common interests.

At the deliberation stage in the legislature, lawmaking players conflicted once again. That is, the SCA and the Industrial & Commercial Administration Bureau argued for their case, while the Education Committee and the Public Health Bureau of government and relevant social organizations strongly opposed the SCA's argument. Facing strong objections, the Bureau and the Association had to withdraw some of their original demands. Most of all, education and medical services were finally excluded from mediation; only "commercial" houses remained in the draft. The main reason education and medical services were excluded while houses remained within the mediation items was that the lobbying power of the education- and medical-related coalition was far stronger than that of the construction- and sales-related coalition.[57] The introduction of the three systems had been deleted as well. But the Bureau and the Association maintained their firm stance toward the introduction of a recall system with strong support from the public.[58]

The legislative committees also confronted each other when they deliberated the draft revision. The Financial & Economic Affairs Committee, responsible for preliminary deliberation, supported the arguments of the SCA as anticipated: education and medical services as well as houses should be included in mediation.[59] In contrast, the Education, Science, Culture & Health Committee (*jiaokewenweiwei*), which has a close relationship with education- and medical-related executive agencies and social organizations, opposed this. Meanwhile, the Legislative Committee adopted a position close to the education and medical coalition: it excluded education and medical services from mediation and rejected the three systems. The Committee, however, agreed to the introduction of a recall system and included "commercial" houses within the mediation items.[60]

---

[56] Interview with senior leaders of the SCA: Shanghai, February 2004.

[57] Ibid.

[58] Ibid.

[59] Shanghaishi renda, *An Interpretation on the Shanghai Consumers' Rights Protection Regulation*, pp. 162–65.

[60] Ibid., pp. 166–75.

In sum, the lawmaking processes of the Labor Contract and the Consumers' Right Protection Regulations indicated a common characteristic of lawmaking politics in Chinese local legislatures. Executive agencies, legislative committees, and social organizations formed alliances or confronted each other at every stage of the lawmaking process, and the legislature played a coordinating role. The final versions of the two Regulations reflect these conflicts and compromises.

EVALUATING LEGISLATIVE DEVELOPMENT IN CHINA

The status of local people's congresses in the politics of lawmaking has been highly enhanced since the 1990s. In the Party-legislature relations, local legislatures have been able to enact most local laws without the prior review and approval of the Party. The Party has also shifted its means of exercising leadership from directly interfering with individual lawmaking cases to comprehensive oversight and coordinating the organs concerned. In legislative-executive relations, Chinese legislatures have begun to take the initiative in lawmaking processes since the late 1990s. The legislatures have made several attempts to institutionalize the lawmaking process in order to cope with "department protectionism." Changes to lawmaking guidelines and the resultant intensification of legislative plans, the diversification of drafters, the "opening-up" of the lawmaking process and the increased participation of social organizations and ordinary people, the introduction of the multi-step and unified deliberation systems, and the increase of legislative capability are representative examples of this.

In addition, legislation has become a significant political process against the backdrop of a changing political and socioeconomic environment. With a market economy having taken hold and the governance according to law policy widely implemented, laws have become a vital tool to rule the country. Government agencies and social organizations accordingly would be willing to participate in the lawmaking process so that they can extend their interests. In particular, the "opening-up" of the lawmaking process has provided social organizations and even ordinary people with a new opportunity to take part in the process. During lawmaking, government agencies, legislative committees, and social organizations frequently make alliances and confront each other in order to advance common goals. In this way, a new political arena in the Chinese party-state, a lawmaking politics, has emerged. As a result, Chinese policymaking processes have become more diversified, open, and consultative, and some important conflicts of interest among government agencies and social groups can be controlled and coordinated in this lawmaking politics.

Chinese local legislatures play two roles in lawmaking politics. They coordinate conflicts of interest among government agencies and social groups. Although legislature committees tend to represent the voices of certain executive agencies and social groups in the deliberation of draft laws, the final results reflect a series of compromises of conflicting opinions. In other words, there are no outright winners or losers in the lawmaking politics led by legislatures. The legislatures also represent various social groups' interests. Chinese legislatures' ongoing attempts to cope with "department protectionism" of government agencies which take powerful positions in society, and to check the initiatives of certain coalitions or forces in the lawmaking process, invalidate the legislatures' roles. This indicates that Chinese legislatures have begun to secure their own independent jurisdiction, different from the jurisdictions of the Party and governments.

Meanwhile, we should not overestimate the roles of legislature and social organizations, and the confrontational aspect of legislative actors in lawmaking processes. In a word, the relations between the legislative and the executive, from a comprehensive perspective, are cooperative and harmonious relative to those in legislative supervision, while social organizations' active participation in lawmaking tends to be limited to a few cases that are directly concerned with their critical interests. Significantly, the majority of enacted local laws deal with economic matters that require specific technical knowledge. And these cases do not contain so many sensitive issues that can induce interest conflicts between government agencies and legislative committees. In fact, legislature and government, under the leadership of the territorial Party in a province, have made concerted efforts to promulgate economic-related local laws in order to speed up regional economic development. In this sense, we cannot overestimate the distinguished roles of legislatures and social organizations in lawmaking politics.

At the same time, we should not neglect the evident constraints on laws and lawmaking politics in the Chinese party-state, notwithstanding their increasing significance. The actual significance of laws and lawmaking politics in China is still qualified. The Party and governments have various channels and measures to influence policymaking other than laws and lawmaking politics. Even in lawmaking politics per se, the Party and governments wield great authority. The Party, as previous analysis proves, has the final say on "important" and "sensitive" legal bills, and governments still take the initiative in agenda-setting and drafting. Finally, the making of laws and their implementation are often two different stories. Government agencies may not faithfully implement laws initiated by and reflecting the interests of legislatures and social organizations.[61]

Finally, an evaluation of legislative development in China is in order. A balanced view on the strengthening roles of the legislature is needed. Chinese legislatures, like representative bodies in other countries, fulfill four functions: legislation, supervision, representation, and regime-maintenance. To put it simply, the roles of Chinese legislatures have been unevenly strengthened: their lawmaking power has already been recognized as their own proper authority, and Chinese legislatures can exercise it in a stable fashion; and local legislatures, but not the NPC, have begun to exert substantive power in overseeing state organs while their roles are still very limited in representation. Therefore, we should not think of the strengthened lawmaking role of Chinese legislatures as the emergence of representative politics. In particular, caution in this regard is necessary given that the main functions of legislatures in liberal democracies have shifted from legislation to supervision and representation since the 1970s.

Chinese legislatures, however, can be considered to have successfully strengthened their lawmaking roles through institutionalization prior to liberalization.[62] Established powers' recognition of the lawmaking authority of legislatures, the intensification of legislatures' initiative in lawmaking processes, and the coordinating and representative roles of legislatures reflect this path of Chinese legislative development.

---

[61] Kevin O'Brien, "Hunting for political change," *China Journal*, No. 41 (1999), pp. 167–68.

[62] See O'Brien, *Reform without Liberalization*, pp. 3–8; Murray Scot Tanner, "The National People's Congress," in Merle Goldman and Roderick MacFarquhar (eds.), *The Paradox of China's Post-Mao Reforms* (Cambridge, MA: Harvard University Press, 1999), pp. 101–4, 125–28.

3

Supervising Governments and Development Strategies

Legislative supervision over governments, along with legislation, is one of the most important roles of Chinese local people's congresses. So after investigating the lawmaking role of Chinese legislatures, we need to analyze their supervision over governments in order to understand roles that they have actually played in local politics and political implications for the Chinese political system. This chapter addresses two research questions. The first is determining whether Chinese local legislatures have played a meaningful role in the arena of legislative supervision over governments, just as they do in the lawmaking arena. The second is finding out what kinds of development strategies they have employed to cope with resistance and obstacles from governments during the periods of supervision.

The chapter argues that Chinese local legislatures have chiefly used the support they gained from the CCP and cooperation with governments as their priority strategy, instead of confrontation, to overcome their lower political status. That is, as Kevin O'Brien explains it, local legislatures pursued a kind of "embeddedness" strategy to get clarified and expanded jurisdiction, and organizational capacity, in which they would be "entwined" with the CCP (subordination) rather than distanced from it (autonomy).[1] But after achieving most of these goals by the early 1990s, while firmly pursuing increased Party support, the legislatures have also begun to employ a confrontational approach to local

---

[1] Kevin O'Brien, "Chinese People's Congresses and legislative embeddedness: Understanding early organizational development," *Comparative Political Studies*, Vol. 27, No. 1 (April 1994), pp. 80–109.

governments. At the same time, local people's congresses have actively pioneered new supervisory measures with the intention of overcoming problematic legal and legislative obstacles. As a result, legislative supervision began to significantly influence governments and officials in the early 1990s. Therefore, Chinese local people's congresses, along with the CCP and governments, have become important political actors in local politics, even though they are not as influential as the last two.

This chapter focuses on county-level legislatures' supervision over governments, and two areas of supervision: examination of law enforcement (*zhifa jiancha*), and appraisal of government bureaus and officials (*pingyi*), which have been the most active and representative forms of legislative supervision since the early 1990s. In contrast to lawmaking, in which cooperation between political actors is prevalent, supervision frequently entails conflicts, because it involves controlling the power of governments and sometimes that of the Party. Analyzing these conflicts reveals the real status and role of local legislatures with respect to the Party and governments. Besides, compared with the NPC, which has concentrated on lawmaking, local legislatures have regarded supervision as their most important role since the early 1980s.[2] In particular, because county-level legislatures do not enjoy local legislative power, they have to concentrate on supervision. So focusing on the oversight activities of county-level legislatures is one of the best ways to examine legislative supervision at different levels (hereafter local legislatures are county-level unless otherwise indicated).

POWER RELATIONS AND DEVELOPMENT STRATEGIES

Chinese legislatures are regulated as "organs of state power" at each level, not just legislative organs, according to the Constitution. However, the real power relations between legislatures, the CCP, and governments seriously affect local legislatures' supervision over governments regardless of the formal regulations. And local legislatures have a less powerful political status than governments, not to mention the Party. To overcome difficulties caused by their weaker political position, they have adopted two strategies: gaining Party support and

---

[2] Quanguorenda changweihui bangongting (ed.), *Guojia quanli jiguande jiandu zhidu he jiandu gongzuo* (*The Supervisory Systems and Work of State Power Organs*) (Beijing: Zhongguo minzhu fazhi chubanshe, 1999), pp. 44–46; Yang Fengchun (ed.), *Zai shengji renda gongzuo gangweishang* (*On the Posts of Provincial People's Congresses*) (Beijing: Zhongguo minzhu fazhi chubanshe, 1996), pp. 378–79.

cooperating with governments. But with the accumulation of supervisory experiences and under encouraging Party policy in the 1990s, local legislatures have gradually employed a confrontational strategy against governments.

GAINING SUPPORT: LOCAL LEGISLATURES AND THE CCP

The success of Chinese local legislatures' supervision over governments relies heavily on gaining Party support. Local legislatures are almost impossible to conduct without this support in a party-state. Therefore, legislative leaders emphasize that they should stick to the principle of Party leadership during supervision.[3] For Chinese legislatures, adhering to this principle is not rhetoric, but a necessity, for two reasons.

First, local legislatures need to cope with the resistance of governments during supervision. Governments do not always agree to the requests of local legislatures. In extreme cases, they openly challenge legislatures' authority.[4] Two conditions allow governments to behave in this way. The political status of governments, as measured by the standing of their leaders in the Party hierarchy,[5] is much higher than that of local legislatures. According to a 1994 report, in sixty-one local legislatures surveyed, only 28 percent of chairpersons for local people's congresses served concurrently as (vice-)secretaries of Party committees.[6] Consequently, most legislative leaders had only limited influence on Party decision making since they attended Party standing committee

---

[3] Interview with leaders and staff of local legislatures: Tianjin and Shijiazhuang of Hebei, July and August 2000; Quanguorenda changweihui bangongting yanjiushi (ed.), *Difang renda shi zenyang xingshi zhiquande (How Local People's Congresses Exercise Their Power)* (Beijing: Zhongguo minzhu fazhi chubanshe, 1992), p. 296; Quanguorenda changweihui bangongting yanjiushi (ed.), *Difang renda jiandu gongzuo tansuo (An Exploration for the Supervisory Works of Local People's Congresses)* (Beijing: Zhongguo minzhu fazhi chubanshe, 1997), pp. 148–49, 231.

[4] Quanguorenda changweihui bangongting yanjiushi (ed.), *Woguo dangqian falü shishide wenti he duice (Problems and Countermeasures in Law Enforcement in China)* (Beijing: Zhongguo minzhu fazhi chubanshe, 1997), p. 105.

[5] In China, an institution's political status tends to be decided not by its legal regulation but by its leaders' position inside the Party hierarchy. Cai Dingjian, *Zhongguo renmin daibiao zhidu (People's Congress System in China)* (Revised edition) (Beijing: Falü chubanshe, 1998), p. 38.

[6] Quanguorenda changweihui bangongting yanjiushi (ed.), *Renmin daibiao dahui chengli sishi zhounian jinian wenji (Papers on Commemorating the 40th Anniversary of People's Congresses)* (Beijing: Zhongguo minzhu bazhi chubanshe, 1995), pp. 327–28.

meetings only as nonvoting members (*liexi*). In contrast, all government chiefs were Party deputy secretaries and usually ranked number two in command in the Party hierarchy. This situation has not yet changed, and the status of legislative leaders inside the Party, it is insisted, should be enhanced to a level at least equal to that of government chiefs.[7] So people say, "Legislatures supervise governments in the state, but governments supervise legislatures in the Party."[8] Also, most important government policies are decided in advance at Party meetings, and Party committees and governments sometimes jointly issue policies. Therefore, governments can reject the requests of local legislatures under the pretext that the Party decided and supported their policy.

Furthermore, local legislatures have to abide by the "request and report system" (*qingshi huibao zhidu*), as other state and major social organizations do. Local legislatures should report and wait for Party instructions before making such important decisions as dismissing leading officials during supervision.[9] In principle, local legislatures do not need the instructions because they are not subordinate to the Party. But Party groups (*dangzu*), which are formed in local people's congress standing committees and lead the work of legislatures, are directly subordinate to the Party and they must obey Party rules.

Taking these conditions into account, it is necessary and rational for local legislatures to endeavor to be entwined with the CCP rather than keep it at a distance. To this end, local legislatures always conduct supervision in accordance with Party policy. When the local Party committees urge governments to observe certain economic laws, local legislatures supervise governments to ensure that they implement these laws properly.[10] They also request the Party to take part in their supervision, by for instance asking Party leaders to attend appraisal conferences, or

---

[7] Some legislative leaders and staff consider that the recent power balance among the Party, legislature, and government of the Center is ideal: the General Secretary of the CCP (Jiang Zemin) was the "number one man," and the Chairman of the NPC Standing Committee (Li Peng), not the Premier of State Council (Zhu Rongji), was the "number two man." Interview with legislative leaders: Tianjin, March 2001.

[8] Hubeisheng Wuxueshi renda changweihui (ed.), *Xianxiang renda gongzuo yanjiu* (*A Study on the Works of County- and Township-level People's Congresses*) (Beijing: Zhongguo minzhu fazhi chubanshe, 1994), p. 24.

[9] Quanguorenda, *Problems and Countermeasures in Law Enforcement in China*, pp. 148–49, 160.

[10] Interview with legislative leaders and staff of local legislatures: Tianjin and Shijiazhuang of Hebei, July and August 2000; Bai Guangquan (ed.), *Kaichuang chengshi quji renda gongzuode xinjumian* (*Pioneering New Situation of Big City District People's Congresses*) (Beijing: Zhongguo minzhu fazhi chubanshe, 1997), pp. 78, 316–20.

asking them to act as heads of ad hoc supervisory groups.[11] Whenever they encounter difficulties caused by governments, local legislatures report and follow Party instructions instead of acting of their own volition. In this way, local legislatures save the face of the CCP and avoid confrontation with governments.[12]

During the 1990s, the attitude of the CCP toward legislatures changed. The Party came to consider legislative supervision as a useful means of checking and preventing corruption in governments. A decision issued by the CCP Central Committee in 1990 illustrates this point well. The Party decided to strengthen the supervisory functions of all state organs as well as Party apparatuses to control cadre corruption and restore people's confidence.[13] Thereafter, the provincial Party committees throughout the country held legislative work conferences to solidify the central policy in their regions. They usually emphasized two points: the Party committees at all levels should put legislative works on their agenda and fully support local legislatures to exert their power according to laws; and local legislatures should toe the Party line when improving legislative activities.[14] In addition, since the CCP launched the governance according to law policy in the early 1990s, which was formalized at the 15th Party Congress in 1997, local Party leaders have encouraged local legislatures to supervise officials more rigorously. As a

[11] Interview with legislative leaders and staff of local legislatures: Tianjin and Shijiazhuang of Hebei, July and August 2000; Bai, *Pioneering New Situation of Big City District People's Congresses*, p. 78; Quanguorenda, *An Exploration for the Supervisory Works*, p. 187.

[12] Bai, *Pioneering New Situation of Big City District People's Congresses*, p. 160; Chen Yaoliang (ed.), *Ruiyi jinqude xianji renda gongzuo* (*Resolute Progress of the Works of County-level People's Congresses*) (Beijing: Zhongguo minzhu fazhi chubanshe, 1997), p. 227.

[13] "Zhonggong zhongyang guanyu jiaqiang dang tong renmin qunzhong lianxide jueding" (A decision of the CCP Central Committee on strengthening the connection between the Party and mass), Zhonggong zhongyang wenxian yanjiushi (ed.), *Shisanda yilai zhongyao wenxian xuanbian (zhong)* (*Selections of Important Documents since the 13th Party Congress*) (Vol.2) (Beijing: Renmin chubanshe, 1991), p. 935.

[14] Li Bojun, "Ge sheng zizhiqu zhixiashi dangwei zhaokai renda gongzuohuide qingkuang" (The situations of people's congress work conferences held by provincial Party committees), *Zhongguo renda*, No. 3 (February 2000), pp. 19–20; Tianjinshi difangzhi bianxiu weiyuanhui (ed.), *Tianjin tongzhi: zhengquan zhi renmin daibiao dahui juan* (*Overall Annals of Tianjin: Regime Annals People's Congress Volume*) (Tianjin: Tianjin shehui kexueyuan chubanshe, 1997), pp. 482–83.

result, some Party committees have taken pride in "supporting" legislatures to exercise their powers according to pertinent laws.[15]

At the same time, local legislatures have gained more autonomy with respect to the CCP. Except for important items, they can decide and handle their own matters without prior Party approval. When they need Party approval and support, they actively strive to get them, rather than passively waiting to receive them. In this regard, the status and autonomy of local legislatures have been markedly strengthened since the 1990s.[16]

COOPERATION: LOCAL LEGISLATURES AND GOVERNMENTS

According to the Chinese Constitution and pertinent laws, local governments should function as the executive branches of local legislatures. In other words, local governments are legally responsible to local legislatures and subject to legislative supervision. At the same time, because local legislatures and governments are state organs that carry out Party policy, they should complement each other and cooperate on an equal footing.[17] The legislative-executive relations are thus considered a division of labor, not a separation of powers, from this point of view. Of these two potentially contradictory regulations, the actual political status and capacities of local legislatures and governments make the second set of relations surpass the first, so local legislatures are forced to use cooperation rather than confrontation as their priority strategy with governments.

As mentioned earlier, since government leaders are well represented in the Party hierarchy, they play a decisive role in whether the Party supports legislative supervision over governments. Therefore, local legislatures should consider the position of governments if they want to gain Party support. If local people's congresses' chairpersons are

[15] "Liangou xianwei: womenshi ruhe zhichi renda jiqi changweihui yifa xingshi zhiquande" (Liangou county Party committee: how we support people's congress and its standing committee to use their power according to the law), *Zhongguo renda xinwen* (*News of Chinese People's Congresses*), September 16, 2000 (available at http://zgrdxw.peopledaily.com.cn/gb/paper7/2/class000700005/hwz3003.htm).
[16] Interview with leaders and staff of local legislatures: Tianjin and Shijiazhuang of Hebei, July and August 2000.
[17] Hangzhoushi renda (ed.), *Zhongxin chengshi renda gongzuode xinjinzhan* (*New Developments in the Works of Core City People's Congresses*) (Beijing: Zhongguo minzhu fazhi chubanshe, 1997), pp. 191, 251.

(vice-)secretaries of Party committees, as they increasingly are in some regions, local legislatures can more easily make governments accept their supervision.[18]

In addition, governments have a decisive advantage over legislatures in terms of capacity. Local legislatures began to establish standing committees and bureaucratic systems in the early 1980s, and the number of standing committee members and staffers increased thereafter.[19] But they are not sufficiently well equipped to conduct supervision properly. The core members of standing committees are still relatively old, for they are mostly transferred from Party and government leadership positions just before retirement.[20] Also, only about 30 percent of standing committee members serve on a full-time basis.[21] There are problems with the offices and staff as well. In general, local legislatures have about three offices, three to five work committees (*gongzuo weiyuanhui*),[22] and fifteen to thirty-five permanent staff members.[23] These are not large enough to monitor the work

---

[18] Interview with legislative leaders and staff: Tianjin, March 2001.

[19] Interview with leaders and staff of local legislatures, Tianjin and Shijiazhuang of Hebei, July and August 2000; Jinniuqu rendazhi biancan weiyuanhui (ed.), *Chengdushi Jinniuqu rendazhi* (*Gazette of Jinniu District People's Congress in Chengdu City*) (Chengdu: Sichuan renmin chubanshe, 1995), pp. 163–74.

[20] A local people's congress standing committee is composed of three groups. The core group of chairperson and vice-chairpersons is transferred from the Party committee and government as usual. The second group are representatives of social classes (such as workers, peasants, and intellectuals). The third comes from mass organizations (trade unions, women's federations, and communist youth leagues). The last two groups are better educated and younger than before, but most of them are part-timers.

[21] Interview with leaders and staff of local legislatures: Tianjin and Shijiazhuang of Hebei, July and August 2000; Guangdongsheng renda zhidu yanjiuhui (ed.), *Yifa zhishengde tantao* (*An Inquiry into the Governance of Province According to the Law*) (Beijing: Zhongguo minzhu fazhi chubanshe, 1997), pp. 164–65; Hubeisheng Wuxueshi, *A Study on the Works of County- and Township-level People's Congresses*, p. 166.

[22] Offices include general office (*bangongshi*), research office (*diaoyanshi*), and deputy liaison office (*daibiao lianluoshi*). Work committees are interior and legal affairs (*neiwu sifa*); financial and economic affairs (*caizheng jingji*); education, science, culture, and public health (*jiaowei kexue wenhua weisheng*); city construction and management (*chengjian chengguan*); and rural areas (*nongcun*). Interview with leaders and staff of local legislatures: Tianjin and Shijiazhuang of Hebei, July and August 2000.

[23] Zhuzhoushi rendazhi biancan weiyuanhui (ed.), *Zhuzhoushi rendazhi* (*Gazette of Zhuzhou City People's Congress*) (Changsha: Hunan chubanshe, 1991), p. 191; Chuanzhoushi Lichengqu rendazhi biancan weiyuanhui (ed.), *Chuanzhoushi Lichengqu rendazhi* (*Gazette of Licheng District People's Congress in Chuanzhou City*) (Beijing: Zhongguo minzhu fazhi chubanshe, 1994), p. 173.

of a local government that has as many as fifty to sixty bureaus and 700–1,000 officials.[24]

Finally, local legislatures have financial problems. They have the right to review draft budgets and oversee the implementation governments. But legislature budgets are not independent of those of governments. Government financial bureaus – not local legislatures – manage and control legislature expenditures. Therefore, local legislatures have to get approval from governments to pay for their work. This financial dependency discourages local legislatures from resolutely supervising governments.[25] To solve this problem, for example, the Weishi County Party Committee in Henan Province required the government to increase and guarantee legislature expenditures as a measure to strengthen the legislature's capacity in 2000.[26]

These factors have forced local legislatures to use a cooperation strategy. For example, local legislatures discuss schedules and agendas with governments before implementing supervision, to avoid unnecessary conflicts. They also try to resolve problems in advance. For instance, the financial and economic committees (*caijingwei*) of legislatures usually take part in or observe government drafting of budgets. Local legislatures give their opinions, and differences of opinion between the two institutions are usually resolved through this process before draft budgets are presented at legislatures' plenary sessions.[27] Finally, local legislatures sometimes conduct joint oversight with governments. During supervision, government officials explain their behavior to legislators and address small issues on the spot as they arise.[28] While it may seem strange that the objects of supervision also act as supervisors, this practice persists in many areas.[29]

[24] Niao Jie (ed.), *Zhongguo zhengfu yu jigou gaige (shang)* (*Chinese Government and Structural Reform*) (Vol.1) (Beijing: Guojia xingzheng xueyuan chubanshe, 1998), p. 1051.

[25] Interview with legislative leaders and staff: Tianjin, March 2001; Zhou Wenxian (ed.), *Difang renda gongzuo lilun yu shiwu* (*Theory and Practice of the Works of Local People's Congresses*) (Beijing: Zhongguo minzhu fazhi chubanshe, 2000), pp. 385–86.

[26] "Weishi xianwei duofangwei jiaqiang renda jianshe" (Party committee of Weishi County takes various actions to strengthen people's congress construction), *Zhongguo renda xinwen*, February 21, 2001 (available at http://zgrdxw.peopledaily.com.cn/gb/paper7/7/class00070005/hwz91725.htm).

[27] Interview with leaders and staff of local legislatures: Tianjin and Shijiazhuang of Hebei, July and August 2000.

[28] Ibid.

[29] Interview with leaders and staff: Tianjin and Shijiazhuang of Hebei, July and August 2000; Quanguorenda, *Papers on Commemorating the 40th Anniversary of People's*

In addition, local legislatures and governments use various official and unofficial systems (*lianxi zhidu*) to communicate with each other.[30] But there have been important changes in legislative-executive relations since the early 1990s, especially after the governance according to law policy, which emphasizes that government, as an executive branch of legislature, should accept legislative supervision in compliance with laws. In a word, local legislatures, not governments, have begun to take the initiative in these relations. They can require governments to convene joint meetings when necessary. Government officials willingly attend these meetings and prepare the required materials. Government leaders usually instruct agencies and officials to execute the requirements of legislatures faithfully and to accept supervision calmly.[31] Within these changed relations, local legislatures have dared to dismiss leading officials during supervision, and to employ stronger supervisory measures like interpellation (this is discussed in more detail below). This reveals that local legislatures have gradually used confrontation in conjunction with cooperation as they have become more firmly embedded in the Chinese political system.

PIONEERING NEW SUPERVISORY MEASURES

Local legislatures conduct supervision in the legal and legislative systems. But due to problems with these systems, they have been unable to fulfill their delegated duties. Therefore, at the same time as local legislatures have tried to activate supervisory measures provided by the Constitution and pertinent laws, they have had to pioneer "new forms" of strong measures that are not described in laws. These new measures have become their main methods for supervising governments since the early 1990s.

The Chinese Constitution and Local Organic Law provide local legislatures with supervisory measures, including hearing and reviewing government work reports, socioeconomic development plans, and draft budgets, questions and interpellation (*zhixun*), special investigative commissions, and inspection (*shicha*).[32] From a purely legal

---

Congresses, pp. 375–76; Quanguorenda, *An Exploration for the Supervisory Works*, p. 121.

[30] Ibid.

[31] Ibid.

[32] Sun Weiben (ed.), *Renda gongzuo shouce* (*Handbook for the Works of People's Congresses*) (Beijing: Zhongguo minzhu fazhi chubanshe, 1997), pp. 164–71; Zhang

viewpoint, Chinese legislatures enjoy as many supervisory methods as their counterparts in liberal democracies. But these measures have two serious weaknesses.

First, these measures exceed the present capacities of local legislatures. Most of them are used in annual plenary sessions, which last three to five days, and at bimonthly local people's congress standing committee meetings, which last one to two days. Local legislatures can thus use them for a total of fewer than twenty days a year. Also, deputies to local people's congresses need specialized knowledge to examine government work reports and draft budgets, as well as sufficient time to investigate certain matters. But most deputies lack knowledge and time because they are amateurs (*jianzhi daibiao*). As stated previously, local people's congress standing committee members and staff are better equipped than deputies, but they do not have sufficient capacities either, especially in financial and economic areas.

Besides, the laws concerning these measures were too ambiguous for local legislatures to use, so the tools were less effective than intended. For example, it was not clear who would be responsible if the work reports of state organs were not ratified in legislature meetings. When the Shenyang People's Congress in Liaoning Province did not ratify the annual work report of the Intermediate Court in February 2001, no one knew which procedures to follow and who was responsible.[33] In a similar way, the Baoshan City People's Congress in Yunnan Province could not punish officials when it rejected a government work report on implementing suggestions from legislature deputies in February 2001.[34] For this reason, NPC deputies had petitioned their leaders to enact a supervision law since the mid-1980s, but the Supervisory Law was promulgated only in August 2006, more than two decades after the need for legislation was raised. As an emergency action, most provincial local legislatures

Wei, *Renda jiandu zhineng yanjiu* (*A Study on the Supervisory Function of People's Congresses*) (Beijing: Zhongguo falü chubanshe, 1996), pp. 14–21.

[33] "Shenyang Zhongji Fayuan baogao weihuo shirenda tongguo" (A work report of Shenyang Intermediate Court didn't pass Municipal People's Congress), *Zhongguo renda xinwen*, February 15, 2001 (available at http://zgrdxw.peopledaily.com.cn/gb/paper6/6/class000600002/hwz87453.htm); "Baogao weihuo renda tongguo zenmeban" (If a work report doesn't pass people's congress, what's to be done), *Zhongguo renda xinwen*, March 27, 2001 (available at http://zgrdxw.peopledaily.com.cn/gb/paper6/7/class000600002/hwz107837.htm).

[34] "Yunnan Baoshanshi zhengfu yi xiang baogao weihuo shi renda changweihui tongguo" (A report of Baoshan City Government didn't pass City People's Congress Standing Committee), *Zhongguo renda xinwen*, February 24, 2001 (available at http://zgrdxw.peopledaily.com.cn /gb/paper7/7/ class000700001/hwz91720.htm).

enacted supervisory regulations in the 1990s.[35] But local laws did not solve the problems either, because they lack the legal authority that only the NPC and its Standing Committee can exercise, and because they are so ambiguous that local legislatures cannot punish governments.

Instead of grumbling about problematic legislative and legal systems, local legislatures have worked to develop new supervisory measures since the early 1980s, without either direction from the NPC or concrete legal regulations. This is the most important characteristic of legislative supervision. So people say, "Legislatures do not go along a highway but a path."[36] These new measures include examination, appraisal, the responsibility system of department law enforcement (*bumen zhifa zerenzhi*), law supervision papers (*falü jiandushu*), and individual case supervision (*gean jiandu*).

Not all local legislatures have tried to explore new supervisory measures, however. There are regional disparities in adopting new measures, and local legislatures can be classified into three categories in terms of their commitment to adopting new measures. The first is "pioneer." The role of both legislature and Party leaders is the most important factor in the adoption of new measures. Pioneering can entail political risks because of the lack of legal guarantees, so both resolute legislative leaders and accompanying Party support are necessary. A former vice-chairman of the Shanxi Provincial People's Congress summed up their experiences of introducing appraisal by commenting at a 1992 legislative work conference that "appraisal is not the work of legislatures, but both Party committee and legislatures."[37] So there are few pioneers. The second category is the "bandwagoner," who emulates other local legislatures only after being assured that carrying out new measures is politically safe. Most local legislatures belong to this category. Bandwagoners frequently become more active legislatures as they accumulate experience. The third category is "inactive," which does not try to use new measures for fear of legal and political problems. Few local legislatures fell into this category in the 1990s.[38]

---

[35] Quanguorenda changweihui bangongting yanjiushi (ed.), *Difang renda 2onian (Twenty Years of Local People's Congresses)* (Beijing: Zhongguo minzhu fazhi chubanshe, 2000), p. 88.

[36] Zhou Wenxian, *Theory and Practice of the Works of Local Legislatures*, pp. 398–403.

[37] Quanguorenda neiwu sifa weiyuanhui sifashi (ed.), *Shehuizhuyi minzhu fazhi jianshede youyi tansuo (A Beneficial Exploration of Socialist Democratic and Legal System Construction)* (Beijing: Zhongguo minzhu fazhi chubanshe, 1993), p. 58.

[38] Quanguorenda, *Problems and Countermeasures in Law Enforcement in China*, p. 255.

As local legislatures have received more political support from the CCP, and accumulated supervisory experiences and self-confidence through new measures, they have also dared to activate the strong weapons (e.g., interpellation, special investigative commissions, and veto of work reports) that pertinent laws provide and that can be exercised by deputies only in plenary sessions or standing committee meetings. For example, according to a 1994 report, of sixty-one local legislatures surveyed, 20 percent (twelve local legislatures) supervised governments twenty-five times in total by use of interpellation for three years from 1991 to 1993. And 12 percent (seven local legislatures) also formed special investigative commissions a total of sixty-seven times to investigate important matters during the same period.[39] By the late 1990s, even provincial local people's congresses began to employ interpellation for overseeing governments: Hunan Province in 1998, Sichuan Province in 1996 (to the Higher Court) and 1999, Henan Province in 1999, and Hainan and Guangdong Provinces in 2000, respectively.[40]

In addition, local legislatures have resolutely vetoed the work reports of state organs since the late 1990s whenever they believe these organizations did not make best efforts to do works or did not listen to their requests faithfully. Apart from the above-mentioned cases of Shenyang and Baoshan cities, the People's Congresses of Chongqing, Wuhan, and Shiyan cities in Hubei Province did not approve government work reports in 1999: a report on implementing suggestions of legislative members (Chongqing), the situation of implementing a re-employment project (Wuhan), and settling the problems of misappropriation of a poverty relief fund (Shiyan).[41] In these ways, local legislatures sometimes do

---

[39] Ibid., pp. 330–31.

[40] "Sichuan renda daibiao zhixun shebaoju" (Deputies to the Sichuan Provincial People's Congress took an interpellation to Social Insurance Bureau), *Renmin zhi you* (*People's Friend*), No. 3 and 4 (April 1999), p. 55; Chu Yang, "Weiyuan nu ti zhixunan" (Members angrily introduced an interpellation bill), *Renmin zhi you*, No. 3 and 4 (April 1999), pp. 20–22; Wang Caiwei, "Yipian kaikuo er qinglangde tiankong: jiqi zhixunan jishi" (Open and clear sky: Records on several interpellation cases), *Renmin zhengtan* (*People's Political Forum*), No. 6 (June 2001), pp. 10–13; Ren Tianyang and Wang Diao, "Guangdongsheng renda daibiao zhixun sheng huanbaoju shimo" (The whole story on the interpellation to the Environmental Protection Bureau of government by deputies to Guangdong Provincial People's Congress), *Renda yanjiu* (*Studies on People's Congresses*), No. 4 (April 2000) (available at http://www.rdyj.com. cn/2000/rdqk-4–7.html). In 1989, Hunan Provincial People's Congress introduced an interpellation bill to provincial government, but it was a rare case at that time.

[41] Yun Wanbang, "Liangge xiao gushi, yipian da wenzhang" (Two small stories and one big essay), *Zhongguo renda*, No. 16 (August 2000), pp. 33–34; "Wuhanshi renda

not hesitate to confront governments, even though they more frequently cooperate with governments.

LEGISLATIVE SUPERVISION OF THE GOVERNMENT IN THE 1990S

Examination and appraisal are the most important and typical types of supervision that local legislatures have conducted nationwide since the early 1990s. They have some problems, but they have real supervisory effects in controlling government officials.

EXAMINATION OF LAW ENFORCEMENT

Examination shows local legislatures whether government officials faithfully enforce laws and central policies. It has two main aims: to understand law enforcement conditions and identify problems, and to urge governments to address these problems.[42] Some local legislatures carried out examination in the early 1980s, and most used it by the early 1990s under the encouragement of the CCP.[43] The NPC also enacted a detailed regulation for examination in 1993 and declared that it regarded examination to be as important a duty as lawmaking. Local legislatures also put it at the top of their agendas.[44]

---

changweihui foujue zhengfu yifen gongzuo baogao" (Wuhan Municipal People's Congress Standing Committee vetoed a government work report), *Jilin renda gongzuo (Works of People's Congresses in Jilin)*, No. 4 (April 1999), p. 26; Sun Tianfu, "Shiyanshi renda changweihui yanshen fupin gongzuo baogao" (Shiyan City People's Congress Standing Committee strictly deliberated a report of poverty relief work), *Zhongguo renda*, No. 4 (February 2000), pp. 13–14.

[42] "Quanguorenda changweihui guanyu jiaqiang dui falü shishi qingkuang jiancha jiandude ruogan guiding (1993)" (The NPC Standing Committee's several regulations on strengthening the examination of law enforcement), *Renda gongzuo tongxun*, No. 13 (July 1994), p. 5.

[43] Quanguorenda, *How Local People's Congresses Exercise Their Power*, pp. 156–58; Chen Yong, "Guanyu falü zhixing jiandude jige wenti" (On the problems of the examination of law enforcement), *Renda gongzuo tongxun*, No. 2 (January 1994), p. 30; Quanguorenda, *The Supervisory System and Works of State Power Organs*, pp. 44–46.

[44] "Tian Jiyun fu weiyuanzhang zai Quanguorenda changweihui mishuzhang huiyi shangde jianghua" (An address of the Vice-Chairman of Tian Jiyun at the NPC Standing Committee secretaries' meeting), *Renda gongzuo tongxun*, No. 4 (February 1997), p. 6; Liu Fusheng, "Renqing xingshi, mingque renwu, nuli kaichuang difang renda gongzuode xinjumian" (Clearly understanding situations and duties, endeavoring to open new prospect of the works of local legislatures), *Renda gongzuo tongxun*, No. 4 (January 1997), p. 9.

Examination generally involves three steps: preparation, investigation, and addressing problems. At the close of an annual plenary session of a local legislature, the standing committee makes a plan and organizes supervisory groups composed of its members and ordinary deputies. Party policy usually determines which laws will be supervised. After collecting materials and listening to comprehensive reports from government officials, supervisory groups conduct field research for up to several months, by visiting government bureaus and interviewing residents. Afterward, the groups submit inspection reports to the standing committee. Finally, the standing committee notifies the government of the results and requires it to address problems and to report the results within a certain period. When necessary, it reassembles supervisory groups and conducts an examination to verify that the government has corrected problems as reported.[45]

The supervisory effect of examination can be evaluated from two aspects of its publicized aims: one is to oversee the enforcement of laws and to urge governments to execute laws; the other is to urge them to correct problems. Local legislatures can check how laws are being implemented and urge government officials to implement them by use of several tactics. For instance, local legislatures at various levels in a province simultaneously conduct examination for certain designated laws under the leadership of the provincial legislature. When the Henan Provincial People's Congress conducted examination in 1992 to determine whether governments had implemented agriculture-related laws and central policies properly, 77 percent of county-level legislatures and 91 percent of township-level legislatures participated in this examination, mobilizing some 70,000 deputies at all levels.[46] Other regions did the same.[47] Most local legislatures also conduct examination for certain laws (e.g., the Compulsory Education Law and Environment Protection Law) for several consecutive years in order to repeatedly urge governments to implement the laws.

---

[45] Quanguorenda, *How Local People's Congresses Exercise Their Power*, pp. 284–85; Sun Weiben, *Handbook for the Works of People's Congresses*, p. 165.

[46] Quanguorenda, *Papers on Commemorating the 40th Anniversary of People's Congresses*, p. 239.

[47] Quanguorenda changweihui bangongting yanjiushi (ed.), *Difang renda xingshi zhiquan shilie xuanbian* (*Selected Cases on Local People's Congresses Exercising Their Power*) (Beijing: Zhongguo minzhu fazhi chubanshe, 1996), pp. 159–63; Yang, *On the Posts of Provincial People's Congresses*, pp. 48–49, 104, 197, 290.

Local legislatures cannot force government officials to correct problems faithfully in many cases, however. A 1994 report, based on the investigation of examination executive situations in Anhui Province, said that governments faithfully corrected only about 30 percent of the problems identified.[48] Other local legislatures experienced similar problems.[49] Officials were usually willing to address visible and minor issues immediately, but not complex ones. For instance, when Dongcheng District People's Congress in Beijing required the district government to devote more funds to education in accordance with the Compulsory Education Law in 1987, the district government had to fulfill the request, for it was a clear violation of the law.[50] But peasant problems are different. Most local legislatures repeatedly conducted examination into the implementation of the Agriculture Law and related central policies in the 1990s. But the excessive burdens on peasants have not yet been lifted, even though governments took some action to relieve these burdens whenever local legislatures raised the issue. In a similar fashion, governments only took action to implement the Environment Law and related policies when local legislatures urged them to do so.

Local legislatures have difficulties in forcing government officials to correct these complicated problems through examination. As mentioned above, local legislatures usually occupy lower political status than governments in the Party hierarchy. To faithfully carry out laws and central policies that local legislatures demand, governments often have to find extra money or adjust spending priorities. But in existing power relations, local legislatures do not have enough power to force both the Party and governments to adjust their priorities. At the same time, governments are adept at escaping criticism about poor policy implementation. They concentrate a large part of their budgets on industrial projects to follow Party policy about developing regional economies. This sometimes means sacrificing investment in the environment and agriculture, resulting in complaints from local legislatures and the public. Therefore, local legislatures cannot force governments to correct problems through examination without an improved overall system of policy implementation.[51]

[48] Quanguorenda, *An Exploration for the Supervisory Works*, pp. 119, 123.
[49] Quanguorenda, *The Supervisory System and Works of State Power Organs*, pp. 81, 88; Quanguorenda, *An Exploration for the Supervisory Works*, p. 99.
[50] Quanguorenda, *How Local People's Congresses Exercise Their Power*, pp. 171–72.
[51] Interview with legislative leaders and staff: Tianjin, March 2001; Quanguorenda, *Problems and Countermeasures in Law Enforcement in China*, pp. 60–64, 85–89;

Examination also has some problems in terms of procedure. Local legislatures do not officially have the right to treat problems directly, only to make suggestions. That is, examination per se carries no legally binding force because suggestions are not orders.[52] Besides, local legislatures conducted examination so often that they could not execute it properly. Most local legislatures conducted examination about five to ten times annually up until the mid-1990s, to follow the requests from higher authorities and to show that they were doing something.[53] But they could not fulfill these duties properly.

Local legislatures take some action to enhance the supervisory effects of examination. For example, in Guangdong and Hubei Provinces, some local legislatures have used law supervision papers since the late 1980s: the standing committee, after examination, issues supervision papers to a government, clearly stating specific problems to be corrected, bureaus to implement, and deadlines to be met. Upon receiving the paper, the bureaus should address the problems without reservation; otherwise, the appropriate officials should take legal responsibility.[54] Many local legislatures also connect examination with appraisal of officials. Local legislatures consider whether governments implement their suggestions as a criterion of appraisal. As a result, officials cannot neglect a legislature's suggestions and supervisory effects of examination are enhanced, as discussed below.

In sum, local legislatures can check and urge governments to execute laws and central policies through examination. They can also sometimes force governments to correct the problems identified during examination.

APPRAISAL OF GOVERNMENT AGENCIES AND OFFICIALS

Local legislatures use appraisal to supervise the performance of government bureaus and officials. The terms and procedures of appraisal differ from place to place, but there are two main types: self-reporting of

---

Guangdongsheng, *An Inquiry into the Governance of Province According to Law*, pp. 89–91.

[52] Quanguorenda, *The Supervisory System and Works of State Power Organs*, pp. 8, 81, 88.

[53] Quanguorenda, *Problems and Countermeasures in Law Enforcement in China*, p. 355.

[54] Quanguorenda, *The Supervisory System and Works of State Power Organs*, p. 45; Quanguorenda, *An Exploration for the Supervisory Works*, pp. 340–51.

performance appraisal (*shuzhi pingyi*) and deputies' appraisal (*daibiao pingyi*). Local people's congress standing committees use the first type to examine leading officials elected or appointed by the legislatures. Legislature deputies mainly use the second to oversee the conduct of government bureaus.[55] Some local legislatures started appraisal in the early 1980s and it extended nationwide after a former vice-chairman of the NPC Standing Committee, Peng Chong, publicly approved it in 1992. Now most local legislatures conduct it. According to one 1995 report, all local legislatures in Hebei and Shaanxi Provinces used appraisal; in Zhejiang Province, the figure was 88 percent.[56]

Appraisal focuses on three aspects: first, how faithfully government bureaus and officials implement laws and central policies; second, how honestly and sincerely officials work; and third, how faithfully they implement the legislature's suggestions.[57] This shows that appraisal, like examination, is carefully set to target certain aims. The first two aspects can meet the Party's expectation by helping address poor policy implementation in localities and anti-corruption policies. The third can satisfy local legislatures' desire by strengthening their status with regard to governments.

Appraisal usually has four steps: preparation, investigation, appraisal, and execution. A local people's congress standing committee makes a plan and assembles an appraisal group composed of its members and ordinary deputies. The group conducts investigations for several months by visiting relevant officials and interviewing residents. It then submits an appraisal report to the standing committee. At the appraisal stage, the standing committee convenes appraisal conferences, which Party and government top leaders attend. The agendas of the conferences proceed as follows: officials' self-evaluation report, questions and answers, the appraisal group's comments, and final evaluation of performance. In some regions, local legislatures put appraisal to a secret vote and release the voting results. After the conferences, the standing committee

[55] Sun Weiben, *Handbook for the Works of People's Congresses*, pp. 167–68; Meng Liankun, "Renzhen zongjie jingyan, tuidong pingyi gongzuo jiankang kaizhan" (Sincerely summarizing experiences, promoting the works of appraisal healthily), *Renda gongzuo tongxun*, No. 24 (December 1995), pp. 9–12; Yun Wanbang, "Shilun renda daibiaode pingyi gongzuo" (On Appraisal works of legislative deputies), *Renda gongzuo tongxun*, No. 13 (July 1994), pp. 27–32.
[56] Quanguorenda, *The Supervisory System and Works of State Power Organs*, p. 239; Quanguorenda, *An Exploration for the Supervisory Works*, p. 207.
[57] Quanguorenda, *The Supervisory System and Works of State Power Organs*, pp. 217, 225–26; Yun Wanbang, "On Appraisal works of legislative deputies," p. 28.

reports the result to the Party committee and takes action. If a majority of appraisal members do not approve the officials supervised, the standing committee punishes them severely, for instance by dismissing them. If officials commit trivial mistakes, the committee advises them to address these mistakes and requires them to report the results within a certain time frame.[58]

The supervisory effects of appraisal are much greater than examination of law enforcement.[59] Several factors make this possible. Most important, appraisal is closely connected with the system of Party cadre management. The results of appraisal are reported to Party committees, who use them as important materials for future personnel transfers, and are sometimes recorded in personnel files (*dang'an*).[60] Some Party committees send leading cadres in organization departments to participate in legislative appraisal.[61] In this case, local legislatures and the Party conduct appraisal together. Negative appraisals can thus fatally affect officials' career prospects, even though they are not discharged from office immediately.

In addition, appraisal has legally binding force; local legislatures can dismiss leading officials based on the supervisory results. Officials were actually dismissed from office after appraisal in the 1990s. For instance, the Yiliang County People's Congress in Yunnan Province discharged the director of the Forestry Bureau in 1994. The director received only one vote of "worked well," thirty-three votes of "worked badly," and

---

[58] Quanguorenda, *The Supervisory System and Works of State Power Organs*, pp. 226–28, 243–45; Sun Weiben, *Handbook for the Works of People's Congresses*, pp. 166–68; Yun Wanbang, "On Appraisal works of legislative deputies," pp. 28–29; Hangzhoushi renda, *New Developments in the Works of Core City People's Congresses*, p. 74.

[59] Interview with leaders and staff of local legislatures: Tianjin and Shijiazhuang of Hebei, July and August 2000; Tian Jiwun, "Fahui renda jiandu zuoyong, cuijin minzhi fazhi jianshe" (Displaying the supervisory role of people's congresses, promoting the construction of democracy and legal system), *Renda gongzuo tongxun*, No. 12 (June 1995), p. 3; Men, "Sincerely summarizing experiences," pp. 7–8; Yun Wanbang, "On Appraisal works of legislative deputies," pp. 30–31; Quanguorenda, *The Supervisory System and Works of State Power Organs*, pp. 245–47; Yang, *On the Posts of Provincial People's Congresses*, pp. 433–34.

[60] Interview with leaders and staff: Tianjin and Shijiazhuang of Hebei, July and August 2000; Quanguorenda, *The Supervisory System and Works of State Power Organs*, pp. 228–29; Quanguorenda, *An Exploration for the Supervisory Works*, pp. 217–18, 255.

[61] "Tengchong shixing renda pingyi yu dangwei kaocha xiang jiehe" (Tengchong County put together the appraisal work of people's congress and cadres investigation of Party committee), *Zhongguo renda xinwen*, March 1, 2000 (available at http://www.peopledaily.com.cn/zgrdxw/news/200003/01/30107.html).

seventeen votes of "worked average" in secret voting. The Xiacheng District People's Congress in Hangzhou City discharged the director of the Culture Bureau after appraisal in 1993. The Pan'an and Tiantai County People's Congresses in Zhejiang Province also dismissed the directors of the Grain and Tourism Bureaus in 1993 and 1994, respectively.[62] Mayang County People's Congress in Hunan Province appraised ten leading officials in 2000 and dismissed two directors of the Forestry and Water & Electricity Bureaus.[63] Local legislatures, of course, should gain prior consent from Party committees before dismissing officials.

Finally, by targeting certain government bureaus or officials, not laws and policies, the procedure of appraisal differs from examination. Officials cannot escape responsibility if they carry out their duties in substandard fashion. In contrast, examination targets certain laws and policies; officials can shift responsibility back and forth. And local legislatures usually select five to ten objects for annual appraisal so that they can supervise most officials within a five-year term of office.[64] So, even officials who are not currently being supervised should follow the requests of local legislatures because their turn will come soon. Examination usually concentrates on bureaus related to economic matters and to hot issues about which the public files complaints, like education and pollution. Consequently, other bureaus can avoid examination if they perform their duties without committing any serious errors.

There are still problems in appraisal. Because local legislatures occupy lower political status, conflicts can occur if they attempt to dismiss leading officials without strong Party support.[65] For example, a county Party committee in Yunnan Province reassigned an official dismissed by a legislature to another position.[66] There are also problems in terms of procedure. Local legislatures generally laud the achievements of government bureaus and officials, rather than criticize them. In more infrequent but serious cases, governments ask local legislatures to conduct appraisal to

[62] Quanguorenda, *The Supervisory System and Works of State Power Organs*, pp. 232–33; Chen, *Resolute Progress of the Works of County-level People's Congresses*, p. 221; Quanguorenda, *Selected Cases on Local People's Congresses Exercising Their Power*, p. 300.

[63] "Xingshi shenshengde zhiquan" (Exercising a sacred power), *Zhongguo renda xinwen*, February 28, 2001 (available at http://zgrdxw.peopledaily.com.cn/gb/paper7/7/class000700004/hwz93804.htm).

[64] Interview with leaders and staff of local legislatures: Tianjin and Shijiazhuang of Hebei, July and August 2000.

[65] Quanguorenda, *Twenty Years of Local People's Congresses*, pp. 89–90.

[66] Quanguorenda, *Problems and Countermeasures in Law Enforcement in China*, p. 294.

publicize their achievements.[67] In these cases, appraisal is no more than a political stunt.

In sum, legislative supervision has exerted real effects to control governments and officials since the early 1990s, and as a result, local legislatures have become important players in local politics. For this reason, some deputies to the NPC were able to criticize the NPC Standing Committee for not supervising the State Council as thoroughly as local legislatures supervised local governments.[68] In addition, people have visited local legislatures and their deputies more frequently to express their complaints and demands.[69]

IMPLICATIONS FOR LEGISLATIVE DEVELOPMENT IN CHINA

When local people's congresses were reorganized around 1979, occupying a political space in an already crowded power structure was a challenging task. Because of their lower political status, the legislatures were vulnerable to the encroachment of the Party and governments. Problematic legal and legislative systems were not able to provide local legislatures with appropriate institutional guarantees necessary to face governments. Poor organizational capacity and weak popular support also added to the problems.

In these conditions, it was dangerous as well as unrealistic for local legislatures to pursue only autonomy by confronting the established powers. Instead, local legislatures have adopted gaining the support of the CCP and cooperating with governments as their priority strategy. In retrospect, as this chapter showed, this strategy has been successful: legislative supervision exerts real influence on the control of government bureaus and officials, and accordingly, legislatures have emerged as a new political power in local politics. This shows that "embeddedness" is not merely expedient but also strategically optimal for newly emerging social forces.[70]

[67] Quanguorenda, *Twenty Years of Local People's Congresses*, p. 90.
[68] "Daibiao shenyi fayan zhaideng" (A summary of deputies' speeches), *Renda gongzuo tongxun*, No. 6 and 7 (May 1997), pp. 78–79.
[69] Tianjian Shi, "Mass political behavior in Beijing," in Merle Goldman and Roderick MacFarquhar (eds.), *The Paradox of China's Post-Mao Reforms* (Cambridge, MA: Harvard University Press, 1999), p. 155.
[70] Richard Baum and Alexei Shevchenko, "The 'state of the state'," in Goldman and MacFaquhar, *The Paradox of China's Post-Mao Reforms*, pp. 358–59.

However, with the accumulation of experiences and self-confidence, and in the improved political environment, which is attributable to the Party, the development strategy gradually changed throughout the 1990s. Local legislatures have taken a more assertive attitude toward governments by use of a confrontation strategy: dismissing leading officials after appraisal, introducing interpellation bills, and disapproving government work reports in legislature meetings. This shows that local legislatures have begun to argue and pursue independence as well as cooperation concerning governments, and they are entering a new developmental stage. This also reveals that the power balance between political actors can be readjusted without radical reforms of the Chinese one-party system.

On the other hand, the Chinese legislatures still stick to the strategy of gaining Party support (that is, entwinement with the CCP) as a vital weapon to cope with governments, and this will not change in the foreseeable future. This limits the potential development of Chinese local legislatures: they risk becoming merely legal arms that the Party can use to control more differentiated and sophisticated government bureaucrats, and to supplement its ideological and personnel controls.[71] In fact, most Chinese researchers and people involved with legislatures have argued in this way. The CCP has experimented with this possibility in certain areas since the late 1980s: all Party leaders except those responsible for government work served concurrently as legislative leaders.[72] Therefore, for further legislative development in China, readjusting the relations between the Party and legislatures becomes a central problem: until this problem is resolved, we should not simply regard the legislative development itself as democratization in China.

[71] Peter Vanneman, *The Supreme Soviet: Politics and the Legislative Process in the Soviet Political System* (Durham, NC: Duke University Press, 1977), pp. 101, 141; William A. Welsh, "The status of research on representative institutions in eastern Europe," *Legislative Studies Quarterly*, Vol. 15, No. 2 (May 1980), p. 290.

[72] On the experiments in Baiyin city in Gansu, see Cai Dingjian and Wang Chenguang (eds.), *Renmin daibiao dahui ershinian fazhan yu gaige* (*Twenty-Years' Development and Reform of People's Congresses*) (Beijing: Zhongguo jiancha chubanshe, 2001), pp. 410–13.

4

Supervising Courts and the Development of New State Organs

The past three decades' economic reform in China has impacted the political system. For example, the introduction of a market economy created an urgent need for a lawmaking system, and thereby the NPC and local people's congresses were able to strengthen their roles, as Chapter 2 analyzed in detail. Similarly, Chinese courts received more attention than ever with the increasing importance of judicial functions in resolving civil and economic disputes.[1] In this way, new state organs in the reform era, like legislatures and courts, have had the opportunity to become more important political actors in the Chinese political system.

Legislatures and courts, however, as latecomers and weaker forces compared to the CCP and governments, have encountered challenges. On the one hand, they should secure clarified jurisdiction against the obstruction of established powers, while on the other, they should increase the organizational capabilities necessary to fulfill their functions. This can also apply to the legislative-judiciary relationship. This does not matter in common-law or continental European legal systems, because these courts have a great deal of independent authority guaranteed by a separation of powers and a system of checks and balances. In contrast, Chinese people's congresses are not just lawmaking bodies, but organs of state power that exercise the rights of supervision and personnel appointment over courts. Judges are thus elected or appointed

---

[1] Stanley B. Lubman, *Bird in a Cage: Legal Reform in China after Mao* (Stanford, CA: Stanford University Press, 1999), pp. 253–55; Xin Chunying and Li Lin (eds.), *Yifa zhiguo yu sifa gaige* (*Governance According to Law and Judicial Reform*) (Beijing: Zhongguo fazhi chubanshe, 1999), p. 1; Wang Liming, *Sifa gaige yanjiu* (*Research on Judicial Reform*) (Revised edition) (Beijing: Falü chubanshe, 2001), pp. iii, 30–31.

by local legislatures, and courts are responsible to the legislatures.[2] Furthermore, with the strengthening of the status of local legislatures in the 1990s, legislative supervision has an important effect on the work of courts. So now courts should adeptly deal with legislatures as well as the Party and governments for the sake of ensuring their jurisdiction and improving their capacities.

This chapter explores legislative supervision over courts in an attempt to understand the pattern of the new state organs' development in the reform era. Analyzing this can tell us an interesting story about how newly emerging forces have dealt with each other to further their own interests and ultimately to become embedded in the political system. This study tries to answer several questions. With respect to people's congresses, why are they so enthusiastic to supervise courts to the extent that they occasionally interfere with the adjudication process, and how do they supervise courts? With respect to courts, what attitudes do they adopt toward legislative supervision, and how do they deal with it? In this regard, it is worth noting that the CCP and governments have already encroached upon the authority of the courts to a significant extent, and courts have strongly argued that judicial independence (*sifa duli*) – that the courts should operate without interference from external powers in terms of personnel, finance, and adjudication – is a precondition for realizing judicial fairness (*sifa gongzheng*).[3]

---

[2] *Constitution of the People's Republic of China* (Beijing: Foreign Languages Press, 1999), pp. 44, 46, 48, 55.

[3] Tan Shigui (ed.), *Zhongguo sifa gaige yanjiu* (*A Study on Judicial Reform in China*) (Beijing: Falü chubanshe, 2000), pp. 21–49; Hu Xiabing and Feng Renqiang (eds.), *Sifa gongzheng yu sifa gaige yanjiu zongshu* (*Summary on the Researches of Judicial Justice and Reform*) (Beijing: Tsinghua daxue chubanshe, 2001), pp. 38–70; Liu Lixian and Zhang Zhihui (eds.), *Sifa gaige redian wenti* (*Hot Issues on Judicial Reform*) (Beijing: Zhongguo renmin gong'an daxue chubanshe, 2000), pp. 16–48. On laws and court systems in the reform era, see Anthony Dicks, "The Chinese legal system: Reforms in the balance," *China Quarterly*, No. 119 (September 1989), pp. 540–75; Edward J. Epstein, "Law and litigation in post–Mao China," in Potter, *Domestic Law Reforms in Post–Mao China*, pp. 19–55; Stanley Lubman, "Introduction: The future of Chinese law," *China Quarterly*, No. 141 (March 1995), pp. 1–21; Lubman, *Bird in a Cage*, pp. 298–319; Margaret Y. K. Woo, "Law and discretion in contemporary Chinese courts," in Karen G. Turner, James V. Feinerman, and R. Kent Guy (eds.), *The Limits of the Rule of Law in China* (Seattle and London: University of Washington Press, 2000), pp. 163–95; Pitman B. Potter, "The Chinese legal system: Continuing commitment to the primacy of state power," *China Quarterly*, No. 159 (September 1999), pp. 673–83; Pitman B. Potter, *The Chinese Legal System: Globalization and Local Legal Culture* (London and New York: Routledge, 2001), pp. 4–15.

TAKING LEGISLATIVE SUPERVISION OVER
COURTS SERIOUSLY

Legislative supervision over courts was almost nonexistent in the 1980s: Chinese local legislatures heard the annual work reports of courts only at annual plenary sessions and asked them to act on demands that residents made through letters and visits (*xinfang*) to the legislatures.[4] But since the early 1990s, local legislatures have put the supervision over courts at the top of their agenda and have actually spent a lot of time and effort in overseeing courts. There is every reason for them to do so.

Most of all, local legislatures found that courts were easier to supervise than governments in the 1990s because of the inferior political status of courts. In the case of supervision, it is political, not legal, status that is important, because supervision implies a degree of control over the power of supervised organs. For this reason, even now local legislatures occasionally encounter difficulties in the process of supervising governments (see Chapter 3). In contrast, they can wield supervisory power more aggressively with regard to courts. In the 1980s, both legislatures and courts, along with the public security and judicial bureaus of governments, were under the control of the Party's political-legal committees (*zhengfawei*). But in the 1990s, legislatures were elevated to the jurisdiction of Party committees, while courts are still under the control of the political-legal committees. That is, legislatures are now placed one level above courts in the Party hierarchy. As a result, the chairpersons of people's congresses can attend Party standing committee meetings as full or nonvoting members, and they are in direct contact with Party committees, rather than through the political-legal committees. Therefore, legislatures can more "comfortably" oversee courts than they can governments.[5]

[4] Li Tian, "Cong gean jiandu kan jiandu lidude jiada" (Seeing the strengthening of supervisory power in terms of individual case supervision), *Renmin zhi sheng* (*People's Voice*), No. 7 (July 1999), p. 11; Quanguorenda neiwu sifa weiyuanhui sifashi (ed.), *Shehuizhuyi minzhu fazhi jianshede youyi tansuo* (*A Beneficial Exploration of Socialist Democratic and Legal System Construction*) (Beijing: Zhongguo minzhu fazhi chubanshe, 1993), p. 111.
[5] Interview with leaders and staff of local legislatures: Tianjin, Shijiazhuang of Hebei Province, July and August 2000 and January 2002. On the same change in the central level, see Murray S. Tanner, "The erosion of Communist Party control over law-making in China," *China Quarterly*, No. 138 (June 1994), pp. 393–95; Wang Jianying (ed.), *Zhongguo gongchandang zuzhishi ziliao huibian* (*The Compilation of Documents of*

Increasing demands from the public have also encouraged people's congresses to pay more attention to the supervision of courts. As the status of local legislatures has been enhanced, residents more frequently visit them when facing trouble.[6] Most local legislatures across the country have witnessed a sharp increase in the volume of public letters and visits (*xinfang*). For example, local legislatures in Guangdong Province have had an increase of 25 percent annually since 1993, and Heilongjiang Provincial People's Congress has recorded an increase of about 50 percent since the mid-1990s.[7] A majority of complaints are about law enforcement departments (courts, procuracies, and public security bureaus), and more than half of these are aimed at courts.[8] Public complaints about courts cover all aspects of judicial problems in China (see Table 4.1).

These increasing demands provide local people's congresses with a chance to get public support. Such support, together with the political backing of the Party and legal guarantees, plays a crucial role in extending the legislatures' sphere of authority. In fact, local legislatures, some legislative leaders and staff note, were able to cleanse their tarnished image of being "rubber stamps" through the supervision of courts rather than that of governments, and to impress upon the public the authority of

---

the CCP Organizational History) (Beijing: Zhonggong zhongyang dangxiao chubanshe, 1994), pp. 1182–1293.

[6] According to Shi, between 1988 and 1996, the percentage of the public who complained through people's congress deputies increased from 8.6 to 14.1 percent. Tianjian Shi, "Mass political behavior in Beijing," in Merle Goldman and Roderick MacFarquhar (eds.), *The Paradox of China's Post-Mao Reforms* (Cambridge, MA: Harvard University Press, 1999), p. 155.

[7] "Shensheng quanli" (Sacred power), *Renmin zhi sheng*, No. 1 (January 2000), p. 39; Chen Xin, "Yifa guifan renda changweihui xinfang gongzuo" (Standardizing people's congress standing committee's works of letters and visits), *Fazhi (Rule of Law)*, No. 1 (January 2001), p. 12.

[8] Yun Zhiqiang, "Qianghua lingdao lidu, gaohao gean jiandu" (Strengthen leadership power and conduct individual case supervision well), *Liaoning renda jianshe (Construction of People's Congresses in Liaoning)*, No. 2 (February 1999), p. 25; Fang Zhongbing and Wang Zhiming, "Cong renda xinfang gongzuo kan renmin fayuan gongzuo zhong cunzaide jige wenti" (Some problems in the works of people's courts in terms of letters and visits to people's congresses), *Renmin zhengtan (People's Political Forum)*, No. 6 (June 1999), pp. 8–9; "Yifa kaizhan xinfang gongzuo weihu renmin hefa qaunyi" (Conduct the works of letters and visits according to law, and defend people's legal rights and interests), *Zhongguo renda*, No. 14 (July 2001), pp. 18–19; Dong Shouan (ed.), *Minzhu fazhi jianshede zuyin (The Footmarks of Democracy and Legal System Construction)* (Beijing: Zhongguo minzhu fazhi chubanshe, 2000), pp. 262–63.

TABLE 4.1. *Court-related public letters and visits to people's congresses: Heilongjiang Provincial People's Congress, 1998*

Categories of complaints: numbers (%)		Numbers of cases (%)
Unfairness of adjudication and refusal to accept judgments	Criminal 959 (38.4) Civil 887 (35.5) Economic 592 (23.7) Other 60 (2.4)	2,498 (67.5)
Difficulty in court judgments' enforcement		722 (19.5)
Delay of adjudication		296 (8)
Irregularities for favoritism and violating laws		185 (5)
Total		3,701 (100)

Source: Fang Zhongbing and Wang Zhiming, "Cong renda xinfang gongzuo kan renmin fayuan gongzuozhong cunzaide jige wenti" (Some problems in the works of people's courts in terms of letters and visits to people's congress), *Renmin zhengtan* (*People's Political Forum*), No. 6 (June 1999), pp. 8–9.

state power organs.[9] In particular, because people in most cases resort to legislative authority only as a final solution after exhausting other means, local legislatures can make a stronger impression on the public when they successfully address problems through the supervision over courts.

Finally, local people's congresses can more easily get expected results in the case of oversight over courts than in the case of governments. There are a considerable number of delayed, mishandled, and unenforced legal cases in China. In 1998 alone, for instance, courts across the country redressed more than 10,000 misjudged cases by vetting previous judgments.[10] As a result, local legislatures are sure to produce results once they undertake supervision over courts. For example, people's congresses in Sichuan Province conducted deputies' appraisal (*daibiao pingyi*) of courts for one-and-a-half years during 1998 and 1999. About 70,000 deputies to local legislatures at various levels investigated about 2,000 doubtful judgments on the basis of public complaints, and

[9] Lao Luo, "Renda jujiao: sifa jiandu" (The focusing of people's congresses: judicial supervision), *Renmin zhi you* (*People's Friends*), No. 2 (February 2000), pp. 6–7, 37; Li Tian, "Seeing the strengthening of supervisory power," p. 11; Quanguorenda, *A Beneficial Exploration of Socialist Democratic and Legal System Construction*, p. 124; Quanguorenda changweihui bangongting (ed.), *Guojia quanli jiguande jiandu zhidu he jiandu gongzuo* (*The Supervisory Systems and Work of State Power Organs*) (Beijing: Zhongguo minzhu fazhi chubanshe, 1999), p. 202.

[10] Wang, *Research on Judicial Reform*, p. 485.

they required courts to redress about 500 misjudged cases and punish about 200 judicial officers.[11] In a similar fashion, some 70,000 legislative members in Henan Province were able to address about 2,000 mishandled legal cases through deputies' appraisal of courts in 1999.[12]

By the late 1990s, local legislatures even seemed to shift the focus of supervision from governments to courts in an effort to further their interests and to implement the Party center's policy. After the five-year "anti-corruption struggle" from 1993 to 1997, the CCP center began to intensively tackle the issue of "judicial corruption" (*sifa fubai*). This started with Jiang Zemin's demand for judicial reform at the 15th Party Congress in September 1997.[13] In 1998, courts launched a nationwide campaign to educate and rectify judicial cadres.[14] China declared 1999 as a "judgments enforcement year" and waged a "grand war on unenforced court decisions" under the direction of Jiang Zemin in January and a special party circular called "CCP Center Document Number 11 (1999)" in July.[15] Finally, the Supreme People's Court itself released a master plan on judicial reforms entitled "An outline on the five-year reforms of people's courts" in October 1999.[16] These policies from the Party center boosted local legislatures' enthusiasm and legitimacy in relation to supervising courts.

SUPERVISORY MEASURES AND STRENGTHS OF LOCAL LEGISLATURES

The strengthening of legislative supervision over courts has been achieved by the use of new forms of supervisory measures that

---

[11] "Weile tianping bu qingxie: Sichuan quansheng pingyi fayuan gongzuo zongshu" (In order not to make scales tilted: Summary on the appraisal of court works in Sichuan), *Minzhu fazhi jianshe* (*The Construction of Democracy and Legal System*), No. 10 (October 1999), pp. 11–13.

[12] Kong Fanping, "Jiandu kuangfeng qi zhongyuan: Henansheng renda pingyi fayuan jingji shenpan gongzuo zoubi" (Supervision hurricane swept over central plains: Quick writing on the Henan province people congresses' appraisal over court works of economic adjudications), *Renda jianshe* (*The Construction of People's Congresses*), No. 1 (January 2000), pp. 13–16.

[13] Wang, *Research on Judicial Reform*, p. 36.

[14] Xin and Li, *Governance According to Law and Judicial Reform*, p. 93.

[15] Ren Keli, "Quebao zhixing gongzuo shunli jinxing" (Ensure the successful progress in enforcement works), *Renda jianshe*, No. 10 (October 1999), pp. 7–8. On the difficulty in enforcement of court decisions, see Donald C. Clarke, "The execution of civil judgments in China," *China Quarterly*, No. 141 (March 1995), pp. 65–81.

[16] Zuigao renmin fayuan yanjiushi (ed.), *Renmin fayuan wunian gaige gangyao* (*An Outline of the Five-Year Reforms of People's Courts*) (Beijing: Renmin fayuan chubanshe, 2000), pp. 59–72.

Chinese local legislatures have pioneered since the 1980s. They include appraisal (*pingyi*) of judicial officers and work, individual case supervision (*gean jiandu*), and the system of investigating the responsibility for misjudged cases (*cuoan zeren zhuijiuzhi*). Most local legislatures now use them.

Appraisal is one of the most effective measures that local people's congresses can apply to state organs. As mentioned above, for instance, most local legislatures and their members in Sichuan and Henan Provinces appraised courts under the leadership of provincial-level legislatures and investigated allegedly mishandled cases for up to one-and-a-half years. Investigations involved all the courts in those provinces, and numerous cases were investigated and intensively appraised. For example, local legislatures in Henan Province investigated 27,964 cases of economic disputes handled by courts, and intensively estimated 3,055 selected cases in 1999 (see Table 4.2). And they forced courts to redress problems and punish related personnel after the supervision.[17] In this way, appraisal, some reports argue, plays an important role in correcting misjudgments and enhancing judicial efficiency.[18]

Individual case supervision was invented as a specialized weapon for overseeing courts and other law enforcement departments in the 1990s. While appraisal is aimed at unspecified judicial work, it focuses on misjudged individual cases. As a result, there are suspicions that the individual case supervision infringes upon judicial independence, as discussed below. However, most local legislatures competitively conducted it with the formal encouragement and endorsement of Li Peng, the Chairman of the NPC Standing Committee during the 9th period from 1998 to 2002.[19]

For individual case supervision, local people's congresses first carefully select targets among public complaints and serious cases that are

[17] Kong Fanping, "Supervision hurricane swept over central plains," pp. 13–16; "In order not to make scales tilted," pp. 11–13; Cui Jianhua, "Pingyi zhi hua zai Shuzhong zhandi diankai (1)(2) (The flowers of appraisal evolved in the Sichuan area), *Minzhu fazhi jianshe*, No. 8 (August 1999), pp. 8–10 and No. 9 (September 1999), pp. 9–11; Quanguorenda, *A Beneficial Exploration of Socialist Democratic and Legal System Construction*, pp. 56–211.

[18] Dong, *The Footmarks of Democracy and Legal System Construction*, pp. 272–76; Quanguorenda, *A Beneficial Exploration of Socialist Democratic and Legal System Construction*, pp. 121–24, 130–36, 144–48.

[19] On the dissemination of individual case supervision in the 1990s, see the reports of 31 provincial-level people's congresses in Quanguorenda changweihui bangongting (ed.), *Difang renda 20 nian (shang)* (*Twenty Years of People's Congresses*) (Volume 1) (Beijing: Zhongguo minzhu fazhi chubanshe, 2000), pp. 114–265.

TABLE 4.2. *Appraisal of courts: People's congresses in Henan Province, 1999*

Level of courts and numbers of cases investigated (%)	Numbers of cases intensively appraised and rectified (%)
Higher court 109 (0.4)	Rectified 1,440 (47)
Intermediate courts 2,058 (7.6)	Partly rectified 562 (19)
Basic-level courts 25,797 (92)	Processing or maintained 1,053 (34)
Total: 27,964 (100)	Total: 3,055 (100)
Number of judicial officers punished: 39 persons	

Source: Kong Fanping, "Jiandu kuangfeng qi zhongyuan: Henansheng renda pingyi fayuan jingji shenpan gongzuo zoubi" (Supervision hurricane swept over central plains: Quick writing on the Henan province people's congresses' appraisal over court works of economic adjudications), *Renda jianshe (The Construction of People's Congresses)*, No. 1 (January 2000), pp. 13–16.

identified through other forms of supervision. Generally, targets include typical misconduct by judges, such as accepting bribes, and notorious cases that cause widespread public complaints. Then legislature committees on interior and judicial affairs (*neiwu sifa weiyuanhui/neisiwei*) investigate the cases for at least several months. When the cases are believed to be extraordinarily serious or strong resistance from courts is expected, local legislatures organize joint investigative teams with the CCP and procuracies.[20] Finally, they require courts to correct problems within a certain time, and punish related persons, for instance by dismissal. Courts generally accept the demands of local legislatures when these demands are based on clear evidence obtained through intensive investigation.[21] So the supervision is evaluated as the most effective measure of dealing with courts.

[20] Zhou Yisong, "Faguan weifa xingquan renda lingqi xiagang" (People's congress fired a judge who illegally wielded power), *Chutian zhuren (Masters in Hubei)*, No. 4 (April 1999), p. 11; Zhang Youzhi, "Jianchi sige yuanzhe gaohao gean jiandu" (Do individual case supervision well, holding up the four principles), *Guangxi renda (People's Congresses in Guangxi)*, No. 8 (August 1999), pp. 15–16; Wang Zhonglu, "Fayuan zuochu sixing panjue zhi hou" (After a court sentenced a death penalty), *Renda jianshe*, No. 2 (February 1999), pp. 35–38; Yun Jun, "Kaizhan gean jiandu quebao sifa gongzheng" (Launch individual case supervisions and ensure judicial fairness), *Yunnan renda (People's Congresses in Yunnan)*, No. 12 (December 1999), pp. 4–5.

[21] Zheng Guofeng, "Pingan tuxian jiandu lidu" (Appraisal of cases highlights supervisory strength), *Renmin zhengtan*, No. 5 (May 2001), pp. 11–13; Su Li, "Yifa jiaqiang dui dianxing anjiande jiandu" (Strengthen supervision on typical cases

A district court in Hebei Province pioneered the system of investigating the responsibility for misjudged cases in 1990,[22] but this system spread nationwide under legislative supervision and the encouragement of the Supreme People's Court.[23] In contrast to other supervision systems, it is praised as a more institutionalized and court-centered regime. Under this system, courts themselves should establish subsystems for investigating misjudged cases and punishing responsible personnel.[24] Local legislatures enact local laws and regulations and conduct supervision to verify whether or not courts establish necessary systems and observe pertinent regulations. This system, several reports argue, plays a certain role in correcting mishandled cases and enhancing the efficiency of adjudications.[25] More and more judicial officers are reportedly being punished under this system: for example, 185 judicial officers involved in 211 mishandled cases in Shaanxi

according to law), *Liaoning renda jianshe*, No. 6 (June 2000), pp. 4–6; Zhou Huizong, "Guanzhu baixing" (Pay close attention to common people), *Renmin zhi you*, Nos. 1 and 2 (February 2001), pp. 7–8; Jing Quan and Ning Tao, "Xinjishi renda kaizhan gean jiandu e shan shi" (Several cases of Xinji City People's Congress's individual case supervision), *Difang renda jianshe* (*Construction of Local People's congresses*), No. 10 (October 2000), pp. 23–24; Rui Siwei, "Shenshou bi beizhua" (Stretched hands should be arrested), *Renmin yu quanli* (*People and Power*), No. 2 (February 1999), pp. 20–22; Liu Hanlong, "Yiqi bijiao chenggongde gean jiandu" (A relatively successful case of individual case supervision), *Shidai zhuren* (*Master of Times*), No. 3 (March 2001), p. 3; Zhang Bohou and Zhen Shubin, "Sheng renda shishi gean jiandu jiuzheng yiqi cuoan" (Provincial people's congress conducted individual case supervision and corrected a misjudged case), *Shandong renda gongzuo* (*The Works of People's Congress in Shandong*), No. 1 (January 2001), pp. 6–7, 28.

[22] Hebeisheng shehui kexueyuan ketizu, "Jianshe shehuizhuyi fazhi guojiade youyi tansuo" (A beneficial exploration to build socialist legal system state), *Zhongguo renda*, No. 8 (April 2001), pp. 17–20.

[23] Quanguorenda changweihui bangongting yanjiushi (ed.), *Difang renda jiandu gongzuo tansuo* (*An Exploration for the Supervisory Works of Local People's Congresses*) (Beijing: Zhongguo minzhu fazhi chubanshe, 1997), pp. 301–39; Quanguorenda changweihui bangongting yanjiushi (ed.), *Woguo dangqian falü shishide wenti he duice* (*Problems and Countermeasures in Law Enforcement in China*) (Beijing: Zhongguo minzhu fazhi chubanshe, 1997), pp. 312–20.

[24] In 1998, the Supreme People's Court itself promulgated a regulation on this system. See Zuigao renmin fayun, *An Outline of the Five-Year Reforms of People's Courts*, pp. 180–85.

[25] Quanguorenda, *The Supervisory Systems and Work of State Power Organs*, pp. 200–203; Quanguorenda, *An Exploration for the Supervisory Works of People's Congresses*, pp. 310–12; Dong, *The Footmarks of Democracy and Legal System Construction*, pp. 96–97.

Province were punished by criminal responsibility (three persons), dismissal (eleven), and party discipline (five), in 1994 and 1995.[26]

Finally, to what degree can local people's congresses supervise courts? Do they exert real power in making courts correct problems? This study suggests that they do. They can force courts to act. First, local legislatures can and did dismiss more and more judicial officers after supervision. For example, in 2000 alone, people's congresses in Huaihua City of Hunan Province discharged three judges.[27] Even a judge who was absent from an appraisal conference without getting the prior permission of the legislature was dismissed in Gaoan City of Jiangxi Province.[28] And local legislatures in many regions tie judicial appointments to courts' fulfillment of their demands: that is, they turn down courts' requests for personnel appointments when the courts do not execute their demands faithfully.[29] Finally, some local legislatures even veto the work reports of courts: this occurred in Gonghe County in Qinghai Province in 2000, and Shenyang Municipality in Liaoning Province and Dengcheng County in Shaanxi Province in 2001, among others.[30]

---

[26] Quanguorenda, *An Exploration for the Supervisory Works of People's Congresses*, p. 311.

[27] "Yanming fadu tuijin fazhi" (Strict and impartial laws advance rule of law), *Zhongguo renda xinwen*, April 4, 2001 (available at http://zgrdxw.peopledaily.com.cn/gb/paper6/7/class00060002/hwz111533.htm). For other cases, see "Wuxiangxian fayuan yitingzhang tuola zhixing bei chezhi" (The first chamber chief of Wuxiang county court was discharged after delaying implementation), *Shandong renda gongzuo*, No. 11 (November 2000), p. 62; Zhang Liuli, "Limou dizhi renda jiandu bei chezhi shenpanyuan zhiwu" (Li so-and-so resisted people's congress supervision and was discharged from judicial office), *Jilin renda*, No. 3 (March 2000), p. 21; "Fujian Shanghangxian renda changweihui yifa bamian yi shizhi faguan" (Shanghang County People's Congress in Fujian dismissed a judge accused of misconduct), *Zhongguo renda xinwen*, August 13, 2001 (available at http://zgrdxw.peopledaily.com.cn/gb/paper7/9/class00070001/hwz165193.htm).

[28] "Jiangxisheng Gaoanshi yi faguan bu chanjia pingyi bei chezhi" (A judge who did not attend an appraisal was dismissed in Gaoan city of Jiangxi province), *Zhongguo renda xinwen*, November 7, 2001 (available at http://zgrdxw.peopledaily.com.cn/gb/paper7/11/class00007.../hwz181840.htm).

[29] "Dui gean jiandu jige wentide sikao" (A consideration on the several questions of individual case supervision), *Zhongguo renda xinwen*, March 30, 2001 (available at http://zgrdxw.peopledaily.com.cn/gb/paper7/7/class000700001/hwz109555.htm).

[30] "Cong foujue dao zancheng: Shenyang renda liangci shenyi fayuan gongzuo baogao" (From veto to approval: Shenyang People's Congress considered court work report twice), *Zhongguo renda xinwen*, August 10, 2001 (available at http://zgrdxw.peopledaily.com.cn/gb/special/class00000.../hwz164763.ht); "Shenyang zhongyuan shijian yinfa shenceng falü wenti" (Shenyang incident caused serious legal problems), *Zhongguo renda xinwen*, August 13, 2001 (available at http://zgrdxw.peopledaily.com.cn/gb/special/class00000.../hwz165058.ht); "Shaanxi Dengchengxian fayuan

JUDICIAL RESPONSES TO LEGISLATIVE SUPERVISION

In principle, most jurists acknowledge the legitimacy of legislative supervision over courts, cognizant as they are of Article 104 of the Constitution, which allows people's congresses to oversee courts. Some even argue that the supervision should be augmented since serious judicial problems have caused widespread public outcry and courts alone have not been able to redress the problems. But jurists have a much different attitude toward individual case supervision. Most legal scholars object to this form of supervision on the grounds that it can obstruct judicial independence and fairness, because it oversees individual cases – even though currently under trial – instead of the general work of courts. In other words, under this system, judges should consider local legislatures in addition to the Party and governments when they examine cases; this could seriously influence the ruling process.[31]

Judicial officers, who could be directly subject to supervision, oppose it even more strongly.[32] Some cynically ask why local legislatures don't supervise governments on a case-by-case basis, even though there are also serious cases of corruption in the executive branch.[33] Some question the quality of legislative members, saying legislators do not necessarily have more legal expertise and ethical standing than judges. In sum,

---

wei tongguo renda pingyi guan" (Dengcheng county court of Shaanxi did not pass the door of people's congress appraisal), *Zhongguo renda xinwen*, December 14, 2001 (available at http://zgrdxw.peopledaily.com.cn/gb/paper7/11/class00007.../ hwz189459.ht).

[31] "Gean jiandu shiye feiye?" (Individual case supervision, right or wrong?), *Minzhu yu fazhi*, No. 3 (March 2000), pp. 4–9; Ye Qing, "Yifa zhiguo yu sifa gongzheng: 1999 quanguo susongfaxue nianhui guandian zongshu" (Governance according to law and judicial fairness: Summary on the viewpoints of a 1999 annual conference of litigation law), *Faxue (Legal Science)*, No. 2 (February 2000), pp. 49–55; Wang, *Research on Judicial Reform*, pp. 510–13; Liu and Zhang, *Hot Issues on Judicial Reform*, pp. 118–27; Hu, *Sifa gongzheng yu sifa gaige*, p. 14; Cai Dingjian and Wang Chenguang (eds.), *Renmin daibiao dahui ershinian fazhan yu gaige (Twenty-Years' Development and Reform of People's Congresses)* (Beijing: Zhongguo jiancha chubanshe, 2001), pp. 351–98.

[32] "Individual case supervision, right or wrong?" p. 9; Yang Tianwu, "Qianyi dangqian renda sifa anjian jiandu gongzuo" (Discussion on the works of present people's congress supervision of judicial cases), *Minzhu fazhi jianshe*, No. 7 (July 2000), pp. 19–21.

[33] Liu Hainian, Li Lin, and Zhang Guangxing (eds.), *Yifa zhiguo yu lianzheng jianshe (Governance According to Law and Building of Honest and Clean Government)* (Beijing: Zhongguo fazhi chubanshe, 1999), p. 630.

judicial officers think that local legislatures only care about increasing their own interests at the expense of courts.[34]

There are grounds to support these complaints and objections. Some members and even staff of local legislatures, like high-level Party cadres and government officials, are reported to improperly intervene in adjudication processes in favor of their friends and relatives, in the name of public interest. So some people warn of "supervision corruption" (*jiandu fubai*) or "legislative corruption" (*renda fubai*).[35] When local legislatures wield their supervisory power collectively, they also frequently interfere with normal ruling processes by knowingly ignoring and sometimes violating related laws and rules.[36] Even legislative leaders have expressed concerns over this phenomenon, and they have advised local legislatures to abide by several principles when they conduct individual case supervision (such as supervision according to laws, collective exercise of power, ex post facto supervision, and respect for the independent adjudication right of courts).[37] However, persons responsible for supervision in many regions seem to be adamant, arguing "no individual case supervision, no effective supervision over courts."[38]

[34] Li Shaopeng and Fei Yongxin, "Dui renda gean jiandude yidian fansi" (Reflections on the individual case supervision of people's congresses), *Renda yanjiu* (*Studies on People's Congresses*), No. 11 (November 1999) (available at http://www.rdyj.com.cn/rdqk-11-5.html).

[35] Li, "Reflections on the individual case supervision of people's congresses"; "Individual case supervision, right or wrong?" pp. 8–9; Xin and Li, *Governance According to Law and Judicial Reform*, pp. 630–31; Liu and Zhang, *Hot Issues on Judicial Reform*, pp. 122–24.

[36] "Guizhou Xishuixian renda changweihui zhuren huiyi zhiding anjian guanxia yinqi yiyi" (Xishui County People's Congress Standing Committee chairmen group assigned the jurisdiction of a case and caused an objection), *Zhongguo renda xinwen*, July 31, 2001 (available at http://zgrdxw.peopledaily.com.cn/gb/paper7/9/class000700001/hwz161403.htm); Li Xuesong, "26li gean jiandu shilide kaocha yu sikao" (Inspection and reflection on 26 cases of individual case supervision), *Renda yanjiu*, No. 8 (August 2000) (available at http://www.rdyj.com.cn/2000/rdqk-8-2.html).

[37] Quanguorenda, *The Supervisory Systems and Work of State Power Organs*, pp. 283–84; Liu, Li, and Zhang, *Governance According to Law and Building of Honest and Clean Government*, pp. 474–75; "Li Peng weiyuanzhang tan renda jiandu" (The Chairman, Li Peng, told about people's congress supervision), *Shandong renda gongzuo*, No. 9 (September 1999), pp. 4–6; Cheng Shiqiang, "Quanli jiguan dui sifa anjian jiandu lifade tantao" (An inquiry into the legislation on the power organ's supervision of judicial cases), *Renda yanjiu*, No. 4 (April 2001) (available at http://www.rdyj.com.cn/2001/rdqk-4-3.html).

[38] Quanguorenda, *An Exploration for the Supervisory Works of People's Congresses*, p. 333; Quanguorenda, *Problems and Countermeasures in Law Enforcement in China*, pp. 271, 389.

Then, what kinds of countermeasures do courts use to cope with individual case supervision? They have two measures. First, they make use of an inner-court machine: the system of request for instructions on cases (*anjian qingshi zhidu*). Under this system, courts can request instructions from higher courts when they hear very "difficult" or "complicated" cases. But this system is alleged to be one of the main causes preventing a transparent adjudication process and the independent ruling of judges and ultimately incapacitating the system of a court of "second instance being of last instance" (*liangshen zhongshenzhi*).[39] So in 1998, the president of the Supreme People's Court, Xiao Yang, instructed that this system should be gradually phased out except for specially regulated cases.[40]

Faced with increasingly aggressive legislative supervision, however, courts willingly resort to this outdated method. For example, upon receiving the requirements of local legislatures, judges ask higher courts to issue instructions that support their judgments. Judges sometimes ask higher-level courts to instruct their rulings in advance when it is expected that judgments will be subject to legislative supervision, and they use instructions as a shield to ward off supervision. Even if courts fail to defend the judges' positions, instructions can still be used as a partial excuse to avoid responsibility for misjudgments, on the grounds that the judge had deferred to a higher court's instructions.[41] In the past, this tactic embarrassed legislatures, because lower-level legislatures cannot review the decisions of higher-level courts.

Recently this system has not worked well. Local people's congresses also have a countermeasure: a joint operation of higher and lower levels (*shangxia liandong*). Now most local legislatures in a province use this tactic when they supervise other state organs.[42] Individual case

---

[39] Tan, *A Study on Judicial Reform in China*, pp. 89–92; Liu and Zhang, *Hot Issues on Judicial Reform*, pp. 210–32; Wang, *Research on Judicial Reform*, pp. 314–65; Xin and Li, *Governance According to Law and Judicial Reform*, pp. 529–36, 629–30.

[40] Zuigao renmin fayun, *An Outline of the Five-Year Reforms of People's Courts*, p. 239.

[41] Yang, "Discussion on the works of present people's congress supervision of judicial cases," pp. 19–21; Liu Jianzhi, "Women shi ruhe jiaqiang sifa gean jiandude" (How we strengthened the supervision of judicial cases), *Difang renda jianshe*, No. 11 (November 1999), pp. 13–14; Wang Xicai, "Zhanzai fazhide qianyan" (Stand on the front line of governance according to law), *Renmin zhi you*, No. 12 (December 1999), pp. 14–15.

[42] Yang Fengchun (ed.), *Zai shengji renda gongzuo gangweishang* (*On the Posts of Provincial People's Congresses*) (Beijing: Zhongguo minzhu fazhi chubanshe, 1996), pp. 48, 63, 177, 300.

supervision is no exception. That is, legislatures can ask their higher-level counterparts to supervise higher-level courts when judges are suspected of obstructing supervision by issuing instructions to lower-level courts. Therefore, higher-level courts cannot easily cover up the misconduct of lower-level courts.[43] Sometimes, legislative members from higher-level legislatures try to defend the supervisory rights of their lower-level counterparts by for instance raising interpellation to higher-level courts, as the Beijing Municipal People's Congress deputies did to the Beijing Higher People's Court in 2000.[44]

Courts also employ a Party channel to avoid supervision: handling legal cases through the coordination of the Party's political-legal committees (*xietiao ban'an zhidu*). Courts should report and request the instructions of the Party when they hear "extraordinarily important" cases or when there are serious disagreements between law enforcement departments. Then the committees play a crucial role as final decision makers, or as coordinators in resolving disputes. This, along with the courts' dependence for their personnel on the Party and for their finances on governments, is alleged to be one of the main external factors that impede judicial independence and foster "local protectionism" or "localization of courts." As a result, most legal academics criticize this system, and some even call for the abolition of the Party's political-legal committees themselves.[45] But individual courts or judicial officers whom local legislatures intend to punish use this tactic to defeat the legislatures.

Once the political-legal committees engage in coordinating certain legal cases alongside courts in the name of Party committees, local people's congresses have difficulty in forcing courts to listen to their demands, because legislatures in this case have to overcome the CCP. If legislatures persist with their arguments, they are accused of not obeying the Party.[46] For this reason, legislatures and courts sometimes compete for Party support, and whichever of the two gets this support will win the game. Therefore, legislative leaders emphasize the importance

[43] Liu, "How we strengthened the supervision of judicial cases," pp. 13–14.
[44] Xu Yijun, *Zoujin renda* (*Entering People's Congress*) (Beijing: Zhongguo minzhu fazhi chubanshe, 2001), pp. 75–76.
[45] Ye, "Governance according to law and judicial fairness," pp. 50–51; Xin and Li, *Governance According to Law and Judicial Reform*, pp. 36–37; Liu and Zhang, *Hot Issues on Judicial Reform*, pp. 34–40; Tan, *A Study on Judicial Reform in China*, pp. 94–95.
[46] Quanguorenda, *Problems and Countermeasures in Law Enforcement in China*, p. 392; Quanguorenda, *The Supervisory Systems and Work of State Power Organs*, p. 287.

of getting the Party's support during supervision: they report their plans and decisions in advance, and actively request Party instructions if they encounter trouble in order to shore up support.[47]

Local legislatures have recently appeared to hold an advantage over courts in this regard. Territorial Party committees cannot easily oppose legislative supervision over courts because of the Party center's policy of encouraging local legislatures to oversee state organs. And, as outlined above, many Party committees participate in united investigation teams at the request of legislatures. In addition, legislatures often employ a mass media ploy, referred to as "connecting legislative supervision with public opinion supervision," in an effort to gain the backing of the local population and to attract support from the Party.[48] This involves publicizing supervisory plans and results in local newspapers and on television networks, as well as through their legislative mouthpieces.[49]

NEW JUDICIAL STRATEGY TOWARD LOCAL LEGISLATURES

In the reform era, courts are no longer a single entity. Courts at the basic level frequently ignore the regulations and directives of higher-level courts to protect the economic interests of their regions.[50] So the Supreme People's Court pinpointed "local protectionism" as the most

---

[47] "Hebeisheng renda changweihui jiaqiang gean jiandu" (Hebei Provincial People's Congress Standing Committee strengthened individual case supervision), *Shandong renda gongzuo*, No. 7 (July 1999), pp. 13–14; Yuan Zongwen, "Yidian yidi zong guanqing" (Every drop of concerns and affections), *Renmin zhi you*, No. 10 (October 2000), pp. 27–28; Guandaoxian renda changweihui, "Shishi gean jiandu zengqiang jiandu shixiao" (Conducting individual case supervision and adding up supervisory effects), *Difang renda jianshe*, No. 7 (July 1999), pp. 23–25; Qinhuangdaoshi renda changweihui, "Qianghua gean jiandu cujin gongzheng sifa" (Strengthen individual case supervision and promote judicial fairness), *Difang renda jianshe*, No. 10 (October 1999), pp. 30–31.

[48] Dai Mingxun, "Sheng renda changweihui 1999nian jiandude dianxing anjian qing-kuang tongbao" (Circular on the conditions of several typical cases supervised by the provincial people's congress in 1999), *Liaoning renda jianshe*, No. 6 (June 2000), p. 7; Liu, "How we strengthened the supervision of judicial cases," pp. 13–14.

[49] Now all 31 provincial-level people's congresses have their own editorials, including newspapers, and about two-thirds of them are published publicly. And national and local mass media have allowed more space to Publicize people's congresses in compliance with the decisions of the NPC and the Party center in 1998 to strengthen people's congress propaganda. So now people's congresses have more opportunities to publicize their activities through the mass media.

[50] Clarke, "The execution of civil judgments in China," p. 81.

serious challenge to the process of court reform.[51] Similarly, there is a cognition gap between higher- and lower-level courts concerning legislative supervision: the higher the level of a court, the more positive and cooperative its attitude. Several factors cause this phenomenon.

Most judicial problems take place in the nearly 3,000 basic-level (city, county, and district) courts. So it is they that receive the most public grievances and resultantly invite legislative supervision. For example, when local people's congresses in Henan Province appraised courts during 1999, 92 percent of investigated legal cases concerned basic-level courts (see Table 4.2). And a survey of 5,526 legislative members in Shaanxi Province in 2001 noted that only 38.5 percent of respondents were satisfied with the work of basic-level courts, while 62.1 percent were satisfied with the Provincial Higher People's Court.[52] Higher-level (intermediate, higher, and the Supreme) courts themselves in many cases cannot control basic-level courts, mainly because of "local protectionism" caused by courts' personnel and financial dependence on territorial Party committees and governments at the same level. So, higher-level courts may cooperate more readily with legislatures in an effort to resolve the problems of lower-level courts. In fact, the Tianjin Municipal Higher People's Court in 1991 – not legislatures – initially asked the Municipal People's Congresses to undertake appraisal of lower-level courts with a view to addressing judicial problems in the region.[53]

In addition, it is not a wise strategy for judicial leadership to confront legislatures in the extant legal and political conditions, even though they may actually detest legislative supervision. Most important, courts have no legal grounds on which to oppose the supervision of legislatures. The principle of independent adjudication, according to Article 128 of the Constitution, does not exclude legislative supervision. Furthermore, the most difficult task for court reform is to resolve "local protectionism."[54] That is, judicial leaders are forced to give priority to

[51] Zuigao renmin fayun, *An Outline of the Five-Year Reforms of People's Courts*, p. 59.

[52] "Shaanxisheng 5,000duo geji renda daibiao pingyi yifu liangyuan gongzuo" (Some 5,000 people's congress deputies at various levels in Shaanxi appraised the works of governments, courts, and procuracies), *Zhongguo renda xinwen*, December 10, 2001 (available at http://zgrdxw.peopledaily.com.cn/gb/paper7/11/class00007.../hwz188661.htm).

[53] Quanguorenda, *A Beneficial Exploration of Socialist Democratic and Legal System Construction*, pp. 162–69.

[54] Zuigao renmin fayuan, *An Outline of the Five-Year Reforms of People's Courts*, p. 59; Xin and Li, *Governance According to Law and Judicial Reform*, pp. 442–43; Liu and

dealing with local Party committees and governments who are the chief causes of "local protectionism," rather than legislatures. Finally, legislatures and procuracies in many regions recently have jointly supervised courts. Procuracies, as state organs for legal supervision (Article 129 of the Constitution), have the right to oversee the courts' adjudication process as well as to carry out public prosecutions. And they have wielded power over courts with the encouragement of legislatures even in civil and economic cases that they did not prosecute.[55] Therefore, courts do not have any other powers to help them if they confront legislatures.

For these reasons, the presidents of the Supreme and higher courts have strongly urged lower-level courts to actively accept the supervision of local people's congresses,[56] and some basic-level courts have changed their attitude markedly since the late 1990s.[57] Judicial leaders argue that courts should combine internal and external supervision to address their problems, and that they can gain the valuable understanding and support of local legislatures by accepting their supervision. To this end, the Supreme People's Court promulgated a regulation on how to accept legislative supervision in 1998, three years after the Supreme People's Procuratorate did.[58] In particular, they emphasize the importance of legislative support in tackling the difficulty in enforcing court decisions (zhixingnan). They are aware that courts alone cannot shield themselves from external influence, such as

---

Zhang, *Hot Issues on Judicial Reform*, pp. 30–31; Tan, *A Study on Judicial Reform in China*, pp. 82–85.

[55] Yang Caifeng and Tian Kaisong, "Dangxin biezai ban cuoan" (Be careful not to misjudge again), *Renmin zhi you*, No. 3 and 4 (April 2000), pp. 24–26; Qinhuangdaoshi, "Strengthen individual case supervision and promote judicial fairness," pp. 30–31; Liu, "How we strengthened the supervision of judicial cases," pp. 13–14.

[56] "Xiao Yang yaoqiu geji fayuan zhudong jieshou renda jiandu" (Xiao Yang required courts at various levels to accept people's congress supervision actively), *Shandong renda gongzuo*, No. 3 (March 1999), p. 61; "Xiao Yang qiangdiao: Geji fayuan yao jinyibu zijue jieshou renda jiandu" (Xaio Yang emphasized: Courts at various level further consciously accept people's congress supervision), *Zhongguo renda xinwen*, October 17, 2001 (available at http://zgrdxw.peopledaily.com.cn/gb/paper7/10/class0007.../hwz177252.htm); Li Daomin, "Renzhen jieshou pingyi jiji gaohao zhenggai" (Earnestly accept appraisal and positively conduct rectification and reform), *Renda jianshe*, No. 5 (May 1999), pp. 7–8.

[57] Interview with legislative leaders and staff: Tianjin, January 2002.

[58] Zuigao renmin fayuan, *An Outline of the Five-Year Reforms of People's Courts*, pp. 197–201; Liu Zheng, Yu Youmin, and Cheng Xiangqing (eds.), *Renmin daibiao dahui gongzuo quanshu* (*Overall Book on the Works of People's Congresses*) (Beijing: Zhongguo fazhi chubanshe, 1999), pp. 292–94.

that of local governments.[59] In fact, courts in many regions, including Yunnan Provincial Higher People's Court, accepted this advice.[60] And local legislatures are willing to support rather than supervise courts, if courts "conscientiously" accept supervision and ask them to help.[61]

DEVELOPING NEW STATE ORGANS

During their development, local people's congresses and courts could not expect to have institutionally based authority in the Chinese party-state. Instead, they have had to make full use of opportunities to expand their jurisdiction and intensify their organizational capacity, coping with each other as well as established powers which incessantly encroached upon their sphere of influence. As a result, the pattern of development of these newly emerging forces becomes more complicated than expected: a series of intertwined relationships of state organs with the CCP at the apex, based on their legal and political status, rather than independent and autonomous development, and their desperate efforts to exploit each and every opportunity.[62]

Even in the reform era, local people's congresses have limited clear-cut jurisdiction, except in legislation. Few question the lawmaking function of legislatures with the advent of a market economy, and the CCP and governments have to a certain degree tolerated the increased power of legislatures in this area, as it does not radically encroach upon their established interests. But supervision is different, because it limits the authority of supervised organs. For this reason, even emerging organizations like courts, not to mention the Party and governments, would not easily acknowledge it. Thus, local legislatures have to take a more assertive attitude toward securing jurisdiction in the area of supervision. Aggressive supervision over courts has been the result. That is, unlike supervision over governments, in which legislatures have been

---

[59] Zuigao renmin fayuan, *An Outline of the Five-Year Reforms of People's Courts*, p. 268.

[60] Ibid., pp. 327–35.

[61] Ren Keli, "Qieshi jiaqiang jiandu baozhang sifa gongzheng" (Surely strengthen supervision and guarantee judicial fairness), *Renda jianshe*, No. 1 (January 2000), pp. 10–12; Xiao Cheng, "Shi jiandu, yeshi zhichi" (Supervision is also support), *Minzhu fazhi jianshe*, No. 7 (July 1999), pp. 8–9.

[62] On the development strategy of Chinese legislatures, see Kevin O'Brien, "Chinese People's Congresses and legislative embeddedness: Understanding early organizational development," *Comparative Political Studies*, Vol. 27, No. 1 (April 1994), pp. 80–109.

very cautious and careful not to confront governments, they actively conducted the oversight of courts in order to secure their authority when the improved political conditions in the 1990s gave them the chance.

Courts are similar, but some differences do exist. The importance of judicial functions was widely acknowledged with the rapid increase in civil and economic litigation cases in the reform era. But courts themselves were not well prepared to take on these tasks due to problems such as a lack of well-educated judicial officers, the bureaucratization of court structures and adjudication procedures, and the dependence of courts on Party committees and governments for personnel and finances. In this context, courts initially opposed legislative supervision, because supervision, in their view, prevented them from realizing their interests such as fair and independent adjudication. But they have gradually changed their attitude after acknowledging both their inability to stand up to legislatures and their rational calculations about the extant legal and political conditions. The result is the entwinement strategy of courts with legislatures rather than confrontation. This strategy will continue until political and legal conditions change in the courts' favor and courts' organizational capacity grows strong enough to confront legislatures, as the legislatures have done with regard to governments since the early 1990s.

5

Role Fulfillment of Deputies to Local Legislatures

In the 1980s, Chinese citizens regarded their legislatures as "rubber stamps" and frequently called legislative members "deputies only in name." Western scholars also had a critical attitude toward the deputies' role fulfillment. For instance, Barrett L. McCormick argued that all deputies whom he had interviewed in the late 1980s and early 1990s did not want to become deputies.[1] In this case, Chinese legislators could not be expected to faithfully carry out their roles. Kevin O'Brien, unlike McCormick, did not find that all legislative members were inactive. But he argued that even active members behaved chiefly as "regime agents," and those who reflected popular interests were best thought of as "remonstrators" rather than representatives.[2]

What changes have there been in the Chinese legislators' role fulfillment since the 1990s? What roles do people's congresses' deputies now perform, and to what degree? In this regard, first, it is worth emphasizing that both the NPC and local legislatures at various levels have become important political actors in the reform era, especially since the 1990s. This hints at the possibility of change in deputies' role fulfillment, because legislative functions could not have strengthened without legislative members themselves being more active.

[1] Barrett L. McCormick, "China's Leninist parliament and public sphere: A comparative analysis," in Barrett L. McCormick and Jonathan Unger (eds.), *China after Socialism: In the Footsteps of Eastern Europe or East Asia?* (Armonk, NY: M.E. Sharpe, 1996), p. 40.
[2] Kevin O'Brien, "Agents and remonstrators: Role accumulation by Chinese people's congress deputies," *China Quarterly*, No. 138 (June 1994), pp. 365–72.

In addition, available evidence notes the changes in public attitude toward deputy status in the 1990s. For example, a 1993 survey conducted in Shuzhu City of Hunan Province showed that about 26 percent of respondents earnestly wanted to be deputies, even though 40 percent of them still did not want to be deputies (the rest said they would serve if elected).[3] Also, more and more influential regional figures, including entrepreneurs and leading cadres in governments and state-sponsored organizations, have asked legislative leaders to help them to become deputies since the mid-1990s.[4] In particular, the "Beijing Phenomena" (*Beijing xianxiang*) and "Shenzhen Phenomena," in which a dozen self-recommended candidates conducted active election campaigns and among them three candidates were finally elected as deputies in the 2003 elections to county-level people's congresses in Beijing and Shenzhen, demonstrate that the attitude of both the public and deputies toward deputy status and role have shifted dramatically.[5]

This chapter argues that the role fulfillment of people's congress deputies has changed since the early 1990s. Most of all, Chinese legislators have performed three roles: supervision, reflection (*fanying*), and policy-providing, with the first two as their dominant roles. That is, they act primarily as "public supervisors" and "opinion reflectors" rather than "regime agents" and "remonstrators." In addition, deputies' role fulfillment has differed depending on their social backgrounds. Legislative members from worker and peasant backgrounds tend to act as opinion reflectors and public supervisors, while legislators with intellectual backgrounds and some official deputies are more oriented to policy-providing. Private entrepreneurs and businesspersons who become

[3] Li Jitai, "Yao zhongshi xuanmin dui daibiao zhixing zhiwude jiandu" (We should pay attention to voters' supervision of deputy's role fulfilment), *Renda gongzuo tongxun*, No. 8 (April 1994), p. 30.
[4] Interview with legislative leaders and senior staff: Tianjin, March 2001; "Renda daibiao bushi hushenfu" (Status of deputy is not an amulet), *Zhongguo renda xinwen*, September 18, 2001 (available at http://zgrdxw.peopledaily.com.cn).
[5] On the concrete cases of these phenomena and the political implications, see Tang Juan and Zou Shulin (eds.), *2003nian Shenzhen jingxuan shilu* (*A Document of 2003 Competitive Elections in Shenzhen*) (Xian: Xibei daxue chubanshe, 2003); Zou Shulin (ed.), *2003nian Beijingshi quxian renda daibiao jingxuan shilu* (*A Document of 2003 Competitive Elections of Deputies to District and County People's Congresses in Beijing*) (Xian: Xibei daxue chubanshe, 2004); Huang Weiping and Wang Yongsheng (eds.), *Dangdai Zhongguo zhengzhi yanjiu baogao IV* (*A Research Report on Contemporary Chinese Politics* (Vol. 4) (Beijing: Shehui kexue wenxian chubanshe, 2004), pp. 224–40.

deputies are more interested in exemplary and economic roles, the closest role to regime agents. In sum, deputies since the early 1990s have become progressively more representative than before, even without the radical change of the Chinese party-state and its legislative system.

This chapter concentrates on the "active" deputies in order to understand roles that they perform and the degree of their performance. Deputies can be placed somewhere along a continuum: at one end are those who play a minimal role (that is, only attending annual plenary sessions and other big events), and at the other are deputies who spend most of their time on legislative duties. The former can be called "inactive." In contrast, active deputies take part in various activities, and they illustrate the kinds and degrees of deputies' role fulfillment.[6] Thus, we need to focus on active deputies. To this end, this study investigated deputies who were featured in journals published by the NPC and provincial-level people's congresses.[7] I have also conducted interviews

---

[6] Now we cannot exactly estimate the proportion of inactive and active deputies because of lack of available statistics. According to some data gathered by Chinese researchers, active deputies are, of course, fewer in number than inactive ones. For example, in a survey of deputies to the Yangzhou City People's Congress conducted in January 1999, about 31 percent of respondents regarded themselves as "deputies who conducted roles well," while about 65 percent replied "generally acted," and 4 percent said that they "did not play any role." And in practice, about 26 percent of deputies did not participate in any kind of legislative activities when the people's congress was not in session. This shows that, in the case of Yangzhou, at best about 30 percent of deputies can be considered as active, and that the same proportion are actually inactive deputies who only attend the plenary sessions and big events (the rest are placed between the extremes). Li Jitai and Zhang Yuanyuan, "Daibiao yanzhongde daibiao gongzuo" (Deputy works in the deputies' eyes), *Renda luntan* (*People's Congress Forum*), No. 8 (August 1999), p. 28. However, now both deputies and the public, according to several survey researchers, think that the roles of both people's congresses and deputies were markedly strengthened in the 1990s. "Baixing xinmu zhongde renda" (People's congresses in the mind of ordinary people), *Shidai zhuren* (*Masters of Times*), No. 11 (November 2000), pp. 26–27; "Guangzhou shimin pubian rentong renda daibiao jianyan" (Citizens in Guangzhou City generally identified with the proposals of people's congress deputies), *Nanfang dushibao* (*Southern City Daily*), March 29, 2001. On the deputies' role fulfillment in the mid-1980s, see Zhao Baoxu (ed.), *Minzhu zhengzhi yu difang renda* (*Democratic Politics and Local People's Congresses*) (Xian: Shaanxi renmin chubanshe, 1990), pp. 87–112, 185–96, 217–41.

[7] Now all the 31 provincial-level people's congresses publish their journals monthly, and every issue carries about two or three articles on deputies' activities. Of these, I investigated 10 journals that are published by relatively active congresses, and I covered the period from January 1999 to June 2001 (30 issues per journal). The journals are: *Shanghai People's Congresses Monthly*; *Renmin zhi sheng* (*People's Voices*) in Guangdong Province; *Renmin zhengtan* (*People's Political Forum*) in Fujian; *Fazhi* (*Rule of Law*) in Heilongjiang; *Renmin yu quanli* (*People and Power*) in Jiangsu;

TABLE 5.1. *Number of people's congress deputies at various levels (November 1, 1994)*

Divisions (number of people's congresses)		Deputies (%)
NPC		2,979 (0.08)
Local people's congresses	Provincial level (31)	20,989 (0.6)
	Cities divided into districts (189) and autonomous prefectures (30)	83,155 (2.8)
	County level (2,897)	651,311 (18.6)
	Township level (48,172)	2,743,378 (78.3)
Total		3,501,812 (100)

Source: Quanguo renda changweihui bangongting lianluoju, "Woguo geji renda daibiao gongyu 350 duowan ming" (Our country has over 3.5 million people's congress deputies at various levels), *Renda Gongzuo Tongxun* (*The Bulletin of the Works of People's Congress*), No. 1 (January 1995), p. 320.

with some legislative leaders, staff, and deputies to complement the documentary surveys.

Finally, in analyzing the deputies' role fulfillment, this chapter does not distinguish among deputies according to their administrative levels for two reasons. First, the deputies to township- and county-level people's congresses comprise about 97 percent of all deputies, as Table 5.1 shows. In other words, the activities of deputies to the NPC and provincial-level people's congresses do not have substantial meaning due to their small number. Second, there are few differences between the NPC and local legislatures' deputies in terms of practical activities when the legislatures are not in session. In a sense, the lower the administrative level the deputies belong to, the more active is their role fulfillment. (This is discussed in more detail later.)

Shandong renda gongzuo (*Works of People's Congresses in Shandong*); *Chutian zhuren* (*Masters in Hubei*); *Renmin zhi you* (*People's Friend*) in Hunan; *Shidai zhuren* (*Master of Times*) in Jiangxi; *Difang renda jianshe* (*Construction of Local People's Congresses*) in Hebei. I also investigated the deputies featured in the NPC's semi-monthly journal, i.e., *Renda gongzuo tongxun* and *Zhongguo renda*, from 1994 to 2001. Finally, I analyzed the most active 100 deputies who were recommended by people's congresses at the request of NPC staff. Quanguorenda changweihui bangongting lianluoju (ed.), *Wo zenyang dang renda daibiao* (*I How to Act as a Deputy to People's Congresses*) (Beijing: Zhongguo minzhu fazhi chubanshe, 2000). In total, I analyzed some 600 cases for which I could confirm both deputies' social backgrounds and role fulfillment.

CHANGED LEGAL-POLITICAL CONDITIONS AND
PUBLIC EXPECTATIONS OF DEPUTIES

Legal and political conditions for the activities of legislatures and public expectations of legislative members have an important influence on roles people's congresses' deputies play and the degree of their performance. Legal and political conditions and the public's cognition have gradually but markedly improved since the early 1990s. Under these more benign conditions, Chinese legislators have become more courageous and active in carrying out their roles.

Legal conditions for deputies' activities have been improved since 1992. Neither legislatures nor their members took root in the 1980s and they frequently encountered difficulties in accomplishing their roles. In particular, Party cadres and government officials frequently infringed upon deputies' powers, and work unit leaders in many cases did not allow legislators enough time to carry out their duties. For this reason, deputies asked legislative leaders to enact a specific law to clearly prescribe their duties and powers.[8] As a result, the NPC enacted the Law of Deputies to the NPC and Local People's Congresses at Various Levels (Deputy Law) in 1992.[9]

This law provides deputies with such guarantees as immunity from arrest. Further, according to the Deputy Law, state institutions, social organizations, and the public should cooperate with deputies to aid them in accomplishing their functions. In addition, work units should provide legislators with compensation for time and income forgone while performing legislative duties. Since the law became effective, incidences of deputies' powers being infringed upon have decreased, and their powers have been better protected. The law's promulgation marks a "new phase" in deputies' work.[10]

There were, of course, continuous infringements of people's congress deputies' powers in the 1990s. In Hunan Province alone from 1992 to 1996, ninety-seven cases of violations of the Deputy Law were reported.[11]

---

[8] Zhao, *Democratic Politics and Local People's Congresses*, pp. 190–91.

[9] Liu Zheng, Yu Youmin, and Cheng Xiangqing (eds.), *Renmin daibiao dahui gongzuo quanshu* (*Overall Book on the Works of People's Congresses*) (Beijing: Zhongguo fazhi chubanshe, 1999), pp. 281–83.

[10] Anhuisheng renda, "Chengxiao xianzhu, renzhong daoyuan" (Achievements are remarkable, but the burden is heavy and the road is long), *Zhongguo renda*, No. 1 (January 2000), p. 14; Interview with legislative leaders and senior staff: Tianjin, March 2001.

[11] Anhuisheng renda, "Achievements are remarkable," p. 14.

However, there are striking differences in the consequences before and after the law's enactment. That is, infringements have been punished since the legislation of the Deputy Law. In those cases, both the Party and legislatures directly participate in the investigations and publicize the results in an attempt to warn other cadres.[12]

In China, political guarantees for people's congress deputies granted by the Party are more critical than legal guarantees. In this regard, Chinese legislators have been able to enjoy markedly improved conditions since the early 1990s. The CCP has taken steps to strengthen the role of people's congresses and their members. After the 1986–87 student movement and the 1989 Tiananmen Incident, the Party center decided to strengthen the supervisory function of all state organs as well as the Party itself in order to control cadre corruption and to restore public confidence. A decision issued by the CCP Central Committee in 1990 was a good example. Support of legislatures in wielding their supervisory powers according to law was an important component of the Party's policy. Since committing itself to the formation of a socialist market economy in 1992, the Party has stressed the policy of governance according to law. This policy, which was adopted as a guiding principle at the 15th Party Congress in 1997 and recorded in the Preamble of the Chinese Constitution through a 1999 amendment, also invigorated legislative members, because legislatures are state power organs with the right to legislate and to supervise the implementation of laws by other state organs.[13]

To implement this policy, the provincial Party committees held work conferences on legislatures across the country throughout the 1990s.[14] The Tianjin Municipal Party Committee, for example, in an unprecedented act, held its conference in July 1994, and it emphasized two points: Party committees should put legislative work on their agenda and fully support legislatures and their members to exercise their powers in accordance with laws; and legislatures should improve their work by

[12] On concrete cases, see Hebeisheng renda changweihui, "Guanyu Fengfengkuangqu fayuan feifa jukao sheng renda daibiao Zhang Fusheng" (A circular on the case of Zhang Fusheng deputy's illegal detention by the Fengfengkuang District Court), *Zhongguo renda*, No. 1 (January 2000), p. 23; "Hunan renda daibiao wugu beida, da renminjing zhong shou chufen" (A Hunan People's Congress deputy was assaulted and assaulter officer was finally punished), *Zhongguo renda xinwen*, September 5, 2001 (available at http://zgrdxw.peopledaily.com.cn).
[13] Interview with legislative leaders and senior staff: Tianjin, March 2001.
[14] Li Bojun, "Gesheng zizhiqu zhixiashi dangwei zhaokai renda daibiao gongzuo huiyide qingkuang" (The situations of people's congress work conferences held by the provincial Party committees), *Zhongguo renda*, No. 3 (February 2000), pp. 19–20.

sticking to the Party line.[15] After this conference, eighteen district and county Party committees in the Tianjin area continued to hold similar meetings to implement this decision, and these measures brought "new winds" to legislative work.[16]

Finally, increased public expectations have encouraged people's congress deputies to play more active roles. In the 1990s, residents more frequently visited their deputies when they encountered difficulties. According to Tianjian Shi's survey of the urban population in Beijing in 1988 and 1996, the percentage of the public who complained through deputies increased from 8.6 to 14.1 percent.[17] Similarly, the volume of public letters and visits (*xinfang*) to legislatures sharply increased. Beginning in the mid-1990s, letters and visits to the Heilongjiang Provincial People's Congress increased by 50 percent annually, and several county-level people's congresses in Guangxi Autonomous Region recorded increases of 20–40 percent in the same period.[18] Consequently, legislatures, along with the Party and governments, became one of the main channels for the public to complain about social problems. As the saying goes, "Call deputies when you have sticky problems."[19]

In line with these greater expectations, the public wants to supervise deputies more strictly. Legislative members who do not appear to fulfill their duties face the prospect of being dismissed from office. Residents in one electorate of Guangxi's Nanning City, for instance, held a meeting in March 2001 and dismissed a deputy who they believed had not carried out the role earnestly.[20] In response to public

---

[15] Tianjinshi difangzhi bianxiu weiyuanhui (ed.), *Tianjin tongzhi: zhengquan zhi renmin daibiao dahui juan* (*Overall Annals of Tianjin: Regime Annals People's Congress Volume*) (Tianjin: Tianjin shehui kexueyuan chubanshe, 1997), pp. 482–83.

[16] Interview with legislative leaders and senior staff: Tianjin, April 2001; Kang Ziming (ed.), *Nankai renda ershinian 1979–99* (*Twenty Years of Nankai People's Congress, 1979–99*) (Tianjin, 1999), p. 4.

[17] Tianjian Shi, "Mass political behavior in Beijing," in Merle Goldman and Roderick MacFarquhar (eds.), *The Paradox of China's Post-Mao Reforms* (Cambridge, MA: Harvard University Press, 1999), p. 155.

[18] Chen Xin, "Yifa guifan renda changweihui xinfang gongzuo" (Standardizing people's congress standing committee's works of letters and visiting), *Fazhi*, No. 1 (January 2001), p. 12; Tan Rifei, "Youwei cai you'wei,' wuwei cai wu'wei'" (If you have something doing, you will have a status, otherwise you won't), *Guangxi renda* (*People's Congresses in Guangxi*), No. 4 (April 1999), p. 5.

[19] Li Zhanggen and Zhang Jihua, "Shuchuanxian rendade xinfang weihe yuelai yueduo" (Why have Shuchuan County People's Congress's works of letters and visiting increased more and more?), *Shidai zhuren*, No. 4 (April 2000), p. 28.

[20] "Guangxi Nanningshi Yongxinqu: Daibiao bujinzhi zhiwu bei zhongzhi" (Yongxin District of Nanning City in Guangxi: A deputy's qualification suspended for not

demands, legislative leaders also begin to suspend the qualifications of ordinary legislators who are absent from plenary sessions twice without prior approval, in line with the Deputy Law. The county people's congresses of Anxiang in Hunan Province, Linqu in Shandong Province, and Pengshan in Sichuan Province all suspended a deputy's qualifications in February 2001.[21] In addition, legislative members have to report their role achievements to voters and face evaluations in voter meetings.[22] From 1994 to 1996 in Chenzhou City of Hunan Province, for example, about 6,500 deputies at various levels reported their accomplishments and were appraised according to this system.[23]

Legislative leaders have not just asked deputies to play their roles more actively, however. That is, they have also strived to motivate legislators by adopting new measures for supervising other state organs since the early 1990s, including the examination of law enforcement and deputies' appraisal of state organ works. These measures have given deputies an expanded and more effective scope for activity than in the 1980s. For instance, when people's congresses in Henan Province conducted examination in 1992 to assess whether governments had implemented agriculture-related laws and central policies properly, some 70,000 members from 77 percent of county-level and 91 percent of township-level people's congresses in the province participated in this

fulfilling deputy's duty), *Zhongguo renda xinwen*, May 23, 2001 (available at http://zgrdxw.peopledaily.com.cn). On other cases, see "Buchengzhi daibiao gaimian" (Incompetent deputies should be dismissed), *Zhongguo renda xinwen*, September 19, 2001 (available at http://zgrdxw.peopledaily.com.cn).

[21] "Hunan Anxiang, Shandong Linqu geyou yi daibiao wugu bucanjia huyi bei zhongzhi zige" (Anxiang in Hunan and Linqu in Shandong had a deputy's qualification suspended for not attending people's congress plenary sessions without reasons), *Zhongguo renda xinwen*, May 23, 2001 (available at http://zgrdxw.peopledaily.com. cn); "Sichuan Pengshan zhongzhi yi xian renda daibiao zige" (Pengshan County in Sichuan suspended the qualification of a county people's congress deputy), *Zhongguo renda xinwen*, April 10, 2001 (available at http://zgrdxw.peopledaily.com.cn).

[22] Some regions started to use it in 1988, and more and more regions have adopted it since the early 1990s. Gan He, "Dangqian difang renda daibiao gongzuode xin jinzhan he xuyao yanjiude yixie wenti" (Contemporary new progresses in the works of people's congress deputies and a few problems need study), *Renda yanjiu* (*Study of People's Congresses*), No. 9 (September 2001) (available at http://www.rdyj.com.cn).

[23] Anhuisheng renda, "Achievements are remarkable," p. 14. On other cases, see Huang Daming, "Xiang xuanmin shuzhi rang xuanmin pingshuo" (Reported duty fulfillment towards voters and let voters appraise), *Shanghai renda yuekan* (*Shanghai People's Congresses Monthly*), No. 2 (February 2000), pp. 12–14; "Renda daibiao zoushang shuzhitai" (Deputies to people's congresses go on self-reporting platforms), *Renmin zhengtan*, No. 8 (August 2001), pp. 38–39.

examination.[24] And annually about 70,000 legislators at various levels in Sichuan Province also engaged in deputies' appraisal of public security systems (1996), procuracies (1997), and courts (1998).[25]

CHANGED DEPUTIES' ROLE FULFILLMENT IN THE 1990S

Under the improved legal and political conditions for legislative activities and higher public expectation since the early 1990s, people's congress deputies have performed three major roles: supervision, reflection, and policy-providing. These roles are different from those in the 1980s.

SUPERVISION

People's congress deputies pay much attention to their supervisory role, regarding it as their most important daily work.[26] As noted before, since the early 1990s, Party and legislative leaders have stressed this role as an effective tool to control cadre corruption in local governments. They also emphasize this role because deputies can help the Party center alleviate the poor implementation of central policies in the localities. In this regard, people's congresses have two advantages: they have a huge supervisory corps of more than three million deputies, and they can wield their supervisory authority in the name of the people.

Generally speaking, legislative members try to supervise the policy implementation of mid- and basic-level state organs, concentrating on such key issues as the "three arbitraries" (*sanluan*, or arbitrary fines, fees, and apportionment) of government agencies and the abuse of power by public security organs. Meanwhile, people's congresses' plenary sessions and standing committee meetings, in accordance with the Constitution and pertinent laws, tend to concentrate on overseeing macro-issues,

---

[24] Quanguorenda, *Papers Commemorating the 40th Anniversary of People's Congresses*, p. 239.
[25] Cui Jianhua, "Pingyi zhi hua zai chuzhong dadi zhankai" (Flowers of appraisal evolved in the Sichuan area) (1) (2), *Minzhu fazhi jianshe (Construction of Democracy and Legal System)*, No. 8 (August 1999), pp. 8–10 and No. 9 (September 1999), pp. 9–11; "Weile tianping buqingxie" (In order not to make scales tilted), *Minzhu fazhi jianshe*, No. 10 (October 1999), pp. 11–13.
[26] Interview with legislative leaders and senior staff: Tianjin, October 2001.

including the overall achievements of state organs, and the drafting and execution of state budgets and socioeconomic plans.

Legislators can conduct supervisory roles both collectively and individually. Since most regions adopted new supervisory measures in the 1990s, most deputies have been able to carry out these activities collectively under the leadership of people's congress standing committees. For instance, when the Nankai District People's Congress in Tianjin Municipality conducted a deputies' appraisal for six months in 2000, 85.6 percent of legislative members participated in inspections, meeting with residents and listening to their opinions.[27] Similarly, about 90 percent of deputies to the Hongkou District People's Congress in Shanghai Municipality have attended deputies' appraisals for several months every year since 1995.[28]

In addition, deputies engage in supervision through deputy small groups (*daibiao xiaozu*). Since the late 1980s, they have had to belong to a region- or trade-based group of this kind. In Beijing, 17,498 people's congress deputies at all levels were organized into 1,734 small groups in 1997: 3 groups for the NPC deputies, 36 for the Beijing Municipal People's Congress, and 471 for county-level and 1,224 for township-level people's congresses.[29] In Tianjin, 77.3 percent of the Municipal People's Congress deputies took part in thirteen groups based on their trades, including economic, financial, education, and urban construction.[30] These groups decide and conduct supervisory activities, such as addressing problems

[27] Su Jingyu and Huang Yumin, "Yici xinde changshi: Nankaiqu zhifa pingyi dahui ceji" (A first new attempt: Sidelights on the appraisal meeting of law enforcement in Nankai District), *Tianjin renda gongzuo (Works of Tianjin People's Congresses)*, No. 12 (December 2000), pp. 8, 17.

[28] Zhou Kecheng, "Fahui daibiao zai pingyi zhongde zhuti zuoyong" (Make deputies play a master role in appraisal activity), *Shanghai renda yuekan*, No. 8 (August 1999), pp. 31–32.

[29] Beijingshi renda changweihui daibiao lianluoshi, "Guanyu renda daibiao xiaozu gongzuode diaocha" (Research on the works of people's congress deputy small groups), *Renda gongzuo tongxun*, No. 8 (April 1997), p. 20.

[30] Yang Fengchun (ed.), *Zai shengji renda gongzuo gangweishang (On the Posts of Provincial People's Congresses)* (Beijing: Zhongguo minzhu fazhi chubanshe, 1996), p. 51. On the activity of deputy small group, see Tianjinshi Dagangqu dijiu daibiaozu, "Baizheng guanxi, gaohao jiehe, nuli fahui daibiaozu zuoyong" (Arrange connections well, collect all efforts well, and display the role of deputy small group), *Renda gongzuo tongxun*, No. 18 (September 1996), p. 31; Hezheshi Nancheng renda lianluochu, "Zhongshi jiaqiang jichu gongzuo, fahui daibiao xiaozu zuoyong" (Emphasis on strengthening basic-level works, to display the role of deputy small group), *Renda gongzuo tongxun*, No. 8 (April 1994), pp. 24–26.

of law enforcement by jointly visiting chiefs of public security and Party leaders.[31]

People's congress deputies also individually visit law enforcement departments, meet leading officials, and demand the resolution of problems. If they directly observe a case of illegal law enforcement, legislative members can protest by showing their identification cards. Furthermore, some deputies concurrently serve as special supervisors of courts, procuracies, and government law enforcement bureaus at the request of these institutions. In 1999, about 12 percent of the Shanghai Municipal People's Congress deputies acted as special supervisors of this kind.[32] And local courts in many regions, under the direction of the Supreme People's Court in 1998, have begun to establish a special office that is specifically responsible for executing deputy's suggestions.

Legislative members occasionally encounter difficulties in conducting their duties, such as assault and arrest. They even risk death while earnestly conducting supervision.[33] There is another problem of relevance here: the supervisory effect was not ideal. However, some evidence supports the claim that the supervisory effect has improved since the 1990s. First, legislative members have resolutely wielded strong powers like interpellation when state organs refused to accept their demands. For example, deputies of the Hunan, Sichuan, Henan, and Hainan Provincial People's Congresses submitted interpellation bills in 1998, 1999, and 2000.[34] Furthermore, leading officials, judges, and procurators were dismissed after supervision. In 2000 alone, people's congresses in Huaihua City of Hunan Province discharged

---

[31] On concrete cases, see Quanguorenda, *I How to Act as a Deputy to People's Congresses*, pp. 270–78.

[32] Hai Yan, "Hu Zhengchang tan xin yinian daibiao gongzuo silu" (Hu Zhengchang explains new year's thinking of deputy works), *Shanghai renda yuekan*, No. 2 (February 1999), pp. 4–5.

[33] On concrete cases, see Xu Yingchong and Zhoubing, "Bingqing yujie xi minxin" (Clear as ice and pure as gem, concerned with people's minds), *Renda gongzuo tongxun*, No. 5 (March 1996), pp. 35–36; Quanguorenda, *I How to Act as a Deputy to People's Congresses*, pp. 212–20.

[34] Chu Yang, "Weiyuan nu ti zhixunan" (Members angrily introduced an interpellation bill), *Renmin zhi you*, No. 3–4 (April 1999), pp. 20–22; "Sichuan renda daibiao zhixun shebaoju" (Deputies to Sichuan People's Congress required social welfare bureau to explain), *Renmin zhi you*, No. 3–4 (April 1999), p. 55; Wang Caiwei, "Yipian kaikuo er qingliangde tiankong: Jiqi zhixunan jishi" (Open and clear sky: Records on several interpellation cases), *Renmin zhengtan*, No. 6 (June 2001), pp. 10–13.

TABLE 5.2. *Implementation of deputy proposals: Shanghai Municipal People's Congress*

		8th (1983–87)	9th (1988–92)	10th (1993–95)	Subtotal
Implemented or	Cases	1,666	3,245	1,228	6,139
implementing	Rate (%)	33.4	48	50.7	43.3
Scheduled to	Cases	734	1,110	429	2,273
implement	Rate (%)	14.8	16.4	17.7	16.1
Conference	Cases	753	1,192	636	2,583
for work	Rate (%)	15.1	17.6	26.3	18.2
Explained to	Cases	1,831	1,214	128	3,173
deputies	Rate (%)	36.7	18	5.3	22.4
Total		4,984	6,761	2,421	14,168

Source: Cai Dingjian, *Zhongguo renmin daibiao dahui zhidu* (*People's Congress System in China*) (Revised edition) (Beijing: Falü chubanshe, 1998), p. 370.

six leading cadres: one county vice-magistrate, three judges, and two procurators.[35]

Second, the implementation rate (*luoshilü*) of people's congress deputies' proposals, through which legislative members express demands on supervision and other matters, has increased. In the case of Shanghai Municipal People's Congress, as Table 5.2 shows, the rate of "implemented or implementing" increased from 33.4 percent in the 8th period (1983–87) to 50.7 percent in the 10th period (1993–95) of the legislature. Likewise, a staff member responsible for deputy liaison work of the Xiangtan City People's Congress in Hunan Province noted that the rate increased from less than 20 percent in the mid-1980s to 48.5 percent in 1999.[36] Further, legislatures have turned down government work reports relating to the implementation of deputies' proposals when governments, they believe, did not sincerely listen to their demands. In

[35] "Yanming falü tuijin fazhi" (Strict and impartial laws advanced rule of law), *Zhongguo renda xinwen*, April 4, 2001 (available at http://zgrdxw.peopledaily.com.cn).

[36] Wang Tingjian, "Rang daibiao manyi" (Make deputies satisfactory), *Renmin zhi you*, No. 11 (November 2000), pp. 23–24. Recently, people's congresses collect and make public the statistics of the implementation rate regularly, and the leaderships of other state organs are very nervous about the results. This is because the Party committees and people's congresses think that a government's low rate of implementation shows the government's "arrogant" attitude toward "people's voices." So other state organs try to raise the rate as high as possible, and as a result, the satisfaction of deputies is elevated. Interview with legislative leaders and senior staff: Tianjin, October 2001.

November 1999, for instance, the Standing Committee of Chongqing Municipal People's Congress vetoed a work report on the implementation of proposals, because about 40 percent of deputies were dissatisfied with the government's handling of their proposals. In these ways, legislative members have forced other state organs to implement their demands more sincerely, and the supervisory effect has been enhanced.

REFLECTION

People's congress deputies are required to maintain contact with the public in order to understand social problems and listen to public demands. At the same time, Chinese legislators should transmit public demands to state organs and urge these organs to carry them out faithfully. In a sense, the reflector roles are similar to that of "remonstrators" posited by O'Brien. This role, a component of the bridge-building (*qiaoliang*) role of deputies, has been regarded as a very important daily task of deputies since the early 1980s. Party leaders emphasize this role, not only because it provides the regime with a trustworthy channel to understand social problems, but also because it enhances social integrity by alleviating public dissatisfaction before an explosion. A case in point is Jiang Zemin's remarks that deputies should maintain contact with the public more earnestly and should more actively reflect public demands.[37] And, in fact, public demands reflected by deputies exerted more and more influential effects on governments in the 1990s, as illustrated by the increased implementation rate of deputies' proposals.

Legislative members reflect various demands affecting people's daily life. Repairing roads and bridges, improving public facilities (e.g., public toilets, street lamps, and water supplies), alleviating environmental pollution, providing better educational and medical services, and preserving public order are the most frequently reflected issues in both urban and rural areas. In the countryside, as a county-level people's congress deputy said, legislators make a special effort to highlight the lack of funds for agricultural construction and the heavy burden on farmers.[38]

---

[37] Jiang Zemin, "Guanyu jianchi he wanshan renda zhidu" (On holding firmly and developing the people's congress system), in Quanguo renda changweihui bangongting yanjiushi (ed.), *Zhonghua renmin gongheguo renmin daibiao dahui wenxian ziliao huibian 1949–90* (*Collections on the Documents of China's People's Congresses 1949–90*) (Beijing: Zhongguo minzhu fazhi chubanshe, 1990), pp. 624–25.

[38] Zhen Yongfu, "Renzhunde shi jiu gan: Yiwei jiceng renda daibiaode zishu" (If you clearly know something, do it immediately: An account in a basic-level deputy's own words), *Renmin zhengtan*, No. 7 (July 2001), pp. 22–23.

Some deputies have attained honorable titles such as "deputy of roads" or "deputy of pollution control" for their achievements in these areas.[39] Deputies also listen to residents' personal problems. They try to find jobs for the unemployed, to resolve disputes between residents, and to raise funds for poor students. So a lot of deputies are affectionately known as "meddlers" (*aiguan xianshi*) because they are willing to interfere in public matters if so requested.[40]

When reflecting demands, people's congress deputies frequently do so collectively. Legislative members have often used the method of jointly submitting bills (*yian*) and proposals (*jianyi*). When the demand needs the approval and support of a higher-level government, it is submitted with the help of that legislature's members. For instance, several deputies to the NPC, the Heilongjiang Provincial and the Hailun City People's Congresses, who were all elected in Hailun City in Heilongjiang Province, submitted a joint proposal to the Provincial People's Congress, not to the city people's congress, in 1993. The proposal urged a Harbin City-owned company to disburse about 3.5 million RMB (yuan) to farmers who lived in the city. Finally, with the strong support of the Provincial People's Congress and Government, deputies could resolve the problem.[41]

Legislative members individually reflect public demands to local Party and government leaders. Since the early 1990s, the Party and governments have established special systems to allow deputies to directly transmit public demands to the leadership. For instance, a deputy of the Guangdong Provincial People's Congress was able to address a serious piracy problem in his region by using the "deputy hotlines" (*zhitong kuaiche*), which were established in 1998 by Li Changchun, then the Party secretary of Guangdong Province.[42] Deputies can also use meetings with top leaders during the plenary sessions of people's congresses or other meetings. An NPC deputy of Jilin Province, for example, actively appealed to several leaders of the State Council and Jilin

---

[39] Quanguorenda, *I How to Act as a Deputy to People's Congresses*, pp. 35–37.

[40] Zhang Zaihua, ""Shuo 'ailao'" (Old man who likes to meddle), *Renmin zhi you*, No. 9 (September 2000), pp. 20–21; Wu Tanchun, "Wukui yu renminde zhongtuo" (Feeling no qualms upon people's great trust), *Renmin zhi you*, No. 12 (December 2000), pp. 12–13; Miu Yichun, " 'Xianshilao' Lai Suping" (Old meddler Lai Suping), *Shidai zhuren*, No. 2 (February 2000), pp. 40–41.

[41] Ma Tianmin, "Pingancun cunmin xinzhongde hao daibiao" (A good deputy in the mind of Pingan villagers), *Fazhi*, No. 5 (May 2000), pp. 14–15.

[42] Chen Yuechan, "Yipian danxin wei renmin" (A leaf of red heart for people), *Renmin zhi sheng*, No. 11 (November 1999), pp. 32–33.

Provincial Government about the economic difficulties of her county during the 1994 NPC plenary sessions in Beijing. Eventually the governor of Jilin Province promised to decrease the amount of money that the county government was required to remit to higher-level governments.[43] Deputies in other regions also frequently use these channels to reflect the public's demands.[44]

POLICY-PROVIDING

Until recently, even the "supreme state power organ in China," the NPC, has played a minimal role in decision making for important state policies except for legislation. For instance, although granted by the Constitution, only since 1998 has the NPC Standing Committee reviewed the issue of emergency national loans requested by the State Council, but without any substantive changes to original proposals. Before then, the NPC in many cases did not even have a chance to review important policies: among fifty-seven huge national infrastructure projects costing more than one billion RMB (yuan) in the 7th (1986–90) Five-Year Plan, none was submitted and considered at the NPC meetings.[45] Similarly, the NPC ordinary deputies play a very limited role in the decision-making process inside the legislature. Only four bills, among 3,667 in total submitted

---

[43] Liu Zhi, "Jiaqiang he gaijin daibiao gongzuo genghaodi fahui daibiao zuoyong" (Strengthen and reform the works of deputy, and better display deputy's role), *Renda gongzuo tongxun*, No. 23 (December 1994), pp. 16–18; Li Guiju, "Woshi zenyang luxing renda daibiao zhiwude" (How I fulfill the duty of deputy), *Renda gongzuo tongxun*, No. 5 (March 1995), pp. 19–20.

[44] For other cases, see Neimenggu zizhiqu renda gongwei bangongshi, "Shendan daibiaozhi, xinji renminshi" (Body burdened with deputy's responsibility, mind concerned with people's affairs), *Renda gongzuo tongxun*, No. 21 (November 1995), pp. 34–35; Xu Xuefeng, "Daibiao shuode hua guanyong" (Deputy's speech was effective), *Renda gongzuo tongxun*, No. 5 (March 1995), p. 22; Xiong Jisheng, "Xinji difang jingji fazhan, fangyan quanguo canzheng yizheng" (Mind concerned with local economy, broadly participating in and discussing national politics), *Renda gongzuo tongxun*, No. 15 (August 1995), pp. 33–34.

[45] Wang Min, *Guojia quanli jiguande guomin jingji jihua he yusuan jiandu jizhi* (*The Supervisory System of State Power Organ over National Economic Plans and Budges*) (Beijing: Zhongguo minzhu fazhi chubanshe, 1993), pp. 253–58. Of course, the NPC reviewed one important issue in 1992: a bill on the Three Gorges dam project introduced by the State Council. But it was a special case, brought about by the coincidence of some deputies' strong requests and government attempts to lessen its burden. See Huang Jiren, *Yige quanguorenda daibiaode riji* (*The Diary of an NPC Deputy*) (Chongqing: Chongqing chubanshe, 1997), pp. 121–263; Zhu Guanglei, *Dangdai zhongguo zhengfu guocheng* (*Contemporary Chinese Government Process*) (Tianjin: Tianjin renmin chubanshe, 1997), pp. 157–65.

by the NPC deputies over ten years from 1983 to 1993, were put on the agenda of NPC meetings, and only one of them was passed with a resolution.[46]

Local people's congress deputies have played a more prominent role than NPC deputies in this area, and their role has been gradually but clearly strengthened since the early 1990s. However, they function mainly as policy "providers," not policy "makers." Policy-providing means that legislative members provide governments with policy proposals on important matters, and that they can sometimes make governments implement their proposals by means of decisions and resolutions that have the same legal effect as local laws in a given region. This role is similar to the policy representation that legislators in liberal democracies perform. In fact, deputies played some role in this area even in the late 1980s, by collecting information and consulting the Party and government on policy implementation. They also acted as opinion leaders in planning for lawmaking by submitting bills and proposals to people's congresses.[47] But they were not able to directly affect the decision making of important policies. It is at this point that deputies have started to break through since the early 1990s.

For example, according to Table 5.3, almost all deputies to Wuxi City People's Congress took part in submitting bills in the 1990s. The legislative leaders more actively put the deputy bills on the agenda of legislative meetings: of 306 bills submitted by the deputies over 16 years from 1983 to 1999, 27 bills (8.8 percent) were considered in the meetings and passed with resolutions and decisions.[48] As a result, Wuxi City Government had to implement them, although some of them needed a large amount of funds and time, as shown in Table 5.4. Other regions show the same trend, although there are disparities between regions. Deputies' bills in the Guangdong Provincial People's Congress, for example, required the

---

[46] Quanguorenda, *Collections on the Documents of China's People's Congresses 1949–90*, pp. 855–57; "Bajie Quanguorenda yici huiyi daibiao tichude yian shenyi baogao zongshu" (Summary on the result of consideration of deputy's bills at the first session of the eighth NPC), *Renda gongzuo tongxun*, No. 3 (February 1994), pp. 14–15, 36. In the same period, the NPC deputies submitted 34,233 proposals in total.

[47] On specific cases, see Compilation group (ed.), *Banli renda daibiao jianyi zhengxie weiyuan ti'an gongzuo ziliao huibian* (*Collections on the Working Materials of Implementing People's Congress Deputies' Proposals and CPPCC Members' Motions*) (Beijing: Zhongguo zhanwang chubanshe, 1989), pp. 41–50, 139–41, 183–93.

[48] Lu Jiebiao, "Liangdian gongcheng" (Enlightened project), *Renmin yu quanli*, No. 8 (August 1999), p. 23.

TABLE 5.3. *People's congress deputy bills: Wuxi City People's Congress, Jiangsu Province*

Year (period)	Deputies registered (1)	Bills submitted	Deputies participated (persons/time) (2)	(2) / (1)
1993 (11th)	596	18	786	1.3:1
1994 (11th)	596	20	846	1.42:1
1995 (11th)	596	12	439	0.74:1
1996 (11th)	596	21	847	1.42:1
1997 (11th)	596	15	1,052	1.77:1
1998 (12th)	418	20	809	1.94:1
1999 (12th)	418	13	553	1.3:1

Source: Lu Jiebiao, "Liangdian gongcheng" (Enlightened projects), *Renmin yu quanli* (*People and Power*), No. 8 (August 1999), p. 22.

TABLE 5.4. *Implementation of deputy bills: Wuxi City People's Congress, Jiangsu Province*

Year	Title of bill	Deputies participated	Period and funds (RMB, yuan)
1995	Strengthening the construction of food basket project	184	3 years 50 million
1996	Firmly controlling water pollution of Tai Lake in Wuxi area	351	8 years 305 million
1998	Accelerating the cleaning of river sediments in the region	189	5–8 years 740 million

Source: Lu Jiebiao, "Liangdian gongcheng," pp. 22–23.

government to start projects in areas like water control, construction of electrical facilities, roads, and housing in the 1990s.

Generally speaking, legislative leaders select deputy bills very strictly, because bills have a legal effect in a given region if they are passed with decisions or resolutions. So they should get the prior approval of the local Party committee at the same level before putting bills on the agenda, and should also consult local governments in advance. For this reason, it is not easy to schedule deputy bills on the agenda. But recently, more and more deputy bills are being considered in legislative meetings. For example, in 2001, Xuhui and Jiabei District People's Congresses in

Shanghai adopted four out of eight deputy bills and three out of seven, respectively.[49]

PROPAGANDA AND EXEMPLARY ROLES

People's congress deputies, as regime agents, are required to promulgate laws and policies, to persuade the public to observe them on behalf of the state. They have performed this role since the early 1980s. However, in the 1990s, first, legislative members did not seem to spend much time and effort in carrying out this role. Strictly speaking, as a legislative leader noted, this is the role of government officials, not legislative members.[50] For this role, deputies generally try to transmit the decisions that are discussed and passed at the plenary sessions of people's congresses to the electorate. They also explain laws and policies when the populace requests this, and sometimes more actively persuade them to observe laws and policies. Second, the content of propaganda has changed since the late 1990s. Deputies pay more attention to publicizing the legislative system itself instead of laws and policies. This is partly because the NPC and the Party center decided to strengthen the propaganda of the legislative system in December 1998.

The exemplary role is similar. Deputies, especially those who come from basic levels, are required to lead the public in carrying out state policies such as economic development. In practice, they actually do this. Most peasant deputies to a county-level people's congress, for example, based on the government's policy of agricultural restructuring, became the first to cultivate economic crops to persuade other farmers to do likewise. Deputies from private business backgrounds also took the lead in paying taxes honestly and cleaning up the environment.[51] But because a lot of deputies, especially basic-level, are role models (*mofan*) in their fields before becoming deputies, this role is not new to them. They perform this duty by continuing in their own occupations as model workers and farmers. It has thus become a far less prominent deputy role than

---

[49] "Shanghai ge quxian renda daibiao yian buxie liushuizhang" (Deputy bills of district and county people's congresses in Shanghai were not day-to-day accounts), *Zhongguo renda xinwen*, March 8, 2001 (available at http://zgrdxw.peopledaily.com.cn).

[50] Interview with legislative leaders and senior staff: Tianjin, October 2001.

[51] Wan Shuming, "Xuan ta dang daibiao meiyou cuo" (Electing her a deputy was not wrong), *Shidai zhuren*, No. 4 (April 2001), p. 31; Huang Hongji and Chen Xianyong, "Ye daibiao texie" (A special writing on deputy Ye), *Renmin zhi you*, No. 1–2 (February 2001), pp. 33–34.

supervision and reflection, even though legislative leaders and members pay lip service to it to go along with the Party's supreme policy of economic development.[52]

DIFFERENTIATION OF DEPUTIES' ROLE FULFILLMENT IN THE 1990S

People's congress deputies come from all major social classes. As Table 5.5 indicates, workers and peasants, intellectuals, and cadres make up 70 to 90 percent of deputies (the rest come from the military, returned overseas Chinese, and minority groups).[53] The Party center and the NPC Standing Committee decide this composition rate before upcoming elections, and provincial Party committees and people's congresses apply the rate to their regions.[54] Thus, the rate does not differ much from province to province, even with variations between regions and periods.

According to the theory of legislator-constituent relationships in China, people's congress deputies should represent the interests of both the entire nation and their specific constituents.[55] Deputies in the 1980s seemed to think this way. A survey conducted in Beijing and Hangzhou Municipalities in 1987 pointed out that about 50 percent of deputies thought they should represent their voters' interests, while a little less than 50 percent said they should serve the national interest.[56] However, Chinese legislators in the 1990s seemed to be more interested in representing the partial and local interests of their social classes and regions. That is, most legislative members tend to consider themselves as "deputy for farmers," "deputy for workers," "deputy for private businessmen," or "deputy for women." Even official deputies (*guanyuan*

---

[52] Interview with legislative leaders and senior staff: Tianjin, October 2001.

[53] On the statistics about people's congress deputies, see Zhi Liu, Shi Weimin, Zhou Xiaodong, and Wu Yunhao, *Shuju xuanju: Renda daibiao xuanju tongji yanjiu* (*Data Elections: Studies on the Statistics of People's Congress Deputy Elections*) (Beijing: Zhongguo shehui kexue chubanshe, 2001).

[54] On the decision of the deputy composition rate, see Quanguorenda, *Collections on the Documents of China's People's Congresses 1949–90*, p. 185; Quanguorenda changweihui bangongting yanjiushi (ed.), *Renmin daibiao dahui wenxian huibian* (*Selections on the Documents of People's Congresses*) (Beijing: Zhongguo minzhu fazhi chubanshe, 1992), pp. 171–78.

[55] Cai Bingwen (ed.), *Shanghai renmin daibiao dahuizhi* (*The Annals of the Shanghai People's Congress*) (Shanghai: Shanghai shehui kexueyuan chubanshe, 1998), pp. 189–91.

[56] Zhao, *Democratic Politics and Local People's Congresses*, p. 180.

TABLE 5.5. *People's congress deputy composition: The NPC, Tianjin Municipal and Nankai District People's Congresses in Tianjin (1993–1997)*

		NPC[a] 2978 (%)	Tianjin[b] 718 (%)	Nankai[c] 265 (%)
Social class	Worker & peasant	612 (20.6)	209 (29.1)	122 (46)
	Intellectual	649 (21.8)	136 (18.9)	67 (25.3)
	Cadre	842 (28.3)	169 (23.5)	46 (17.4)
Party membership	CCP	2,037 (68.4)	500 (69.6)	195 (73.6)
	Democratic parties	572 (19.1)	169 (23.5)	23 (8.7)
Others	Above college-level education (%)	68.74[d]	70.5	75.5
	Average age (years)	53.13	53.1	49
	Re-election (%)	28.05[d]	35.1	N.A.

Notes: In this table, "Social classes" does not include the military, ethnic groups, and returned overseas Chinese because of their small size compared with other categories. "Intellectuals" refers to academics, researchers in state-run institutes, engineers, doctors, and lawyers. "Cadre" mainly refers to senior government officials and Party leaders.

Sources:
[a] Cai Dingjian, *People's Congress System in China*, pp. 227–28.
[b] Tianjinshi difangzhi bianxiu weiyuanhui (ed.), *Tianjin tongzhi: zhengquan zhi renmin daibiao dahui quan (Overall Annals of Tianjin: Regime Annals People's Congress Volume)* (Tianjin: Tianjin shehui kexueyuan chubanshe, 1997), pp. 434–35.
[c] Kang Ziming (ed.), *Nankai renda ershinian 1979–99 (Twenty Years of Nankai People's Congress, 1979–99)* (Tianjin, 1999), p. 273.
[d] *Guangming ribao (Guangming Daily)*, March 1, 1998.

daibiao) regard themselves as representatives for particular areas, such as public security, traffic, or courts.[57] This implies that deputies' role fulfillment has become differentiated in terms of which roles they pay more attention to, mainly depending on their social backgrounds.

WORKERS AND PEASANTS: REFLECTORS AND SUPERVISORS

In general, worker and peasant deputies are most active in reflection and supervision roles. In contrast, few, if any, of these deputies play

---

[57] On the cases of worker and peasant deputies, see Quanguorenda, *How to Act as a Deputy to People's Congresses*, pp. 145–55, 415–17. For cadre deputy cases, see Wang Xiugui, Yue Guoxing, and Ruan Yanxi, "Xuan ta dang daibiao, geng ba ta dang bangyang" (Elect him a deputy, and let him be a model), *Renmin you quanli*, No. 9 (September 2000), p. 16; Su Feng, "Gongpuxin minzuqing" (Mind of public service and ethnic groups), *Shanghai renda yuekan*, No. 7 (July 2000), pp. 45–46.

a prominent role in the policy-providing area. There are, of course, exceptions. A deputy to the NPC and the Zhejiang Provincial People's Congress for fifteen years and accountant of a villagers' committee received the honorable title of "bill champion" (*yian guanjun*) for four consecutive years from 1993 by submitting 61 bills and 157 proposals to the NPC in that period. She was very proud to have subscribed to more than twenty periodicals and academic journals like *Legal Science* and *Administration and Law* at her own expense.[58] But most deputies from worker or peasant backgrounds have not been as active as she was in the policy-providing sphere.

These deputies seem to concentrate on opinion reflection and public supervision roles for two reasons. First, these roles don't need much academic achievement and political resources, only enthusiasm for visiting the public and listening to their demands, and sometimes the courage to stand up to the authorities. Most deputies reported that they knew little about the legal status, powers, and duties of a deputy when they were elected, not to mention how to perform as deputies. After personal study and attending legislatures' training classes for new deputies, they managed to acquire the basic legal knowledge. A deputy to the Fuan City People's Congress in Fujian Province and director of a villagers' committee is one example. He became a role model of legislators with the nickname of "full-time deputy" (*zhuanzhi daibiao*) because of his enthusiastic deputy role fulfillment, even though he was newly elected in 1997.[59] As such, deputies can play these roles successfully if they are willing to do so.

Second, but no less important, the close relationship between deputies and voters forces them to focus on these roles. For worker or peasant deputies, local relationships come first, and that of deputy-to-voter second, because most of them have lived for a long time in their communities before becoming legislative members. In addition, most of these legislators belong to township- and county-level people's congresses and are directly elected by their neighbors. In this situation, if neighbors-cum-voters ask them to do something for the public, they cannot easily refuse, especially when the neighbors ask them after exhausting all other available means. In contrast, the deputies of the NPC and provincial-level people's congresses who are elected by the

---

[58] Quanguorenda, *I How to Act as a Deputy to People's Congresses*, pp. 15–20.

[59] Zheng Guofeng, "'Zhuanzhi daibiao' Ruan Peijin" (Full-time deputy Ruan Peijin), *Renmin zhengtan*, No. 5 (May 2001), pp. 5–9.

deputies of legislatures one level below have a lesser sense of responsibility for residents, because they have no direct relationship with the voters.[60] In short, neighbors' requests and close relationships with them encourage worker and peasant deputies to concentrate on reflection and supervision.

INTELLECTUALS: POLICY-PROVIDERS

Intellectual deputies to people's congresses have an advantage: specialized knowledge and the capacity to use it. And they make full use of this advantage in performing their roles. There are many bill champions among intellectual deputies. Four legislators who won the honorific of bill champions at the 2000 Shijiazhuang Municipal People's Congress in Hebei Province were all intellectuals (three academics and a senior engineer).[61] Also, a senior researcher and deputy to the Hunan Provincial People's Congress for 13 years took pride in having 39 research notebooks and submitting 975 bills and proposals in total to the legislature.[62]

When carrying out the policy-providing role, intellectual deputies tend to concentrate on their areas of research and work specialty. Traditional Chinese medical doctors continuously proposed policy bills on the development of oriental medicine, and other doctors championed medical policies closely related with their jobs.[63] Intellectual legislative members are also interested in such areas as education, the environment, and juvenile delinquency.[64] In addition, they sometimes mobilize their fellow experts to select policy items and conduct joint research, as a doctor in Shanghai and NPC deputy demonstrates. He has organized a "bill think tank" (*yian naoku*) composed of professors, doctors, lawyers, researchers, and entrepreneurs in Shanghai, with whom he has prepared

[60] Interview with legislative leaders and senior staff: Tianjin, May 1998 and October 2001.
[61] Peng Yanfen, "Zuo renminde zhongshi daiyanren" (As faithful spokesmen for people), *Difang renda jianshe*, No. 8 (August 2000), pp. 15–17.
[62] Quanguorenda, *I How to Act as a Deputy to People's Congresses*, pp. 132–36.
[63] Zhou Bing, "Renmin yisheng wei renmin" (People's doctor for people), *Renmin zhi sheng*, No. 9 (September 1999), pp. 28–29; Li Shaojun, "Weile yongbu xiaoqude 'shengbo'" (For the everlasting 'voice wave'), *Renmin yu quanli*, No. 10 (October 2000), p. 15; Quanguorenda, *I How to Act as a Deputy to People's Congresses*, pp. 3–9.
[64] Quanguorenda, *I How to Act as a Deputy to People's Congresses*, pp. 28–34.

policy bills. As a result, he has been able to introduce several legislative bills of high quality.[65]

Compared with deputies from other classes, intellectual legislators appear to devote themselves to deputy roles due to a strong political consciousness. There are many cases of intellectual deputies, especially academics, who were sometimes willing to face political risks for deputy role fulfillment. Wu Qing, an English professor at Beijing Foreign Language University and deputy to the Haidian District and Beijing Municipal People's Congresses for sixteen years, is one of them. She began a weekly reception day for residents the day after the 1984 elections, even though she was originally able to be a deputy by the Party's arrangement. Armed with a copy of the Constitution and deputy's ID card, she has always fought against the authorities to protect the public's rights. She was also one of the prime movers who introduced an interpellation bill against the Beijing Higher People's Court during the 2000 Beijing Municipal People's Congress plenary sessions.[66] Feng Youwei, a professor at the Chinese Academy of Sciences and deputy to the Shenyang Municipal People's Congress, is also well known. He is called "the first deputy of Shenyang" for his resolute and courageous criticism of the works of government and court, even in front of Party and government leaders. In fact, he was at the center of the "Shenyang Incident." He has severely criticized the problems of the court since the 2000 plenary sessions, and has won broad support and sympathy from ordinary people and fellow deputies.

CADRES: POLICY-PROVIDERS FOR SUPPLEMENTATION

Official deputies form an important component of Chinese legislatures, but they are considered to be less active than any other deputies due to role conflict. That is, as officials, they are responsible for implementing laws and policies, while, as legislative members, they should supervise the implementation. Thus, official deputies are placed in a dilemma and many prefer to remain inactive.[67] For this reason, Chinese

---

[65] Xiao He, "Lüye dui gende qingyi" (Green leaves' affection towards root), *Shanghai renda yuekan*, No. 6 (June 1999), p. 29; Quanguorenda, *I How to Act as a Deputy to People's Congresses*, pp. 160–63.

[66] Shou Beibei, "Renda daibiaode tianzhi" (Vocation of deputy), *Renmin yu quanli*, No. 9 (September 2000), pp. 14–15.

[67] Zhao, *Democratic Politics and Local People's Congresses*, pp. 177–78; Quanguorenda, *Papers Commemorating the 40th Anniversary of People's Congresses*, pp. 28, 336–37.

researchers and legislative leaders have called for the reduction of the quota of official deputies, and the NPC and the Party center have also asked local authorities to reduce the quota.[68] Until now, these deputies have represented more than 20 percent of the total (see Table 5.5). In some areas, the real number has been over 50 percent: in 1998, the rate was 55.94 percent in the Putuo District People's Congress in Shanghai Municipality.[69]

Due to role conflict, official deputies pay more attention to policy-providing than supervision, and policies are generally closely related to their work. A deputy-cum-director of agriculture continuously submitted policy bills on agricultural problems, and a military deputy tried to submit military-related bills and proposals.[70] Official deputies from a particular region frequently submitted joint bills and proposals that urged higher-level governments to consider their regions in issues such as financial support, economic development plans, and major construction projects.[71]

Some officials-cum-deputies, of course, supervise fellow officials and superiors. A director of a county government education bureau and deputy to the county people's congress, for instance, successfully led an interpellation bill in 1999 that required the urban construction bureau of the same government to remove an illegal building near a school.[72] And a director of the industrial and commercial bureau of a city government and the city people's congress deputy resolutely introduced an interpellation bill in 2000 opposing the city court in an attempt to protect state assets.[73] Even in these cases, however, official deputies wielded

---

[68] Shou Beibei, "Vocation of deputy," p. 15; Liu, Yu, and Cheng, _Overall Book on the Works of People's Congresses_, pp. 949, 958.

[69] Zhang Hanghua, "Xinyijie renda daibiao qingkuang fenxi ji gaohao daibiao gongzuo shexiang" (An analysis on the composition of newly elected deputies and a tentative plan for doing deputy works well), _Shanghai renda yuekan_, No. 7 (July 1998), p. 25.

[70] Chen Mengzhi, "'Nongguan' daibiao xinxi nongye" (An agricultural official deputy concerned with agriculture), _Renmin zhengtan_, No. 5 (May 2001), p. 25; Tao Xiao, "Wang Fuqingde 'daibiao qingjie'" (Deputy's affection of Wang Fuqing), _Renmin zhengtan_, No. 8 (August 2001), p. 24.

[71] Luo Tanping, "Daibiao yao chang zheyangde 'ge'" (Deputies should sing such a song), _Renmin zhi you_, No. 3–4 (April 1999), pp. 38–39; Huang Shupei, "Laoji zhongtuo shi-wunian" (Firmly remembered heavy trust for 15 years), _Chutian zhuren_, No. 7 (July 2000), pp. 22–23; Lin Kemin, "Xinde qidian" (New start point), _Renmin zhengtan_, No. 3 (March 2001), p. 24.

[72] Xie Senchuan, "Gongpuxin" (Mind of public servants), _Renmin zhi you_, No. 9 (September 2000), pp. 19–20.

[73] Bin Wenyou, "Zuishi nanwang gongshangqing" (Most unforgettable is industrial and commercial affection), _Renmin zhi sheng_, No. 3 (March 2001), pp. 32–33.

their power against other bureaus or state organs mainly to help their own bureaus' work. Most official deputies hesitate to use this weapon for fear of "offending people" (*dezuiren*).

Since the 1990s, according to some legislative leaders and staffers that I interviewed, most senior government officials and other state organ leaders want to be elected as people's congresses deputies. Why do leading cadres want to be deputies? Apart from the fact that being elected deputies proves officials' credibility with the public, and that deputy status gives them the opportunity to develop personal networks with regional leaderships, the role can actually help them to do their own jobs.[74] For example, when official deputies submit policy proposals to other government agencies or state organs using administrative channels, they can only ask and wait for a reply. In contrast, when they propose the same things through legislative channels by bills or proposals with fellow legislative members, other agencies and state organs cannot easily ignore them, because in this case they are the business of legislature, not that of a government bureau. At least, they should explain why they could not accept the policy in writing via people's congress standing committees. Also, officials can sometimes accomplish their goals by using weapons like interpellation. In addition, officials-cum-deputies can voice the demands of their bureaus or organs when legislatures hear and review related matters. Or they can have a chance to skillfully defend their positions during legislative supervision of their bureaus or organs. With the rise of Chinese legislatures' status in the 1990s, these opportunities became more important resources for protecting and furthering organizational interests.

Similarly, directors of residents' committees in urban areas or villagers' committees in rural areas, and leaders of social organizations (e.g., trade unions, women's federations, and communist youth leagues) also want to be elected deputies and prefer to raise problems through legislative channels. For example, when a residents' committee director asked the district government for financial support to repair the sewerage system, he only got the reply: "Your committee should try to find a solution itself." When he raised the same matter at a people's congress plenary session as a legislative member, district government leaders were willing to accept his request.[75] And a trade union leader used a similar tactic to

---

[74] On the general motivations of deputies' role fulfillment, see O'Brien, "Agents and remonstrators," pp. 375–77.

[75] Ren Li and Yan Chunping, "Pingfan zhongde guanghui" (Glories among commons), *Renmin zhi sheng*, No. 12 (December 1999), pp. 32–33.

enforce the Labor Law and to address illegal labor practices at foreign-affiliated companies. That is, when he raised the problems as a trade union leader, the companies would not accept his requests. However, when he argued as a legislative member, the companies changed their attitude, and he achieved his goals relatively easily.[76]

PRIVATE ENTREPRENEURS AND BUSINESSPERSONS: EXEMPLARY LEADERS

Of all social classes, private entrepreneurs (*siying qiyezhu*) and businesspersons (*getihu*) seem to aspire to become people's congress deputies the most, perhaps in order to make up for their weak and unstable political status.[77] As legislative members, they can meet Party and government leaders by attending legislature plenary sessions and other events, which can help them to develop a valuable resource, *guanxi* ties. The status of deputy can also function as an "amulet" (*hushenfu*) when they are forced to face arbitrary law enforcement officials and appear in court.[78] According to a survey of private entrepreneurs conducted nationwide by the Chinese Academy of Social Sciences in 1999 and 2000, entrepreneurs think of being legislative members as the most preferable political measure to enhance their social status, although they much prefer to employ socioeconomic measures like maximizing business size, participating in public projects, and establishing a good image to this end.[79]

In practice, with the rapid expansion of the private economic sector in the 1990s and accompanying entrepreneurs' efforts to secure their political status, these deputies have increased in number in many regions, although we cannot exactly estimate the number due to the lack of available statistics. For example, only 1 percent of deputies to the Haidian

---

[76] Quanguorenda, *I How to Act as a Deputy to People's Congresses*, pp. 384–87. For this reason, social organizations that have their quota in people's congresses try to actively participate in congressional activity of lawmaking and supervision. Interview with staff of the Tianjin Communist Youth League: Tianjin, May 2001; Interview with a staffer of the Shanxi Women's Federation: Tianjin, July 2001.

[77] Lu Xueyi (ed.), *Dangdai Zhongguo shehui liudong* (*Social Mobility in Contemporary China*) (Beijing: Shehui kexue wenxian chubanshe, 2004), pp. 263–65; Wu Bo, *Xin jieduan Zhongguo shehui jieji jieceng fenxi* (*An Analysis on Classes in Contemporary Chinese Society*) (Beijing: Qinghua daxue chubanshe, 2004), pp. 223–26.

[78] Interview with legislative leaders and senior staff: Tianjin, March 2001.

[79] Lu Xueyi (ed.), *Dangdai zhongguo shehui jieceng yanjiu baogao* (*A Research Report on Contemporary Chinese Social Classes*) (Beijing: Shehui kexue wenxian chubanshe, 2002), p. 221.

and Dongcheng District People's Congresses in Beijing Municipality came from private business in 1987.[80] In contrast, now 23.5 percent of deputies to the Taizhou City People's Congress in Jiangsu Province and about 30 percent of deputies to the Jinghai County People's Congress in Tianjin Municipality are actually private entrepreneurs.[81] There are regional disparities that originated from the development of private economy and the attitudes of Party leaders toward the raising of entrepreneurs' political status. For instance, of all deputies to the Huaihua City People's Congress in Hunan Province in 1998, only 2 percent were private entrepreneurs and businesspersons, while people involved in private businesses in the region comprised about 8 percent of the total population.[82]

Legislators from the private sector, unlike deputies from other classes, pay much more attention to the dissemination of state policies and exemplary roles (i.e., regime agent roles). They frequently become the first to carry out government policies such as cleaning up marketplaces and paying taxes honestly. They sometimes enthusiastically help to persuade fellow businesspeople to observe government policy. As business spokespersons, they also try to protect and to further corporate interests, sometimes to the detriment of their own business. In these cases, it is relatively easy to get government support because of their exemplary role.[83] In this

---

[80] Zhao, *Democratic Politics and Local People's Congresses*, p. 199.

[81] Zhonggong zhongyang zuzhibu ketizu (ed.), *Zhongguo diaocha baogao 2000–2001: Xin xingshi xia renmin neibu maodun yanjiu* (*Research Reports on China 2000–2001: Studies on Contradictions among the People in New Situations*) (Beijing: Zhongyang bianyi chubanshe, 2001), p. 158; Interview with legislative leaders and senior staff: Tianjin, January 2002.

[82] Quan Xinlin and Song Tianan, "You zuoweide renda daibiao" (A deputy to people's congress who had actions), *Renmin zhi you*, No. 12 (December 2000), p. 47. There is a caveat regarding these statistics. A large number of Chinese people and the Party leaders still don't like to see rich persons attain a higher political status in addition to wealth. So, the public and the Party leaders in some regions would not recommend private entrepreneurs as candidates in deputy elections. For the same reason, people's congresses try to conceal the true number of deputies-cum-entrepreneurs by, for example, counting them as "worker," "cadre," or "intellectual" when they collect statistics on deputies' social backgrounds. Therefore, the true number of deputies from the private sector is generally much larger than the formal statistics that people's congresses gathered. Interview with legislative leaders and senior staff: Tianjin, October 2001.

[83] Wan, "Electing her a deputy was not wrong," p. 31; Huang, "A special writing on deputy Ye," pp. 33–34; Su Zhangmiao, "Shanguangde zuji" (Gleaming footsteps), *Renmin zhi sheng*, No. 5 (May 2000), pp. 30–31; Fan Chuchu, "Laoji daibiao shensheng zhize, quanxin quanyi wei renmin fuwu" (Firmly remembering sacred duty, wholeheartedly served for people), *Difang renda jianshe*, No. 7 (July 1999), pp. 35–36.

respect, these deputies are the closest to the agent type of deputies which O'Brien describes.[84]

In addition, deputies-cum-entrepreneurs tend to contribute a share of their income to public projects like building schools and cultural centers, repairing roads and bridges, and helping poor students and the needy. They take pride in their contribution to the socioeconomic development of their communities.[85] In fact, they contribute to the community even before becoming legislative members in an attempt to improve their social status and image, and they often seem to be elected as deputies for their generous behavior as well as for their success in business. Nonetheless, they regard these duties as important to their functions.

Finally, these deputies actively participate in economic-related activities both individually and jointly. One example is the Deputies' Friendly Society for Economic Development of the Taihe City People's Congress, Heilongjiang Province, which deputies-cum-leaders of economic development established in 1995. It has been praised for its prominent role in regional economic development by disseminating experience and economic and technological information, by attracting foreign investment, and by helping poor peasants make money. It started with nine members from the Jiazihe District People's Congress in 1995 and rose to 156 deputies across the city in 2001.[86] A deputy small group in Didao District of Jixi City, Heilongjiang Province, composed of ten entrepreneur deputies to provincial, city, and district people's congresses, conducted similar activities.[87]

---

[84] O'Brien, "Agents and remonstrators," p. 373.

[85] Sun Shan, "Zhuan Jinchengde 'shuo' he 'zuo'" (Speeches and behaviors of Zhuan Jincheng), *Renmin zhengtan*, No. 20 (January 2001), p. 20; Zheng Zichang, "Wo shi zenyang dang renda daibiaode" (How I became a deputy to the people's congress), *Shandong renda gongzuo*, No. 9 (September 1999), pp. 49–50; Da Jia, "Yige shiyejiade zuiqiu" (An entrepreneur deputy's pursuit), *Fazhi*, No. 10 (October 2000), pp. 10–11; Chen Jianshi, "Rongyu zeren yiwu" (Honor, responsibility, and duty), *Fazhi*, No. 7 (July 2000), pp. 14–15; Xiao Yan, "Keji chongde fengxian rensheng" (Scrupulously esteemed virtue and offered life as a tribute), *Renmin zhi sheng*, No. 6 (June 2001), pp. 36–37, 40.

[86] Zheng Chunqiao, "Daibiao huodong yu jingji jianshe jiehe cujin quyu jingji fazhan" (Union of deputy activity and economic construction promoted region's economic development), *Fazhi*, No. 8 (August 1999), p. 19; Shi Jinhua, "Qitaiheshi renda daibiao fazhan jingji lianyihui" (A friendly society for developing economy of deputies to Qitaihe City People's Congress), *Fazhi*, No. 7 (July 2001), p. 6.

[87] Jixishi Didaoqu geti siying qiye renda daibiao xiaozu, "Chongfen fahui zishen youshi, renzhen lixing daibiao zhize" (Fully displayed advantages, earnestly fulfilled deputy's duty), *Fazhi*, No. 11 (November 2000), p. 19.

IMPLICATIONS OF NEW ROLE FULFILLMENT

Even now, ordinary deputies cannot control the legislative system, much as Chinese legislatures per se cannot control the polity. Most deputies, as amateurs and sometimes role models in their fields, suffer from the lack of time, information, and material resources necessary for active participation in legislative work. In particular, legislators from peasant backgrounds, who comprise the majority of deputies in basic-level people's congresses, are said to be passive and incapable of fulfilling their roles due to insufficient political consciousness and poor education. This came to light when government leaders in some rural areas used bribery to get elected to higher positions at plenary sessions. In contrast, many official deputies, even when equipped with various kinds of political resources and capacities, are unwilling to perform their deputy duties because of role conflict. Legislative members cannot easily overcome these problems without fundamental political and legislative reforms.

Chinese legislators, however, have moved nearer to the center of the legislative system since the early 1990s, and have become more representative than before even without the radical change of a Chinese party-state and legislative system. They have conducted supervision, reflection, and policy-providing roles more than regime agent and remonstrator roles in the improved legal and political conditions. Role differentiation between deputies has also taken place according to their social backgrounds. Worker and peasant deputies pay more attention to reflection and supervision, while intellectual legislators and some cadre deputies tend to focus on the policy-providing role. Deputies-cum-entrepreneurs are more likely to concentrate on exemplary and economic-related roles.

What implications does deputies' changing role fulfillment have for the Chinese political process? For the Party top leadership, legislative members have become important assistants to supervise inadequate policy implementation by local governments and to control the corruption of mid- and low-level officials. For legislatures, ordinary members, together with legislative leaders and staff, have joined the powers of improving legislative status and performance by overcoming the resistance of governments and squeezing support from the Party in the name of the people. Finally, for the populace, deputies have become an important channel for expressing public demands and complaints, and are sometimes more effective than the Party and government. In this sense, the

Party, legislatures, and the public all benefit from changes to deputies' role fulfillment.

Finally, these changes are significant with regard to legislative development in China. The main forces in the development of Chinese legislatures have historically come from above. The present Chinese legislatures are unimaginable without the efforts of legislative leaders like Peng Zhen and the support of the Party leadership. Legislative and Party leaders promoted the development of people's congresses because it was beneficial for both the Party and legislatures: it strengthened the power base of legislative leaders and supported Party reform policy by lawmaking and supervisory functions. As a result, legislative development in China, as O'Brien and Tanner noted, has an interesting characteristic: that is, institutionalized influence with little liberalization.[88] However, in the future, power from below – deputies and the public – will be the primary force in legislative development, and thereby Chinese legislatures will be more representative or liberalized than they are now. The last decade's role fulfillment of Chinese legislators highlights the potential for further development of legislatures in that direction.

---

[88] Kevin O'Brien, *Reform without Liberalization: China's National People's Congress and the Politics of Institutional Change* (New York: Cambridge University Press, 1990), pp. 3–8; Murray Scot Tanner, "The National People's Congress," in Merle Goldman and Roderick MacFarquhar (eds.), *The Paradox of China's Post-Mao Reforms* (Cambridge, MA: Harvard University Press, 1999), p. 126.

6

Symbiosis between Local Legislatures and Social Organizations

All aspects of Chinese society have undergone remarkable change since the introduction of reform policies three decades ago. One such change has involved state-society relations, which now allow greater autonomy for society. The explosive increase in the number of social organizations (*shehui tuanti*) and their activities illustrates society's growth relative to the state. For example, the Ministry of Civil Affairs announced that the total number of registered social organizations was about 246,000 in 2002; one Chinese media report even goes on to argue that the real number including nonregistered organizations was about eight million in 2006.[1]

With the increasing number of social organizations and their activities, analyzing the potential for social organizations to influence Chinese politics has become an important research topic. The 1989 Tiananmen Incident alerted China watchers to the political role of social organizations. The Incident likely indicated that various informal intellectual groups were already active in urban areas and that workers swiftly formed autonomous organizations and pursued their own agenda

---

[1] Wang Ming, *Minjian zuzhi tonglun* (*General Discussion on Civil Organization*) (Beijing: Shishi chubanshe, 2004), p. 15; Zhu Jiankang, "Minjian liliang tuidong Zhongguo she-huide gaige kaifang" (Civil powers promote reform and opening-up of Chinese society), *Chinese News Net*, January 23, 2007 (available at http://www2.chinesenewsnet.com/MainNews/Opinion/2007_1_23_8_41_23_267.html). In conference, according to Pei, there were only 103 national associations in the late Mao era. Minxin Pei, "Chinese civic associations: An empirical analysis," *Modern China*, Vol. 24, No. 3 (July 1998), pp. 290–91.

during the Incident.[2] Furthermore, the rise of private entrepreneurs as an important class in Chinese society and the vigorous activities of social organizations that claim to further the interests of the private economy in the 1990s have drawn much more attention to changes in state-society relations.[3]

This chapter explores relations between local people's congresses and social organizations in order to understand changes in relations between the state and Chinese society. The development of local legislatures as important political forces provides social organizations with a good opportunity to further their rights and interests by participating in legislation and supervision. Capitalizing on these opportunities, social organizations have earnestly taken part in legislative activities, and this has facilitated the formation of a distinct relationship between legislatures and social organizations. To this end, this chapter briefly examines previous studies on state-society relations, focusing on two approaches (i.e., civil society and state corporatism). Then, it analyzes the reciprocal relations between local legislatures and social organizations. Finally, it investigates social organizations' participation in legislative activities.

This research, first, argues that we need to pay more attention to the legalization and marketization perspectives when analyzing state-society relations. At the same time, the "state" as a unit of analysis needs to be extended not only in a vertical direction (i.e., from the central to the local) but also in a horizontal direction (i.e., from the Party/governments to legislatures and courts). Second, viewed in this way, a new form of state-society relations, distinguishable from relations between the CCP/governments and social organizations, has developed between legislatures and social organizations. Social organizations can enter a new political arena (legislative activities) to further their interests with little or no control

[2] Barrett L. McCormick, Su Shaozhi, and Xiao Xiaoming, "The 1989 democracy movement: A review of the prospects for civil society in China," *Pacific Affairs*, Vol. 65, No. 2 (Summer 1992), pp. 182–202; Andrew G. Walder and Gong Xiaoxia, "Workers in the Tiananmen protests: The politics of the Beijing Workers' Autonomous Federation," *Australian Journal of Chinese Affairs*, No. 29 (1993), pp. 1–29.
[3] Kelle S. Tsai, *Capitalism without Democracy: The Private Sector in Contemporary China* (Ithaca, NY and London: Cornell University Press, 2007); Scott Kennedy, *The Business of Lobbying in China* (Cambridge, MA: Harvard University Press, 2005); Bruce J. Dickson, *Red Capitalists in China: The Party, Private Entrepreneurs, and Prospects for Political Change* (Cambridge: Cambridge University Press, 2003); David L. Wank, *Commodifying Communism: Business, Trust, and Politics in a Chinese City* (Cambridge: Cambridge University Press, 1999); Margaret M. Pearson, *China's New Business Elite: The Political Consequences of Economic Reform* (Berkeley: University of California Press, 1997).

from the state (legislatures). Furthermore, cooperation and competition between different state agencies and social organizations frequently occurs when social organizations participate in these new forms of political activity. These new state-society relations go beyond the patterns that civil society theory and state corporatism have suggested.

NEW PERSPECTIVES ON STATE-SOCIETY RELATIONS IN CHINA

Previous approaches to the study of Chinese state-society relations can be divided into two categories: civil society and state corporatism. Following the collapse of the socialist bloc and the 1989 Tiananmen Incident, civil society theory was applied to the analysis of China's state-society relations. It first assumes that civil society could develop in isolation from the state in China with the introduction of a market economy. And this development, it predicts, could eventually lead to Chinese democratization by limiting the extent of state power, just as it did in the former socialist countries in Eastern Europe. In fact, some China researchers in the early 1990s cautiously suggested that civil society was already evolving and could play a significant role in the democratization of China.[4]

Criticism of civil society theory has increased with the accumulation of empirical data, however. The crux of the criticism is that most social associations in China have been organized under the strict control of the state. Consequently they enjoy little autonomy from the state, which is the minimum condition and critical indicator of the formation of civil society. In addition, it is stressed that state-society relations in China are not as antagonistic as civil society theorists presuppose.[5] Studies on private entrepreneur associations in the 1990s cast further doubt

---

[4] Martin K. Whyte, "Urban China: A civil society in the making," in Arthur Lewis Rosebaum (ed.), *State and Society in China: The Consequences of Reform* (Boulder, CO: Westview Press, 1992), pp. 77–101; McCormick, Su, and Xiao, "The 1989 democracy movement."

[5] Mary E. Gallagher, "China: The limits of civil society in a late Leninist state," in Muthiah Alagappa (ed.), *Civil Society and Political Change in Asia: Expanding and Contracting Democratic Space* (Stanford: Stanford University Press, 2004), pp. 419–52; Tony Saich, "Negotiating the state: The development of social organizations in China," *China Quarterly*, No. 161 (March 2000), pp. 124–41; Timothy Cheek, "From market to democracy in China: Gaps in the civil Society model," in Juan D. Lindau and Timothy Cheek (eds.), *Market Economics and Political Change: Comparing China and Mexico* (Lanham, MD: Rowman & Littlefield, 1998), pp. 219–52; Timothy Brook and B. Michael Frolic (eds.), *Civil Society in China* (Armonk, NY: M.E. Sharpe, 1997).

upon the assumptions of civil society arguments.[6] As a consequence, various qualified theories of civil society emerged, including "semi" civil society,[7] "incipient" civil society,[8] "state-led" civil society,[9] "embryonic" civil society,[10] and "unofficial" civil society.[11]

Instead of civil society, many researchers have analyzed China's state-society relations in terms of state or socialist corporatism. Drawing on the work of Philippe C. Schmitter, these scholars have argued that the relations between the state and social organizations in China can be regarded as a variation of state corporatism. First, the state takes the initiative in establishing and running social organizations. Second, the state exerts enormous influence on the personnel (especially leadership), structure, finance, and policy of social organizations. Third, the state grants social organizations a near-monopoly of representation in specific functional and territorial areas; social organizations thereby mediate between the state and their members.[12] Furthermore, the perspective distinguishes itself from civil society theory in that it views state-society relations not as confrontational but as cooperative. In other words, mainly due to the Chinese polity's being a party-state, social organizations seek to cooperate with, rather than gain

[6] Bruce J. Dickson, "Do good businessmen make good citizens? An emerging collective identity among China's private entrepreneurs," in Merle Goldman and Elizabeth J. Perry (eds.), *Changing Meanings of Citizenship in Modern China* (Cambridge, MA: Harvard University Press, 2002), pp. 255–87; Jonathan Unger, "'Bridges': Private business, the Chinese government and the rise of new associations," *China Quarterly*, No. 147 (September 1996), pp. 795–819; Christopher Earle Nevitt, "Private business associations in China: Evidence of civil society or local state power?" *China Journal*, No. 36 (July 1996), pp. 25–43; David L. Wank, "Private business, bureaucracy, and political alliance in a Chinese city," *Australian Journal of Chinese Affairs*, No. 33 (January 1995), pp. 55–71.

[7] Baogang He, *The Democratic Implications of Civil Society in China* (London: Macmillan Press, 1997).

[8] Gordon White, Jude Howell, and Shang Xiaoyuan, *In Search of Civil Society: Market Reform and Social Change in Contemporary China* (Oxford: Clarendon Press, 1996).

[9] B. Michael Frolic, "State-led civil society," in Timothy Brook and B. Michael Frolic (eds.), *Civil Society in China* (Armonk, NY: M.E. Sharpe, 1997), pp. 46–67.

[10] Pei, "Chinese civic associations."

[11] Gallagher, "China: The limits of civil society."

[12] Pearson, *China's New Business Elite*, p. 130; Unger, "'Bridges'," p. 818: Saich, "Negotiating the state," pp. 129–32; Gallagher, "China: The limits of civil society," pp. 420–21; Jonathan Unger and Anita Chan, "Corporatism in China: A developmental state in an East Asian context," in Barrett L. McCormick and Jonathan Unger (eds.), *China After Socialism: In the Footsteps of Eastern Europe or East Asia?* (Armonk, NY: M.E. Sharpe, 1996), p. 96.

autonomy from, the state. In this way they attempt to garner resources and authority from the state.[13]

There are four main strands of criticism about state corporatism, however. The first calls for a complementary or hybrid perspective on state-society relations. This view acknowledges the relevance of state corporatism in analyzing China's state-society relations, but also highlights its lack of comprehensiveness. Some scholars, who study private entrepreneurs and business elites in the 1990s, suggest that notions such as "informal personal ties" (*guanxi*) and "clientelism" can complement and thereby strengthen the explanatory value of state corporatism. Clientelism can help explain interactions both between business associations and the state and between private entrepreneurs and the state.[14]

The second criticism involves state corporatism's lack of utility. That is, state corporatism – and, for that matter, civil society – cannot be applied to Chinese state-society relations. A corporatist relationship, Ray Yep argues, has two requirements: an organizational framework for effective communication and strong internal solidarity on the part of the concerned social interest. But China meets neither of these conditions.[15] Likewise, Kenneth F. Foster argues that Chinese social organizations, as appendages of governments or the CCP, have little involvement in what is conventionally known as interest representation or interest intermediation. So although Chinese state-society relations can be seen as the structural form of corporatism on the surface, they are not in essence corporatist.[16]

The third line of argument is that state corporatism has evolved. That is, the past pattern of state-society relations in China was state corporatist, but a new pattern has recently emerged that falls outside preexisting boundaries. For instance, although very small in number, some genuine nongovernmental organizations (NGOs) and other civil organizations

---

[13] Edward Gu, "State corporatism and the politics of the state-professional {AU: OK to add?}relationship in China: A case study of three professional communities," *American Asian Review*, Vol. 19, No. 4 (Winter 2001), pp. 163–99; Kristen Parris, "Private entrepreneurs as citizens: From Leninism to corporatism," *China Information*, Vol. 10, No. 3/4 (Winter/Spring, 1996), pp. 1–28.

[14] Dickson, *Red Capitalists in China*; Wank, *Commodifying Communism*; Pearson, *China's New Business Elite*.

[15] Ray Yep, "The limitations of corporatism for understanding reforming China: An empirical analysis in a rural county," *Journal of Contemporary China*, Vol. 9, No, 25 (November 2000), pp. 547–66.

[16] Kenneth W. Foster, "Embedded within state agencies: Business associations in Yantai," *China Journal*, No. 47 (January 2002), pp. 41–65.

in marginalized areas, which are completely independent from governments in terms of personnel, finance, and activities, now exist in both
rural and urban China.[17] According to Yijiang Ding, new elements of
civil society in some social organizations have increased within the structure of state corporatism, and as a consequence, the organizations have
exhibited characteristics of "societal" rather than "state" corporatism.[18]
At the local level, as Yunqiu Zhang argues, even trade unions that were
traditionally considered to be firmly under state control have changed
from a state corporatist instrument serving the state's purpose for social
control and mobilization to "social representation" by which they have
represented workers' interests. It is argued that the social representation,
once exercised, could evolve into civil society.[19]

Finally, Mary E. Gallagher stresses the limitation of state corporatism as an analytic framework for Chinese state-society relations. She
acknowledges that state corporatism is relevant and now more dominant
than civil society. However, state corporatism has profound limitations
because it is largely a descriptive model, whereas civil society serves as an
analytic model of social change. That is, state corporatism has difficulty
explaining how authoritarian states such as South Korea and Taiwan,
where national leaders deployed corporatist organizations to control and
coopt society, suddenly became democratic polities.[20]

THE LEGALIZATION PERSPECTIVE AND THE EXTENSION
OF THE STATE

Civil society theory and state corporatism both have their strengths and
weaknesses. Thus, some scholars argue in favor of a hybrid perspective
embracing civil society, state corporatism, and clientelism. This reflects
the reality that state-society relations in China have become much more
complicated in the wake of three decades of capitalist reform. As a
result, a single perspective cannot comprehensively explain the changing

---

[17] Xin Zhang and Richard Baum, "Civil society and the anatomy of a rural NGO,"
    China Journal, No. 52 (July 2004), pp. 97–107; Jude Howell, "New directions in civil
    society: Organizing around marginalized interests," in Jude Howell (ed.), *Governance
    in China* (Lanham, MD: Rowman & Littlefield, 2004), pp. 141–71.
[18] Yijiang Ding, *Chinese Democracy after Tiananmen* (New York: Columbia University
    Press, 2001).
[19] Yunqiu Zhang, "From state corporatism to social representation: Local trade unions
    in the reform years," in Timothy Brook and B. Michael Frolic (eds.), *Civil Society in
    China* (Armonk, NY: M.E. Sharpe, 1997), pp. 124–48.
[20] Gallagher, "China: The limits of civil society," pp. 421–22.

patterns of state-society relations.[21] In my view, two points need to be added to the previous comments on state-society relations.

First of all, a legalization (*fazhihua*) perspective is necessary to ana-lyze Chinese state-society relations, complementing marketization (*shichanghua*).[22] Previous research has focused on how and to what extent the introduction of a market economy has affected state-society relations, regardless of whether it has employed either the civil society or state corporatist perspectives. A case in point are studies on what kinds – and what degree – of changes the emergence of the private entrepreneur class or business elite groups in the 1990s has meant for state-society rela-tions. Studies on how the introduction of a market economy has changed state-labor and state-women relations also belong to this category. It is clear that the introduction of a market economy has brought about tremendous changes in China, and the "bottom-up" pressure of market forces has moved state-society relations in the direction of increasing society's autonomy from the state. Thus, the marketization perspective on state-society relations is relevant and imperative.

We cannot fully understand China's changing state-society relations solely with the marketization perspective, however. This is because state policy, along with market forces, has also played a vital role in shift-ing state-society relations. That is, we should pay attention to "top-down" initiatives of the state as well as "bottom-up" pressure from market forces when analyzing changes in state-society relations. China has indeed implemented political reforms as well as economic reforms. However, in contrast to the former Soviet Union and socialist coun-tries in Eastern Europe, China has approached political reforms from the "institutionalization" of political organizations and procedures, not from the "democratization" of political structures and processes. The repeated implementation of administrative reforms (government reforms) since the early 1980s and governance according to law (i.e., legalization policy) since the early 1990s are clear examples of this phenomenon.

These political reforms have seriously affected state-society relations in China. For instance, since the implementation of the governance according to law policy, laws have come to play a crucial role in deciding

---

[21] Ding, *Chinese Democracy after Tiananmen*, p. 72.
[22] In this regard, a great collective study has been published. Neil J. Diamant, Stanley B. Lubman, and Kevin J. O'Brien (eds.), *Engaging the Law in China: State, Society, and Possibilities for Justice* (Stanford: Stanford University Press, 2005).

the direction of change in state-society relations. On the one hand, the legalization policy requires even the CCP, the sole ruling party (*zhizheng-dang*) in the Chinese political system, to act within certain boundaries set by laws and to rule the country in accordance with laws rather than just Party policy or government decree. In other words, laws became both an important tool with which the Party/state could rule the country and also a constraint on the Party/state. On the other hand, the legalization policy provided ordinary people, social organizations, and business enterprises with a good opportunity to employ laws in securing their rights and furthering their interests. That is, laws became a vital instrument and shield for society to protect their rights and interests from the encroachment of the state. For example, workers have increasingly resorted to the law in labor disputes.[23] In these ways, the legalization policy has influenced the shift in state-society relations, and we need to pay more attention to this trend.

In addition, an extension of our understanding of "the state" is needed in both vertical and horizontal directions. Previous studies have called for the disaggregation or deconstruction of state and society, because the state and society, as Peter Hays Gries and Stanley Rosen argue, are not always unitary.[24] But when arguing for disaggregation, they tend to emphasize vertical disaggregation, that is, a shift in focus from the central/national level to various local levels of state and society. This perspective is relevant and necessary. In fact, following this advice, many scholars have selected certain regions to investigate the changing state-society relations. These studies include the analysis of the entrepreneurial class and its associations, workers and trade unions, environmental NGOs, and rural poverty relief organizations.

[23] Gallagher, *Contagious Capitalism*, pp. 98–132; Feng Chen, "Legal mobilization by trade unions: The case of Shanghai," *China Journal*, No. 52 (July 2004), pp. 27–45.
[24] Joel S. Migdal, Atul Kohli, and Vivienne Shue, "Introduction: Developing a state-in-society perspective," in Joel S. Migdal, Atul Kohli, and Vivienne Shue (eds.), *State Power and Social Forces: Domination and Transformation in the Third World* (Cambridge: Cambridge University Press, 1994), pp. 1–4; Kenneth W. Foster, "Associations in the embrace of an authoritarian state: State domination of society?" *Studies in Comparative International Development*, Vol. 35, No. 4 (Winter 2001), pp. 84–109; Elizabeth J. Perry, "Trends in the study of Chinese politics: State-society relations," *China Quarterly*, No. 139 (September 1994), pp. 704–13; Peter Hays Gries and Stanley Rosen, "Introduction: Popular protest and state legitimation in 21st-century China," in Peter Hays Gries and Stanley Rosen (eds.), *State and Society in 21st-century China* (London: Routledge Curzon, 2004), pp. 1–23; Kevin J. O'Brien, "Neither transgressive nor contained: Boundary-spanning contention in China," in Gries and Rosen, *State and Society in 21st-century China*, pp. 105–22.

But state and society should also be disaggregated in a horizontal direction; that is, we need to shift our focus from a unitary state centering on the Party and governments to a multiple state including legislatures and courts. In fact, previous studies of both civil society and state corporatism have tended to examine state-society patterns with a focus on the CCP and governments. This tendency was not problematic in the 1980s because at that time, Chinese legislatures and courts played a negligible role in the political system. But in the 1990s, when the legislatures and courts grew in influence, Party- and government-centric perspectives were no longer valid. Furthermore, complicated interactions between state and society could be better understood from a horizontal disaggregation perspective. As the politics of lawmaking in provincial legislatures illustrated, cooperation and competition within segments of both state and society became universal in state-society relations during the 1990s.

RECIPROCITY BETWEEN LOCAL LEGISLATURES AND SOCIAL ORGANIZATIONS

Both local people's congresses and social organizations, in an attempt to cope with problems and advance their interests, have striven to intensify their relationship in the reform era. These elaborate efforts from both sides and some changing political conditions have fostered the development of reciprocal relations between them. We can examine them from three aspects.

In terms of legal and political regulations, the relations between legislatures and social organizations differ from those of the CCP/governments and social organizations. The CCP-social organization relations are regulated as "leadership relations" (*lingdao guanxi*), and major social organizations are organized and operated under the firm control of the Party. For example, as a "bridge or link" (*qiaoliang niudai*) between the Party/state and their members, "people's organizations" (*renmin tuanti*), such as trade unions, women's federations, and communist youth leagues, are required to play intermediary roles that convey the Party/state's policy to their members and in turn convey their members' opinions and demands to the Party/state. In addition, the CCP exerts extensive authority over these organizations in the areas of personnel, organization, and policy.[25]

---

[25] Zhonggong zhongyang, "Guanyu jiaqiang he gaishan dang dui gonghui gongqingtuan fulian gongzuo lingdaode tongzhi" (A notice on the strengthening and improvement

Likewise, social organizations are heavily dependent on governments in their establishment and day-to-day functions. For instance,
the Regulations on the Registration and Management of Social
Organizations (1998) require that all social organizations comply with
a two-tier registration system: first, finding professional business units
(*yewu zhuguan danwei*) that will act as a sponsor; and second, applying
for registration and receiving permission from the authorizing government agency (*dengji guanli jiguan*). Under this system, social organizations tend to invite present or former high-level government officials and
Party cadres to serve as leaders in order to gain approval and permission
from sponsors and authorizing agencies more easily. Furthermore, the
government intervenes in and controls social organizations even in their
day-to-day operations and finances.[26] Consequently, social organizations have great difficulty in maintaining equal relations with the CCP
and governments.

In contrast, although legislatures and social organizations are regulated as "supervisory relations" (*jiandu guanxi*), in practice legislatures do not constrain social organizations. According to the Chinese
Constitution, all state organs, political parties, and social organizations
should abide by the law. Local legislatures, as local state power organs,
have the right to supervise the observation of the law by social organizations. In this sense, social organizations are subject to legislatures' legal
supervision. But in reality, the supervisory relations are meaningless;
that is, legislatures rarely supervise social organizations. Social organizations can thus freely and equitably participate in legislatures' lawmaking and supervision, and this facilitates the formation and development
of reciprocal relations between the two entities.

In the reform era, legislatures have also needed the support and
cooperation of social organizations in terms of their increasing

of the Party's leadership toward trade unions, communist youth leagues, and women's
federations) (1989), Zhongguo jinrong gonghui quanguo weiyuanhui (ed.), *Gonghui
gongzuo zhongyao wenjian xuanbian* (*Selections of Important Documents on Trade
Union Works*) (Beijing: Zhongguo jinrong chubanshe, 2002), pp. 195–206; Zhonghua
quanguo zonggonghui, "Guanyu guanche zhixing 'Zhonggong zhongyang guanyu jiaqiang he gaishan dang dui gonghui gongqingtuan fulian gongzuo lingdaode tongzhi'de
yijian" (An opinion on the thorough implementation of 'A notice on the strengthening
and improvement of the Party's leadership toward trade unions, communist youth
leagues, and women's federations') (1991), Zhongguo jinrong gonghui, *Selections of
Important Documents on Trade Union Works*, pp. 247–67.
[26] Saich, "Negotiating the state," pp. 129–32; Gallagher, "China: The limits of civil
society," p. 424.

functions. Chinese legislatures, compared with the CCP and governments, have been able to mobilize only limited resources in personnel,
organizational, and financial aspects. But with their strengthening and
their range of activities widening, legislatures have had to compensate
for poor organizational capacity in any way possible, including the
support of social organizations.[27] And to enhance their political legitimacy, legislatures have sought the participation of social organizations
in their activities. As "people's representative bodies," public attention
on, and participation in, legislative activities are the most important
political resource that legislatures can mobilize. That is, legislatures can
act in the "name of people" to persuade the CCP to support their legislation and supervision when they encounter resistance and obstacles
from governments.

Finally, institutionalized mechanisms linking local legislatures and
social organizations have been formed, and this has facilitated ongoing
reciprocal collaboration. First, because the heads of major social organizations simultaneously serve as leaders of legislatures (such as vice-
chairpersons and members of standing committees), they can mediate
between the two bodies. For example, in the case of the Shanghai legislature, the president of the Shanghai General Trade Union (SGTU) served
as a vice-chairman of the legislature in the 12th period (2003–07), and
three former and present trade union leaders served as members of the
legislature's Standing Committee during the same period. The president
of the Shanghai Federation of Industry and Commerce served as a vice-
chairman, and most leaders of major social organizations also sat on
the legislature's Standing Committee in the 12th period.[28] The situation
in Guangdong Province was similar: in the 10th period (2003–07) of the
legislature, the presidents of the trade union and the women's federation
served as vice-chairpersons of the legislature.[29]

In contrast, the status of social organizations in the Party hierarchy
has declined in the reform era. That is, it has become rare for the presidents of trade unions (the most important mass organizations for the
CCP) to act as standing members of local Party committees since the
1990s. As a consequence, trade unions are less likely to attend Party
meetings as regular voting members and thereby exert influence on Party

[27] Xu Xianghua (ed.), *Xinshiqi Zhongguo lifa sixiang* (*Chinese Lawmaking Thoughts in New Era*) (Shanghai: Xuelin chubanshe, 2004), pp. 156–57.
[28] Interview with senior leaders of the Shanghai legislature: Shanghai, February 2004.
[29] Interview with senior leaders of the Guangdong legislature and social organizations: Guangzhou, August 2004.

policy. Instead, trade unions only regularly report to the Party through Party groups (*tangzu*) in trade unions once or twice a year, or whenever issues arise that require the prior permission of the Party. And when local Party units decide important policies that directly affect workers, trade unions can attend Party meetings as nonvoting members (*liexi*) and raise their own ideas.[30] Women's federations and communist youth leagues face similar conditions.

Second, there are permanent linkages and personnel exchanges between local legislatures and major social organizations. Social organizations maintain ongoing working relations with legislatures through special committees in the legislature. For example, trade unions usually work with the legislative committee (*fazhiwei*) and the interior and judicial affairs committee (*neisiwei*). In addition, the interior and judicial affairs committee generally establishes a labor small group (*laodong xiaozu*) as a subcommittee led by a vice-chairperson of the special committee, and this group is responsible for day-to-day collaborations with trade unions. Women's federations and communist youth leagues have the same type of relationships with legislatures.[31]

Meanwhile, since the 1990s, social organizations have also participated in consultative bodies led by governments. For example, trade unions and government agencies that deal with labor issues run joint conferences (*lianxi huiyi*) where they discuss the government's labor policies and cooperation between the government and trade unions. Trade unions, along with government agencies and business associations, also attend a tripartite labor-management-state dialogue called the three-party coordination on labor relations (*laodong guanxi sanfang xietiao*), in which they also discuss labor-related issues like wage increases and improvements in working conditions.[32] Similarly, the women's and children's affairs committee (*funü ertong gongzuo weiyuanhui*) between government agencies and women's federations, and the juvenile protection committee (*weichengnian baohu weiyuanhui*) between government agencies and communist youth leagues, have been established and run

---

[30] Interview with senior leaders of the trade unions in Shanghai and Guangdong: Shanghai, January 2004; Guangzhou, August 2004.
[31] Interview with senior leaders of the trade unions, women's federations, and communist youth leagues in Tianjin, Shanghai, and Guangdong: Tianjin, May 2001; Shanghai, January 2004; Guangzhou, August 2004.
[32] He Shikun, "Wunianlai gonghui gongzuode zhuyao chengji" (Major achievements of trade unions in the past five years), *Zhongguo gongyun* (*Labor Movement in China*), Additional issue of 2003, pp. 49–56, 96.

since the 1990s. However, because these committees are consultative bodies rather than decision-making forums, and because government agencies use their higher political positions to take the initiative in these bodies when discussing policies and coordinating collaborations, social organizations have a limited capacity to shape government policies to their advantage.[33]

A caveat is in order with regard to relations between legislatures and social organizations. Social organizations cannot maintain a similar degree of reciprocity in their relations with legislatures. That is, the more these social organizations exert social influence by dint of their strong organizational capacities and higher status in the Chinese political system, the greater the position they will enjoy in legislatures and the greater will be their chances to participate in legislative activities. Thus, trade unions and women's federations occupy the most advantageous positions. As discussed previously, the presidents of these organizations concurrently serve as vice-chairpersons or members of the legislature's standing committees and they use their positions to influence legislative decision making in a way that is advantageous to the interests of their organizations. In contrast, new organizations such as consumers' councils, environmental protection associations, and trade associations have lower positions in legislatures and engage in legislative activities only in a limited way. Communist youth leagues, which face declining political and social influence, and federations of industry and commerce, which are experiencing growing status and power in the reform era, have mid-ranking degrees of status in legislatures and participation in legislative activities.

This analysis shows that the political status and social influence of social organizations in China are determined not by the organizations' autonomy from, but by their intimacy with, the political establishment. Therefore, social organizations tend to strive to maintain close relations with political forces rather than to keep distant from them. Cooperating with the political establishment is both an expedient and a necessary survival strategy for social organizations. For this reason, most business organizations (such as federations of industry and commerce, and entrepreneurial associations), of course along with "people's organizations" like trade unions, women's federations, and communist youth leagues,

---

[33] Interview with senior leaders of the trade unions, women's federations, and communist youth leagues in Tianjin, Shanghai, and Guangdong: Tianjin, May 2001; Shanghai, January 2004; Guangzhou, August 2004.

are willing to accept the Party's political leadership and try to toe the Party line in order to increase their authority.

SOCIAL ORGANIZATIONS AND LAWMAKING

As discussed in Chapter 2, the lawmaking power of the NPC and local people's congresses has been remarkably strengthened, and the politics of lawmaking in China has become much more important than before. Under these conditions, social organizations competitively engage in lawmaking processes as an effective means of promoting their interests.

BACKGROUND

Social organizations can actively participate in lawmaking with the strong encouragement of legislatures, the permission of the CCP, and through their own efforts. Since we have already discussed the first factor in Chapter 2, we will examine only the latter two matters here.

In addition to legislatures' request and encouragement, Party policy has also paved the way to widespread and active participation of social organizations in lawmaking. Since the mid-1980s, the CCP has put into practice new social organization policies that have allowed "people's organizations" to get involved in state policymaking processes.[34] This is an inclusion policy aimed at embedding major social organizations into the party-state system. For example, the General Offices of the CCP Central Committee and State Council jointly issued a notice in 1985 ordering that when the CCP and governments decided labor-related policies, they had to allow trade unions to attend meetings and to voice workers' opinions.[35] This notice provided political support for the participation of trade unions in Party and government policymaking processes to protect workers' interests. Since the issuing of this notice,

---

[34] Anita Chan, "Revolution or corporation? Workers and trade unions in post-Mao China," in David S.G. Goodman and Beverley Hooper (eds.), *China's Quiet Revolution: New Interactions between State and Society* (New York: St. Martin's Press, 1994), pp. 162–93; White, Howell, and Shang, *In Search of Civil Society*, pp. 51–55.

[35] Zhonggong zhongyang bangongting and Guowuyuan bangongting, "Guanyu gonghui canjia dang he zhengfu youguan huiyi he gongzuo jigoude qingshide tongzhi" (A notice on the participation of trade unions in Party and government conferences and working organs) (1985), Zhongguo jinrong gonghui, *Selections of Important Documents on Trade Union Works*, pp. 207–08.

trade unions have been actively involved in the making of labor-related policies.[36]

After the 1989 Tiananmen Incident, the CCP intensified efforts to control major social organizations and also to allow them to participate in state decision making to a much greater extent. A notice from the CCP Central Committee in 1989 was a case in point.[37] Soon after the Party notice, trade unions, women's federations, and communist youth leagues across the country prepared and carried out detailed implementation directives. The establishment of joint conferences on labor issues, women's and children's affairs committees, and juvenile protection committees was a result of the 1989 Party policy's implementation.

Finally, social organizations have also striven to engage in state policymaking, including legislation.[38] As the law has come to play a more significant role in resolving social conflicts following the implementation of the legalization policy in the 1990s, social organizations have had to pay much more attention to lawmaking. That is, "people's organizations," including trade unions, women's federations, communist youth leagues, and federations of industry and commerce, have carried out the guideline of "protection of rights and interests through participation from the origin" (*yuantou canyu weiquan*). This policy entails social organizations engaging in the early stages of state policymaking – rather than just the implementation stage – so that policy more clearly reflects the rights and interests of these organizations. This also applies to legislation.[39] As a result, participation

---

[36] Zhonghua quanguo zonggonghui (ed.), *Zhonghua quanguo zonggonghui qishinian (Seventy Years of the All-China Federation of Trade Unions)* (Beijing: Zhongguo gongren chubanshe, 1995), pp. 495–97.

[37] Zhonggong zhongyang, "A notice on the strengthening and improvement of the Party's leadership" (1989).

[38] On the case of the NPC, see Michael William Dowdle, "Constructing citizenship: The NPC as catalyst for political participation," in Merle Goldman and Elizabeth J. Perry (eds.), *Changing Meanings of Citizenship in Modern China* (Cambridge: Harvard University Press, 2002), pp. 330–49.

[39] Biancuan weiyuanhui (ed.), *Shanghai gonghui nianjian 1999 (Shanghai Trade Unions Yearbook 1999)* (Shanghai: Wenhui chubanshe, 1999), pp. 35–36; He, "Major achievements of trade unions in the past five years," p. 49; Meng Yankun, "Yi sange daibiao zhongyao sixiang wei lingdao zai tuijin xiandaihua guoji dadushi jianshe zhong shixian Shanghai fuliande kuayueshi fazhan" (Promoting the leap forward development of Shanghai Women's Federation in the process of constructing a modern and global city by means of Three Represents Thoughts), *Shanghai fuyun (Women's Movement in Shanghai)*, No. 9 (2003), pp. 8–13; Peng Peiyun, "Jiwang kailai tuidong woguo funü yundong shenru fazhan (Promoting Chinese women's movement into a deep

in lawmaking has become "core work" of trade unions and women's federations since the mid-1990s.[40]

For example, the Shanghai General Trade Union (SGTR) established a lawmaking participatory small group (*lifa canyu xiaozu*). The group comprises twelve members in total: a vice president of the SGTR (as chief of the group), the head of the Legal Affairs Department of the SGTR (as vice-chief), researchers from the Legal Affairs Department and Investigation and Research Department, cadres from basic-level trade unions, and professors from law schools in Shanghai. When the legislature enacts labor-related local laws, all members of the small group participate in the preparatory work such as investigation and drafting. In addition, the group is responsible for reviewing and submitting the SGTR's view of draft local laws that the legislature has requested to consider, and in those cases five to six members of the group consider each draft. In these ways, the SGTR has played a part in ten to twenty pieces of legislation per year since the 1990s.[41] The Shanghai Women's Federation has also engaged in lawmaking in a similar way and to a similar degree.

CASE ANALYSES

We can divide the lawmaking participation of social organizations into two categories, mainly according to the features of enacted laws. The first are local laws relating to the vital interests of social organizations. In this case, social organizations, as official or unofficial members of drafting small groups (*qichao xiaozu*), directly participate in the preparation of local laws. The other category is when legislatures send draft laws to social organizations in order to solicit their opinions, even though these laws are not directly related to social organizations. In this case, social organizations review the draft laws and submit their views in written form. Sometimes they attend lawmaking hearings convened by legislatures' special committees or government agencies and express their views.

development in the spirit of carrying on the past and opening a way for future), *Zhongguo fuyun* (*Women's Movement in China*), No. 9 (2003), pp. 4–9.

[40] Interview with senior leaders of the trade unions, women's federations, and communist youth leagues in Tianjin, Shanghai, and Guangdong: Tianjin, May 2001; Shanghai, January 2004; Guangzhou, August 2004.

[41] Interview with senior leaders of the Shanghai General Trade Union: Shanghai, February 2004.

Here we will examine the first category of social organizations' participation in lawmaking in order to address how social organizations engage in lawmaking processes, and to what degree. Participation in lawmaking can be divided into three instances again: the first is when certain social organizations are allowed to almost monopolize the drafting of local laws; the second is when multiple social organizations, along with government agencies and legislative committees, competitively partake in lawmaking; and the third is when social organizations only assist government agencies or legislative committees in lawmaking processes, even though the enacted laws are directly related their critical interests.

First, some social organizations, chiefly trade unions, women's federations, and communist youth leagues, are allowed to take the initiative of drafting. When local legislatures make local laws dealing with matters of workers, women, and juveniles, these organizations initiate the preparation of draft laws. Legislatures in these cases tend to pass the draft laws without substantial revision out of respect for these organizations' opinions. In a sense, the CCP, governments, and legislatures guarantee that "people's organizations" enjoy the lawmaking initiative when they make local laws relating to the affairs of workers, women, and youth. This practice has continued since the mid-1980s.

There are numerous examples of this practice. For example, when the Shanghai legislature formulated the Regulation on Trade Unions in Chinese-Foreign Joint Companies in 1989, the SGTR and the legislature's Legislative Committee were designated as official drafting organs. But in the actual preparatory process, the SGTR led the investigation and drafting with the support of the Committee. A similar situation occurred when the legislature enacted the Trade Unions Regulation in 1995. The SGTR submitted a bill that requested the enactment of trade union regulation to the legislature in 1993. After gaining approval from the legislature, the SGTR, as an official drafting organ, together with the legislature's Legislative Committee, took the initiative of investigating and drafting the regulation.[42] Similarly, the SGTR submitted a lawmaking bill through its deputies to the Shanghai legislature in the 2002 plenary session. The bill requested the revision of the 1995 Trade Unions Regulation. After the legislature approved the request, the SGTR led the

---

[42] Shanghai Labor Movement Compilation Committee, *Shanghai gongyunzhi* (*Annals of Labor Movement in Shanghai*) (Shanghai: Shanghai shehui kexue chubanshe, 1997), pp. 412–13.

preparation of the draft law, and the legislature passed the law without substantive revisions.[43]

The Shanghai Women's Federation (SWF) and Communist Youth League (SCYL) performed similar roles when the legislature enacted local laws dealing with their matters. For instance, the SWF asked the legislature to regulate the protection of women's and children's rights in 1984, and drafted the local law under the authorization of the legislature. The regulation was passed in 1985 without objections. When the legislature promulgated the Implementing Regulation on Women's Rights Protection Law in Shanghai in 1994, the SWF was also responsible for drafting the regulation.[44] The SCYL played a leading role when the legislature enacted the Regulation on Juvenile Protection in 1987. After gaining authorization from the legislature's Legislative Committee in 1985, the SCYL conducted extensive research over one-and-a-half years into the draft regulation. The legislature passed the draft law without substantive revisions in 1987.[45]

The practice is also apparent in other regions. For instance, when the Tianjin legislature enacted the Juvenile Protection Regulation in 1990, the Tianjin Communist Youth League led the preparation of the draft law, even though a legislative committee and a government agency also participated in the drafting small group as co-drafters. Similarly, the Guangdong Women's Federation drafted the Implementing Regulation on Women's Rights Protection Law in Guangdong Province in 1994.[46] This practice is also applied at the national level. When the NPC enacts laws closely related to the vital interests of social organizations, the relevant organizations are allowed to participate in lawmaking processes as major actors. When the NPC enacted the Lawyers Law in 1994, the All-China Lawyers Federation played a vital role in preparing the draft law.[47] The All-China Federation of Trade Unions played a similar role in

---

[43] Tu Guoming, "Tuchu yifa weiquan shixian Shanghai tese" (Highlighting governance according to law and realizing Shanghai characteristics), *Gonghui lilun yanjiu (Studies on Trade Union Theory)*, No. 6 (2002), pp. 22–23, 30; Interview with senior leaders of the Shanghai General Trade Union: Shanghai, August 2003 and February 2004.

[44] Huang Sha and Meng Yankun (eds.), *Shanghai funüzhi (Annals of Shanghai Women)* (Shanghai: Shanghai shehui kexue chubanshe, 2000), p. 274.

[45] Qichao bangongshi (ed.), '*Shanghai qingshaonian baohu tiaoli' lifa jishi (Lawmaking Record on the Shanghai Juvenile Protection Regulation)* (Shanghai: Shanghai shehui kexue chubanshe, 1987), pp. 92–101.

[46] Interview with senior leaders of the women's federations and communist youth leagues in Tianjin and Guangdong: Tianjin, May 2001; Guangzhou, August 2004.

[47] Dowdle, "Constructing citizenship," p. 334; Zhang Geng (ed.), *Zhongguo lüshi zhidu fazhande lichengbei: 'Zhonghua renmin gongheguo lüshifa' lifa guocheng huigu*

the enactment and revision of the Trade Unions Law in 1994 and 2001, respectively.[48]

Second, if local laws affect the interests of several social organizations, some organizations are not allowed to monopolize the preparation of draft laws. Instead, all related lawmaking actors, such as legislative committees, government agencies, and social organizations, are allowed to equitably participate in the lawmaking process. And in these cases, cooperation and conflict between state agencies and social organizations occurs frequently. Laws are ultimately the result of compromise between lawmaking participants. The legislation of the Shanghai Labor Contract Regulation in 2001 and the amendment to the Shanghai Consumers' Rights Protection Regulation in 2002 are good examples. While these cases were examined in detail in Chapter 2 and will not be discussed again in detail here, some points are worthy of mention.

Most notable were the conflicts and confrontation between state agencies and social organizations and also among social organizations themselves in the processes of both framing and amending the regulations. For example, the SGTU had heated disputes with business associations such as the Shanghai Federation of Industry and Commerce, and also with the Labor Bureau and Economy Commission of the government, with regard to the Shanghai Labor Contract Regulation. Likewise, the Shanghai Consumer Association (SCA) clashed with social organizations related to the fields of education and medicine when the legislature amended the Consumers' Rights Protection Regulation. This illustrates that since the introduction of a market economy in China, state-society relations have taken the form of "three force-fields" – state, society, and market – instead of a dyadic structure of state and society.[49]

Furthermore, social organizations were able to compete almost on an equal footing with legislative committees and government agencies to create laws that better reflected their interests. In other words, no one party monopolized the legislative process, and more important, neither the CCP nor the legislature prescribed the contents of laws in advance.

(*A Milestone in the Development of China's Lawyers Institutions: A Retrospect on the Lawmaking Process of the Law of PRC on Lawyers*) (Beijing: Falü chubanshe, 1997), pp. 58–188.

[48] Zhonghua quanguo zonggonghui, *Zhonghua renmin gongheguo gonghuifa jianghua* (*An Explanation on the Law of PRC on Trade Unions*) (Beijing: Zhongguo gongren chubanshe, 2001), pp. 4–5.

[49] Health B. Chamberlain, "Civil society with Chinese characteristics?" *China Journal*, No. 39 (January 1998), pp. 69–81.

Thus, legislation was generally shaped by competition and compromise between the relevant participants. As a consequence, the lobbying by social organizations became widespread and also affected the process and outcome of lawmaking.

For example, when the Shanghai legislature enacted the Consumers' Rights Protection Regulation, the SCA systematically and actively attempted to rally the public and to lobby legislators to their cause. The Association conducted several opinion polls by telephone and publicized the results, which supported the Association's position on major issues. It also held various forums in which representatives of consumers and enterprises, professionals such as lawyers and scholars, government officials, and members of legislative committees were invited to discuss consumer rights issues. The SCA invited the secretary-general of the Hong Kong Consumers' Association to one forum. This official explained the activities of the HKCA in detail, and emphasized the necessity of strengthening the SCA's authority and functions in front of the legislature committee members.[50] This active lobbying by the SCA raised serious concerns among some legislative leaders as to how to deal with the increasing pressure of interest groups in the lawmaking process.[51]

The SGTU also lobbied when the Shanghai legislature drew up the Labor Contract Regulation, even though its lobbying was less extensive than that of the SCA. The Union publicized the results of its research on deteriorating working conditions in the Shanghai region and earnestly publicized its position on the regulation by hosting policy forums. And in order to refute the arguments of business-related associations in legislation hearings held by the legislature, the trade union systematically prepared by collecting raw data from extensive investigations and devising an appropriate division of roles between hearing participants. For example, a lawyer attempted to prove SGTR's case in terms of legal principles, while a female worker tried to demonstrate the relevance of the union's position by revealing her dire working conditions. One union leader argued that these preparations allowed the SGTR to overwhelm the business-related camp in the hearing.[52]

---

[50] Interview with senior leaders of the Shanghai legislature and the Consumers' Association: Shanghai, August 2003 and February 2004.

[51] Shanghai renda changweihui yanjiushi (ed.), *Shijian yu tansuo* (*Practice and Exploration*) (Vol. 4) (Shanghai: Fudan daxue chubanshe, 2003), p. 63.

[52] Interview with senior leaders of the Shanghai legislature and the Trade Union: Shanghai, August 2003 and February 2004.

Third, in some cases, government agencies have initiated legislation while social organizations have played a minor role, even though the relevant laws have impacted on the interests of the organizations in question. A case in point is the Shanghai Regulation on Promoting the Development of Trade Associations (*hangye xiehui*), introduced in 2002.[53] As of 2001, about 160 trade associations existed in Shanghai. But they are small in number and are not representative of their areas. More seriously, most associations function as "second government agencies" (*erzhengfu*) because they are firmly controlled and operated by government. For these reasons, there has been pressure to increase the number of trade associations and broaden their roles. Thus, the Shanghai government promulgated the Temporary Measures for Trade Associations in January 2002, and the legislature decided to enact a related regulation based on the experiences of the Measure's implementation.

Because the Regulation seriously affected their establishment and operation, social organizations were expected to partake in the lawmaking process as major actors. But in practice, government agencies, such as the Legal Affairs Office, the Economic System Reform Office, and the Bureau of Social Organizations Management, initiated the legislation. There were two reasons for this. The first related to the characteristics of the regulation and the objective conditions of social organizations. Because this regulation covered all trade associations in Shanghai, it was inappropriate for some social organizations to lead its drafting. And some people argue that given the present capabilities of trade associations in Shanghai, social organizations might struggle to take responsibility for investigating and drafting the regulation, even though the legislature and government allowed them to do so.

The second reason related to the government's intention, and this factor seems to have been more important. Because government agencies would not relinquish control of trade associations even after the enactment of the regulation, they were reluctant to permit social organizations

---

[53] On the lawmaking process of this regulation, see Zhou Taidan, "Guanyu 'Shanghai cujin hangye xiehui fazhan guiding'de shuoming" (An explanation on the 'Regulation on Promoting the Development of Trade Associations in Shanghai'), *Shanghaishi renda changweihui gongbao* (*Bulletin of Shanghai Municipal People's Congress*), No. 153 (2002) (available at http://www.spcsc.sh.cn); Shen Guoming, "Shirenda fazhiwei guanyu 'Shanghai cujin hangye xiehui fazhan guiding' shenyi jieguode baogao" (A report on the consideration result of the 'Regulation on Promoting the Development of Trade Associations in Shanghai'), *Shanghaishi renda changweihui gongbao*, No. 153 (2002) (available at http://www.spcsc.sh.cn); Interview with senior leaders of the Shanghai legislature: Shanghai, August 2003 and February 2004.

to partake in the legislative process as equal partners. As "second government agencies," trade associations are important to the interests of government agencies. For example, retired high-level cadres and surplus officials after restructuring of government agencies can transfer to trade associations. Government agencies can also use the sizeable revenues that trade associations earn through various activities for their welfare funds. Finally, trade associations are useful means through which government agencies can influence both relevant industrial sectors and individual companies.

Since government agencies led the lawmaking process, some controversial issues between government agencies and trade associations were resolved chiefly in favor of government agencies. For instance, with regard to articles on the jurisdiction and function of trade associations, the associations demanded clearer and more specific statements in order to prevent unnecessary interference from government agencies. Conversely, government agencies argued that detailed articles were unnecessary here because China was still in a transition period. In addition, trade associations argued that in order to activate their roles, the new regulation should clarify that government agencies had to transfer most of their social management functions to social organizations. But government agencies strongly objected to this argument. Only one new article, a measure to enhance the independence of trade associations, was added to the draft during its consideration in the legislature. It specified that incumbent government officials should not serve as leaders in trade associations, but they can do so after retirement. The regulation thus did not address the major problems facing trade associations in Shanghai.[54]

SOCIAL ORGANIZATIONS AND LEGISLATIVE SUPERVISION

Social organizations have partaken less actively in supervision than legislation, for various reasons. Because the supervisory authority of Chinese local legislatures has not been intensified as much as its lawmaking power, social organizations have not had many chances to partake in it. In addition, because social organizations must consider their relations both with governments and with legislatures, they have not been able to take part in legislative supervision over governments as actively as they

[54] Wang Ming, *General Discussion on Civil Organization*, pp. 197–201.

do in lawmaking. However, social organizations place great value on their participation in legislative supervision and engage it in various ways.

As in lawmaking processes, not all social organizations can take part in legislative supervision to the same degree. Only "people's organizations," such as trade unions, women's federations, and communist youth leagues, which enjoy higher political status in the Chinese political system and exert relatively strong influence on society, can partake in legislative supervision. In contrast, the federations of industry and commerce, even though they represent the private economy, rarely participate in legislative supervision.[55]

BACKGROUND

As a legal system has been gradually established with the rapid increase in legislation in the 1990s, the thorough implementation of enacted laws has become a critical political task for both state and society. Notably, the 1989 Tiananmen Incident warned Party leaders that widespread political corruption and power abuses at the local level could threaten the legitimacy of the communist regime if the Party did not respond to these issues. Along with the restructuring of the CCP disciplinary apparatus responsible for supervision over Party cadres and the buttressing of legislative supervision over governments and officials, the ruling Party also considered the strengthening of supervision over state organs by the mass media and social organizations. A decision of the CCP Central Committee in 1990 entitled "A decision of the CCP Central Committee on strengthening the connection between the Party and mass" illustrates this point well.[56]

In terms of social organizations' views, supervision has also become more important. A relatively comprehensive legal system designed to protect the rights and interests of workers, women, and juveniles was already established in the 1990s. The enactment of the Juvenile Protection Law (1991), the Trade Unions Law (1992), the Women's Rights Protection Law (1992), the Consumers' Rights Protection Law (1993), and the Labor Law (1994) is evidence of this fact. Furthermore,

---

[55] Interview with senior leaders of the federations of industry and commerce in Shanghai and Guangdong: Shanghai, February 2004; Guangzhou, August 2004.

[56] "Zhonggong zhongyang guanyu jiaqiang dang tong renmin qunzhong lianxide jueding" (A decision of the CCP Central Committee on strengthening the connection between the Party and mass), Zhonggong zhongyang, *Selections of Important Documents since the 13th Party Congress*, p. 935.

the CCP has made more active attempts to respond to the demands of workers, women, and children who fall into socially weaker groups in the reform era by, for instance, implementing new state policies. However, the fact that state laws and the Party center's policies were not faithfully implemented at the local level was a serious problem. Thus, urging and supervising state organs to execute laws and Party policies has become a major task for social organizations.

To this end, trade unions and women's federations have conducted various supervisory activities since the early 1990s. For instance, in 1997, the SGTU formed the Trade Unions' Supervisory Committees on Labor-Related Laws (*gonghui laodong falü jiandu weiyuanhui*) in major factories and basic units based on articles of the Trade Unions Law and the Labor Law. This allowed trade unions to supervise the implementation of labor-related laws and regulations.[57] The union appointed some 6,500 legal supervisors (*falü jianduyuan*) to committees in the late 1990s, and now about 20,000 supervisors are active. The SGTU has also supervised one major issue every year, such as the implementation of labor contracts and retirement annuities. In 2003, the SGTR supervised about 2,000 companies in Shanghai for a month, focusing on how they had implemented the Trade Unions Law and the Labor Law.[58] Similarly, the Guangdong General Trade Union appointed Labor Supervisors of Trade Unions (*gonghui laoding jiandu weiyuan*) based on the Guangdong Regulation on Trade Unions' Supervision on Labor-Related Laws enacted in 2000. The supervisors, who simultaneously work as trade union leaders at the basic level, oversee the implementation of labor-related laws and regulations.[59]

Social organizations sometimes conduct joint supervision with the CCP and government agencies. Generally speaking, social organizations select the means and targets of supervision, depending on the nature of the issue and targets to be supervised. In the case of serious problems that affect their vital interests, or if government agencies are expected to strongly object during the supervision, social organizations prefer to ask Party committees to carry out joint supervision. If the Party recognizes the seriousness of problems and is willing to join the supervision project, social organizations can expect swift and effective resolution of

[57] Biancuan weiyuanhui (ed.), *Shanghai gonghui nianjian 1998* (*Shanghai Trade Unions Yearbook 1998*) (Shanghai: Wenhui chubanshe, 1998), p. 173.
[58] Interview with senior leaders of the SGTU: Shanghai, February 2004.
[59] Interview with senior leaders of the Guangdong General Trade Union: Guangzhou, August 2004.

problems. However, because the CCP should consider all aspects of the region and coordinate between state organs and social organizations that may come into conflict, it rarely accepts requests from social organizations to conduct joint supervision.

On the other hand, when the issues are relatively trivial and can be easily resolved, social organizations prefer to conduct joint supervision with government agencies. In a sense, this is the most efficient supervisory method for minor issues because government agencies, as the organs chiefly responsible for implementing labor-related laws and Party policies, have the capacity to immediately correct problems. If social organizations cannot compel government agencies to conduct joint supervision, they appeal to local people's congresses – although this is generally seen as a last resort. Since the 1990s, when the political status of Chinese legislatures was enhanced and legislative supervision became more effective, social organizations have been able to pressure government agencies into action by merely mentioning the possibility of referring related matters to legislatures.

PARTICIPATORY METHODS AND EVALUATION OF SUPERVISORY EFFECTIVENESS

Among the major supervisory methods that Chinese local legislatures have adopted, social organizations most frequently engage in the examination of law enforcement. They also participate in the appraisal of government agencies and officials, and individual case supervision.

There are several ways that social organizations partake in legislative supervision. The first is to petition local legislatures to supervise state organs by raising social issues. Major social organizations conduct surveys and research into important issues concerning their missions and publicize the results in order to attract public attention. At the same time, social organizations send the results of their research to local legislatures through their deputies in the form of proposals (*jianyi*) or bills (*yian*). Social organizations can thereby urge local legislatures to pay attention to specific issues that they put forward and to include these issues in the supervisory agenda of legislatures.

For example, the Guangdong Women's Federation has raised some serious issues for women's welfare in the region and urged the Guangdong legislature to take strong measures to address them. These issues include the protection of the rights of female migrant workers, the difficulties of migrant workers' children in getting proper education, and domestic violence. The Guangdong legislature has examined the enforcement of laws and policies relating to women several times at the request of the federation. In particular, the Women's Federation has recently focused on the problems of unfair or prejudicial court decisions, which have been frequent in divorce and inheritance cases. The Federation tends to first request courts to correct these problems by themselves. But if the courts do not accede to these requests, the Federation raises the problems in the legislature and urges it to supervise and investigate the courts. When the legislature acts to supervise the courts, the problems are generally resolved as the Federation expects.[60]

In 2001, the Tianjin Communist Youth League, based on its field research, argued that computer cafés (*wangba*) in the region created serious security and moral problems for students. It requested the legislature to investigate the matter. Upon receiving the League's request, the Tianjin legislature, together with government agencies, carried out a large-scale examination of law enforcement relating to computer cafés. Government authorities subsequently closed down about one hundred establishments.

In addition to raising social issues to local legislatures and influencing the legislatures' selection of supervisory objects, social organizations take part in legislative supervision in direct ways. The most common is participation in the examination of law enforcement. Trade unions, women's federations, and communist youth leagues place great value on the examination process, so they strive to engage in supervision in accordance with the policy of "raising initiatives, participating actively, and concentrating strength" (*zhudong tichu, jiji canyu, jizhong liliang*).[61] In fact, trade unions and women's federations in Shanghai and Guangdong have participated in their legislatures' examination process almost every year by providing relevant materials and sending high-level officials to support investigations. For instance, in June and July 2003, the Guangdong General Trade Union sent eight high-level cadres to the Guangdong legislature when it conducted an examination of the implementation of the Labor Law and the Trade Unions Law. In June 2004, the union also sent five high-level officials to the legislature to support

---

[60] Interview with senior leaders of the Guangdong Women's Federation: Guangzhou, August 2004.

[61] Interview with senior leaders of the trade unions, women's federations, and communist youth leagues in Tianjin, Shanghai, and Guangdong: Tianjin, May 2001; Shanghai, February 2004; Guangzhou, August 2004.

the supervision of the implementation of the Regulation on the Making Public of Factory Affairs.

We cannot uniformly evaluate the supervisory effectiveness of social organizations through participation in legislative supervision because effectiveness varies by region and issue. But we can safely say that supervision by social organizations is much more effective when they jointly supervise with local legislatures.[62] There are several reasons for this. First, because Chinese legislatures are state power organs in the regions, government agencies and other state organs cannot easily ignore the demands of legislatures. Even if state departments cannot properly address problems that legislatures request them to resolve, they should submit explanations in written form with appropriate evidence to legislatures. In contrast, when social organizations act alone to raise issues and ask government agencies to address them, the agencies are likely to respond by merely sending formal replies without taking concrete steps to address the problems.

In addition, since the decisions and demands of legislatures carry legally binding force, government agencies and other state organs have to take some measures to implement them. In particular, it has been difficult for state organs to turn down legislatures' demands since the 1990s, when legislative supervision was noticeably strengthened and the Party began to enforce its governance according to the law policy. As noted in Chapters 3 and 4, local legislatures dismissed the heads of government agencies and courts in some regions for not faithfully implementing the legislatures' demands. Subsequently, social organizations strongly prefer to raise issues through legislative channels rather than by themselves.

Legislative supervision has its limitations, however, and we should not overestimate the effectiveness of social organizations' participation in legislative supervision. That is, because legislatures are still politically less powerful than governments in China, social organizations have limited opportunities to resolve their problems by participating in legislative supervision. Furthermore, social organizations should consider their relations with governments. For social organizations, relations with governments are more important than those with legislatures because governments wield vital powers concerning the establishment and day-to-day operation of social organizations. These organizations engage in legislative supervision over government agencies as long as they do not damage their relations with governments. As a consequence,

[62] Ibid.

social organizations cautiously partake in legislative activities, keeping their participation within the limits set by the law and Party policies.

POLITICAL IMPLICATIONS OF LEGISLATIVE-SOCIAL ORGANIZATION RELATIONS

When examining changes in state-society relations in China, two new perspectives are necessary: legalization and the extension of the "state" in the horizontal dimension. Viewed in these terms, a new state-society relationship can be found between local legislatures and social organizations, different from that between the CCP/state and social organizations. This new relationship does not fit in well with the patterns that state corporatism and civil society theory have predicted. This demonstrates that with the emergence of legislatures as new political forces and the consequent expansion of political arenas like legislative politics, state-society relations in China have moved in a direction that previous studies have not considered.

On the one hand, legislature-social organization relations are inconsistent with the main presumption of state corporatism. State corporatism argues that the state both initiates relations with society and dominates it. Furthermore, social organizations, as official representatives designated by the state in certain functional and regional spheres, behave within boundaries previously prescribed by the state. However, in legislature-social organization relations, social organizations can competitively participate in some lawmaking cases with few restrictions from the state (legislatures), and lawmaking outcomes often reflect both cooperation and confrontation between state departments, legislative committees, and social organizations.

At least in terms of social organizations' participation in lawmaking, legislature-social organization relations go beyond the basic assumptions of state corporatism. This has very important implications because social organizations in these cases refer to "people's organizations," such as trade unions, women's federations, and communist youth leagues, which are traditionally considered to be firmly under state control as pillars of the Party's one-party rule. In a sense, these organizations' relations with legislatures have displayed characteristics of "social representation" rather than state control, as Yunqiu Zhang argues, although we cannot predict at this moment whether the relations could evolve into civil society; or the relations may have increased some new elements of civil society with Chinese characteristics within the structure of state corporatism, as Yijiang Ding insists.

On the other hand, the relations between legislatures and social organizations are incongruent with the major presumptions of civil society theory. Most of all, Chinese legislatures have maintained symbiotic relations with social organizations, rather than the antagonistic relations that civil society theory usually anticipates. Also, social organizations strive to become more embedded in the state (in this case, legislatures), instead of pursuing autonomy from the state. In addition, concerning political change in China, the relations imply that it may occur in a different way than civil society theory predicts. The theory presumes that a market economy will induce the formation of civil society and will lead to democratization by limiting the exercise of state power. Also, it assumes that civil society, in the process of political democratization, both strives for independence from the state and struggles with it to secure political and human rights and to expand the rule of law. The experiences of Third World and former socialist countries, it is argued, provide evidence for the relevance of civil society theory.

Civil society theory, when applied to China, may be flawed in two respects, however. First, it tends to view the state as a unitary entity. Second, it posits that civil society forms and develops outside the state in a "bottom-up" way. But as the development of local legislatures demonstrates, the Chinese state is no longer a monolithic entity composed of only the Party and governments. Furthermore, political arenas have been increasingly enlarged (e.g., the formation of lawmaking politics) with the emergence of new political forces like legislatures and courts. Social organizations can consequently increase their influence by actively engaging in these arenas rather than distancing themselves from legislatures. So in contrast to civil society theory, social forces can induce shifts in state-society relations and political change from within the political regime through proactive cooperation – rather than antagonistic confrontation – with the state, or by intensifying their embeddedness in – rather than increasing independence from – the state.

Relations between legislatures and social organizations also help us to establish a new model of Chinese political processes, including decision making. In the past two decades, "fragmented authoritarianism" has been widely employed to examine Chinese decision-making structures and processes. However, as Michel Oksenberg notes, this is a static model contrived to understand how the Chinese state organs worked in the 1980s. As a consequence, fragmented authoritarianism has limitations insofar as it does not adequately consider changes in Chinese politics since the 1990s, especially the increasing role of society in the political system. In designing a more comprehensive model of Chinese politics, interactions between state and society must be considered.[63] In this regard, legislature-social organization relations are relevant. The participation of social organizations in legislative activities (legislation and supervision) illustrates how social forces have engaged in Chinese politics in a changing political environment, and thereby to what degree Chinese politics in general and state-society relations in particular have been changed.

[63] Michel Oksenberg, "China's political system: Challenges of the twenty first century," *China Journal*, No. 45 (2001), p. 28.

7

The Development of Local Legislatures and Political Leadership

This chapter explores the uneven development of Chinese local legislatures and the main factors that cause the differences in order to understand the features of legislative development in China. It poses two specific questions: to what degree is the performance of local people's congresses different between the legislatures located in the same province, and what factors cause that variation and through what mechanisms? As examined in the previous chapters, the rising status of Chinese local legislatures is a significant step toward a major political reform, and an analysis of the causes and mechanisms of legislative development can provide deeper insights into political change in China.

Previous studies on the democratic election of villagers' committees have paid attention to the uneven dissemination of village democracy and the factors that have brought it about. Focusing on the relationship between economic development and the spread of self-governance, as the modernization thesis does,[1] some studies have examined regional disparity in the development of villagers' committees.

---

[1] For a brief history of studies on the relationship between economic development and political democratization, see Seymour Martin Lipset, "Some social requisites of democracy: Economic development and political legitimacy," *American Political Science Review*, Vol. 53, No. 1 (March 1959), pp. 69–105; Zehra F. Arat, "Democracy and economic development: Modernization theory revisited," *Comparative Politics*, Vol. 21, No. 1 (October 1988), pp. 21–36; Ross E. Burkhart and Michael S. Lewis-Beck, "Comparative democracy: The economic development thesis," *American Political Science Review*, Vol. 88, No. 4 (December 1994), pp. 903–10; Doh Chull Shin, "On the third wave of democratization: A synthesis and evaluation of recent theory and research," *World Politics*, Vol. 47, No. 1 (October 1994), pp. 135–70; Adam Przeworski

For example, Kevin O'Brien argues that self-government autonomy is easiest to promote in the villages that are not among the poorest but have prospering collective enterprises. On the other hand, Susan Lawrence suggests that poor agricultural villages may actually be the pacesetters in village democracy. Empirical evidence produced by Jean Oi confirms Lawrence's view that as income increases, participation in villagers' assemblies and the competitiveness of elections generally decrease.[2]

Meanwhile, Tianjian Shi emphasizes the roles of political leadership in facilitating electoral reform in rural China, like Guillermo O'Donnell and others who previously analyzed the democratization of the Third World and former socialist countries.[3] He has found that democratically committed mid-level officials and their ability to find ways to pursue their goal played a crucial role in the successful implementation of the Organic Law of Villagers' Committees.[4] Furthermore, he observes that the relationship between economic development and village elections appears to be curvilinear; that is, economic wealth increases the likelihood that a village will hold semi-competitive elections for people to choose their leaders, but its impact diminishes as

and Fernando Limongi, "Modernization: Theories and Facts," *World Politics*, Vol. 49, No. 2 (January 1997), pp. 155–83.

[2] Lianjiang Li and Kevin O'Brien, "The struggle over village elections," in Merle Goldman and Roderick MacFarquhar (eds.), *The Paradox of China's Post-Mao Reforms* (Cambridge, MA: Harvard University Press, 1999), p. 130. Also see Susan Lawrence, "Village representative assemblies: Democracy, Chinese style," *Australian Journal of Chinese Affairs*, No. 32 (July 1994), pp. 61–68; Kevin O'Brien, "Implementing political reform in China's villages," *Australian Journal of Chinese Affairs*, No. 32 (July 1994), pp. 33–60; Jean C. Oi, "Economic development, stability and democratic village self-governance," in Maurice Brosseau, Suzanne Pepper, and Tang Shu-ki (eds.), *China Review 1996* (Hong Kong: Chinese University Press, 1996), pp. 125–44; Jean C. Oi and Scott Rozelle, "Elections and power: The locus of decision-making in Chinese villages," *China Quarterly*, No. 162 (June 2000), pp. 513–39.

[3] Guillermo O'Donnell and Philippe C. Schmitter, *Transitions from Authoritarian Rule: Tentative Conclusions about Uncertain Democracies* (Baltimore, MD: Johns Hopkins University Press, 1986); Guillermo O'Donnell, Philippe C. Schmitter, and Laurence Whitehead (eds.), *Transition from Authoritarian Rule: Comparative Perspectives* (Baltimore, MD: Johns Hopkins University Press, 1986); Adam Przeworski, *Democracy and Market: Political and Economic Reforms in Eastern Europe and Latin America* (Cambridge: Cambridge University Press, 1991); Samuel P. Huntington, *The Third Wave: Democratization in the Late Twentieth Century* (Norman: University of Oklahoma Press, 1991).

[4] Tianjian Shi, "Village committee elections in China: Institutionalist tactics for democracy," *World Politics*, Vol. 51, No. 3 (April 1999), pp. 385–412.

economic wealth increases. Rapid economic development may even delay the process of political development, since it may help to consolidate the power of incumbent leaders. Political reform, Shi argues, is a product of interactions between elites and the general populace, rather than the result of economic development per se.[5]

The findings of this research affirm Shi's argument that political leadership plays a crucial role in the process of Chinese legislative development, while economic wealth is negatively associated with it. First, this study has found that the legislative supervision over governments actually differs among legislatures within the same province, as evidenced by the adoption of new forms of supervisory measures and ordinary supervision. Second, the political leadership of both legislatures and the Party at the same level is a vital factor in the faithful carrying out of legislative supervision. If legislative leaders are resolute and Party leaders are willing to support them, the legislatures can employ more effective supervisory measures over governments and successfully fulfill their duty. However, economic development is negatively associated with legislative supervision: local legislatures located in economically more developed areas tend to supervise governments less effectively. Finally, the actual power relations of major political forces (that is, the Party, governments, and legislatures) and institutional constraints make the political leadership the most critical factor in the process of Chinese legislative development.

This study investigates eighteen district and county people's congresses in Tianjin Municipality. Since the policies of territorial Party committees and legislatures at the provincial level differ from one province to another and they have a critical effect on the role fulfillment of lower-level legislatures, we need to limit the investigation to one particular province. In addition, this chapter focuses on legislative supervision of governments because it is the major role of local legislatures, especially at the county level. This chapter begins with a discussion of supervisory measures that people's congresses have used in order to understand how Chinese legislatures have implemented legislative supervision over governments. It then analyzes the different accomplishments of legislative supervision. Finally, it examines the factors and mechanisms that cause the differences.

---

[5] Tianjian Shi, "Economic development and villagers' elections in rural China," *Journal of Contemporary China*, Vol. 8, No. 22 (1999), pp. 425–42.

NEW SUPERVISORY MEASURES AND THEIR
EFFECTIVENESS

People's congresses have been unable to exercise their full constitutional powers because of institutional constraints. Thus, since the early 1980s, they have had to pioneer new supervisory measures that do not appear in the Chinese Constitution and pertinent laws. These measures include the examinations of law enforcement, appraisal of government bureaus and officials, the responsibility system of department law enforcement, and so on.

People's congresses verify whether or not government officials faithfully enforce laws and central policies through examinations. Some people's congresses have used this method since the early 1980s, and it has become a major role of Chinese legislatures since the early 1990s. Official recognition came after the former chairman of the NPC Standing Committee, Wan Li, declared in 1992 that examination was as important a duty as legislation.[6] However, although local legislatures can influence governments to implement laws and central policies more properly through examinations, they have difficulty in forcing governments to correct problems identified during the examination process.[7] Legislatures have thus sought to remedy the supervisory flaws by combining examinations with other supervisory measures, such as appraisals and law supervision papers.

Local legislatures use appraisals to estimate and supervise the performance of government bureaus and officials.[8] There are two main types of appraisals: self-reporting of performance appraisals and deputies' appraisals. Some people's congresses pioneered deputies' appraisals in the early 1980s and the practice spread nationwide after the former deputy-chairman of the NPC Standing Committee, Peng Chong, publicly

---

[6] Wan Li, "Zhifa jiancha he zhiding falü tongdeng zhongyao" (Examination of law enforcement is as important as legislation) (1992), in Liu Zheng, Yu Youmin, and Cheng Xiangqing (eds.), *Renmin daibiao dahui gongzuo quanshu* (*Overall Book on the Works of People's Congresses*) (Beijing: Zhongguo fazhi chubanshe, 1999), pp. 1052–53.

[7] Quanguorenda changweihui bangongting (ed.), *Guojia quanli jiguande jiandu zhidu he jiandu gongzuo* (*The Supervisory Systems and Work of State Power Organs*) (Beijing: Zhongguo minzhu fazhi chubanshe, 1999), pp. 79–89.

[8] Ibid., pp. 217, 225–26; Yun Wanbang, "Shilun renda daibiaode pingyi gongzuo" (On the appraisal works of the deputies to the people's congresses), *Renda gongzuo tongxun*, No. 13 (July 1994), pp. 27–32.

approved it in 1992.[9] Self-reporting appraisals came later, but also rapidly spread throughout China in the 1990s.

The differences between the two appraisals affect their supervisory effect and the diffusion of such practices. In short, self-reporting appraisals are more effective but more difficult to disseminate than deputies' appraisals. Most of all, the two appraisals have different targets for supervision: self-reporting appraisals generally deal with senior officials ("personnel-oriented"/*duiren*); and deputies' appraisals target the work of bureaus ("work-oriented"/*duishi*). Self-reporting appraisals are thus politically risky because appraisal group members can dismiss leading officials. If they are seen to have violated the principle that the Party manages cadres, there exists a real possibility of legislatures coming into conflict with governments and sometimes with the Party. Furthermore, the supervisory subjects differ: self-reporting appraisals generally involve people's congress standing committee members (20–25 persons for a legislature in Tianjin), while ordinary deputies (250–350 persons) participate in deputies' appraisals. Standing committee members are vulnerable to psychological pressure arising from political risk in the case of self-reporting appraisals, especially when they decide to severely punish leading officials.

Finally, the achievements of deputies' appraisals are more visible to both the Party and the public. When the Nankai District People's Congress in Tianjin, for example, conducted a deputies' appraisal for six months in 2000, 280 out of 326 deputies (85.6 percent) participated in a variety of activities, including inspections, meeting with residents, and listening to their opinions. The deputies also made 530 suggestions regarding the problems of three government bureaus and the district people's court. Although these suggestions might have seemed trivial, they were significant in improving the daily lives of the residents. The public and the Party were satisfied with the appraisals, and the legislature took pride in displaying its achievements and authority.[10] But in the case of self-reporting appraisals, the achievements of the legislature are

[9] Cai Dingjian and Wang Chenguang (eds.), *Renmin daibiao dahui ershinian fazhan yu gaige* (*Twenty-Years' Development and Reform of People's Congresses*) (Beijing: Zhongguo jiancha chubanshe, 2001), p. 281.
[10] Su Jingyu and Huang Yumin, "Yici xinde changshi: Nankaiqu zhifa pingyi dahui ceji" (A first new attempt: Sidelights on the appraisal meeting of law enforcement in Nankai District), *Tianjin renda gongzuo* (*The Works of Tianjin People's Congresses*), No. 12 (December 2000), pp. 8, 17.

difficult to publicize unless they openly dismiss leading officials, which rarely occurs due to the aforementioned political risks.

People's congresses created the responsibility system in the late 1980s, and it was gradually disseminated nationwide during the Second Five-Year Plan (1991–95) of Proliferating Legal Knowledge. Under this system, all bureaus (sections and sometimes personnel) of governments, courts, and procuracies are responsible for enforcing laws that are closely related to their missions. They must also establish mechanisms, such as examination, assessment, punishment, and rewards, to help the system work. In the processes of dispersal, legislatures pressure governments to implement the system and to address problems by listening to reports and making inspections.[11] However, as the system has taken hold, legislative supervision has become less important because legislatures are not the major implementing agencies of this system. This role belongs to the governments, courts, and procuracies.[12]

To sum up, the new forms of supervisory measures have uneven supervisory effects and political risk. Among the supervisory measures examined above, self-reporting appraisals are the most effective, and deputies' appraisals, examinations, and the responsibility system come next in a descending order of effectiveness. And the effectiveness of a measure is proportionally correlated with its political risk: the stronger the supervisory effect, the higher the political risk. In this respect, we can estimate the strengths and effectiveness of legislative supervision of governments according to the situation in which a measure is adopted.

UNEVEN ACCOMPLISHMENT OF LEGISLATIVE
SUPERVISION IN TIANJIN

As of 2001, Tianjin was composed of eighteen county-level governments, fifteen districts, and three counties.[13] As Table 7.1 shows, there is a large

---

[11] Quanguorenda, *The Supervisory System and Works of State Power Organs*, pp. 206–12.

[12] Quanguorenda changweihui bangongting yanjiushi (ed.), *Difang renda jiandu gongzuo tansuo (An Exploration for the Supervisory Works of Local People's Congresses)* (Beijing: Zhongguo minzhu fazhi chubanshe, 1997), pp. 279–86.

[13] On Tianjin, see Jane Duckett, *The Entrepreneurial State in China: Real Estate and Commerce Department in Reform Era Tianjin* (London: Routledge, 1998); Brian Hook (ed.), *Beijing and Tianjin: Toward a Millennial Megalopolis* (Hong Kong: Oxford University Press, 1998); Hans Hendrischke, "Tianjin – Quiet achiever?" in Hans Hendrischke and Feng Chongyi (eds.), *The Political Economy of China's*

gap in the level of economic development between districts and counties: in 2000, the value of GDP divided by the registered population of the richest area, Xiqing District (18,149 yuan), was ten times larger than that of the poorest one, Nankai District (1,810 yuan). On the other hand, both the Tianjin Municipal People's Congress and lower-level legislatures have been less active than local legislatures located in other provinces in terms of lawmaking productivity and strength of legislative supervision, as detailed later.

Table 7.1 indicates the disparity between people's congresses in terms of legislative supervision over governments in Tianjin, judging from the adoption of new supervisory measures. First, the entire legislatures in Tianjin adopted both the examination of law enforcement and the responsibility system of department law enforcement. However, only ten out of eighteen people's congresses (55.5 percent) employed self-reporting appraisals, and thirteen (72 percent) used deputies' appraisals. Considering five of the ten people's congresses that adopted self-reporting appraisals did so recently (Tanggu in 1998, Hebei and Baodi in 1999, Hexi and Dagang in 2000), only five legislatures have used them for an extended period of time.

The adoption of examination and a responsibility system by all legislatures in Tianjin was made possible because of the legal guarantee of the NPC and political encouragement of the municipal Party and legislature. After local legislatures in some regions pioneered examinations in the early 1980s, the NPC first implemented them in 1987 and emphasized their importance throughout the 1990s. Subsequently, in 1993 the NPC enacted a regulation for examinations, which gave them the same legal authority as other laws.[14] This legal guarantee from the NPC paved the way for the national diffusion of examinations since the people's congresses in all regions, including legislatures in Tianjin, could adopt them without political repercussions. The development of responsibility systems took a similar path. In 1995, the Tianjin Municipal People's Congress adopted a responsibility system and the Party in Tianjin

---

Provinces: Comparative and Competitive Advantage (London: Routledge, 1999), pp. 183–206; Peter T. Y. Cheung, "Guangzhou and Tianjin: The struggle for development in two Chinese cities," in Jae Ho Chung (ed.), *Cities in China: Recipes for Economic Development in the Reform Era* (London: Routledge, 1998), pp. 18–52.

[14] "Quanguorenda changweihui guanyu jiaqiang dui falü shishi qingkuang jiancha jiandude ruogan guiding" (Several regulations on strengthening the examination of law enforcement) (1993), *Renda gongzuo tongxun*, No. 13 (July 1994), pp. 5–6.

TABLE 7.1. Legislative supervision over governments in Tianjin in 2000

Districts/Counties	Self-Reporting Appraisal	Deputies' Appraisal	Examination of Law Enforcement	Responsibility System of Law Enforcement	GDP Divided by the Registered Population (Standing)[a]
1 Heping			✓	✓	4,957 (yuan) (12)
2 Hedong	✓	✓	✓	✓	2,361 (17)
3 Hexi	✓	✓	✓	✓	2,569 (16)
4 Nankai	✓	✓	✓	✓	1,810 (18)
5 Hebei	✓	✓	✓	✓	2,620 (15)
6 Hongqiao		✓	✓	✓	2,751 (14)
7 Tanggu	✓	✓	✓	✓	4,290 (13)
8 Hangu	✓	✓	✓	✓	6,541 (10)
9 Dagang	✓	✓	✓	✓	7,015 (9)
10 Dongli		✓	✓	✓	15,380 (3)
11 Xiqing			✓	✓	18,149 (1)
12 Beichen			✓	✓	16,535 (2)
13 Jinnan	✓	✓	✓	✓	11,777 (5)
14 Jinghai		✓	✓	✓	10,466 (7)
15 Wuqing			✓	✓	8,117 (8)
16 Ninghe			✓	✓	11,362 (6)
17 Baodi	✓	✓	✓	✓	12,460 (4)
18 Ji	✓	✓	✓	✓	6,426 (11)
Total	10 (55.5%)	13 (72%)	18 (100%)	18 (100%)	
Correlation Analysis[b]		-.521			

Notes:

[a] Statistics for 1998. The value of GDP Divided by the Registered Population (*huji renkou*) is not identical to per capita GDP (GDP divided by the average yearly population) in size. Because we can't find exact statistics for per capita GDP of each district (county), I have no choice but to use this alternative in order to roughly indicate the level of economic development. Therefore, the value might not accurately reflect the level of economic development of each region.

[b] For the correlation analysis between the level of economic development and the strength of legislative supervision, each legislature is given one of three values according to the adoption of self-reporting and deputies' appraisals: when a people's congress adopts both of them, it is 2; when it adopts either of them, it is 1; when it adopts neither of them, it is 0. And I analyze the correlation between the value and GDP divided by the registered population.

Sources: Tianjinshi tongjiju (ed.), *Tianjin tongji nianjian 1999* (*Tianjin Statistical Yearbook*) (*Beijing: Zhongguo tongji chubanshe, 1999*), pp. 393–421; "Jinian difang renda changweihui sheli ershinian zhuanlan" (Special Columns Commemorating the 20th Anniversary of Local People's Congress Standing Committees), *Tianjin renda gongzuo* (The Works of People's Congresses in Tianjin), Nos. 1–12 (January–December 2000), and Nos. 1–3 (January–March 2001); Bianweihui (ed.), *Zhongguo tupian: Jinian Tianjinshi difang renda changweihui chengli ershinian zhuankan* (China in Pictures: Special Issue Commemorating the 20th Anniversary of Local People's Congress Standing Committees in Tianjin) (Beijing: Zhongguo tupianshe, 2000); Interviews with staff of the Standing Committee of Tianjin Municipal People's Congress, May 2001 in Tianjin.

supported it, keeping with the Party center's policy of governance according to law.[15]

The Tianjin legislature's earlier adoption of deputies' appraisals influenced the lower-level legislatures to employ them more easily. When the Tianjin Higher People's Court became worried about problems in the judicial system, particularly with incorrect judgments, delayed trials, and corruption in the lower-level courts, it asked the municipal legislature to introduce deputies' appraisal to correct these problems. After studying the experience of Shaanxi Province and receiving a formal request from the NPC's Special Committee on Interior and Judicial Affairs (*neisiwei*) in 1990, the legislature decided to appraise the judicial operations of the Tianjin Intermediate People's Court in 1991.[16]

Moreover, the Party in Tianjin appears to have encouraged people's congresses to use deputies' appraisals to improve the state of law enforcement in this area. At a legislative work conference (*renda gongzuo huiyi*) in 1994, the municipal Party committee announced a policy for the people's congresses in the Tianjin area to "regard law supervision as the focal point of supervision work," and to promote "work supervision by use of law supervision."[17] The statement revealed the Party's desire for the legislatures to conduct greater "legal" supervision of governments. In an attempt to actualize this policy, the local legislatures strived to hear governments' reports on law enforcement regularly and to conduct examinations of law enforcement more effectively. At the same time, they explored appraisals of law enforcement (*zhifa pingyi*), which combined deputies' appraisals and examination of law enforcement, and concentrated on the supervision of law enforcement agencies, including courts, procuracies, and judicial and public security organs of governments.

Self-reporting appraisals, on the other hand, have not been as attractive to local legislatures in Tianjin. The main reason is that as of 2002,

[15] Quanguorenda, *An Exploration for the Supervisory Works of People's Congresses*, pp. 279–86.

[16] Quanguorenda neiwu sifa weiyuanhui sifashi (ed.), *Shehuizhuyi minzhu fazhi jianshede youyi tansuo (A Beneficial Exploration of Socialist Democratic and Legal System Construction)* (Beijing: Zhongguo minzhu fazhi chubanshe, 1993), pp. 162–69.

[17] Tianjinshi difangzhi bianxiu weiyuanhui (ed.), *Tianjin tongzhi: zhengquan zhi renmin daibiao dahui juan (Overall Annals of Tianjin: Regime Annals People's Congress Volume)* (Tianjin: Tianjin shehui kexueyuan chubanshe, 1997), pp. 482–83.

the municipal legislature itself has not employed them. For the past two decades, in fact, only two out of thirty-one provincial-level people's congresses did not adopt them: Tianjin and Tibet. Even the Beijing Municipal People's Congress has employed them since 1999, and it appraised a deputy-mayor in June 2001.[18] The leaders of the Tianjin legislature maintain that self-reporting appraisals lack concrete legal provisions and therefore can easily clash with the principles of the Party's management of cadres.[19] Likewise, the municipal Party committee also seems to take a negative position toward self-reporting appraisals.

In general, provincial Party committees' support has played a decisive role in the legislatures' adoption of self-reporting appraisal. For example, 91 percent of people's congresses in Zhejiang Province adopted self-reporting appraisal in 1994 with strong support from the provincial Party committee. Furthermore, some legislatures in this province have been able to exercise their personnel power decisively by dismissing leading officials who were deemed to have performed poorly. In 1994, the Pan'an and Tiantai County People's Congresses dismissed directors of the Grain and Tourism Bureaus.[20] People's congresses in Shaanxi Province did the same: in 1995, more than 95 percent of legislatures used self-reporting appraisal with the strong support of the provincial Party committee.[21] But the Party in Tianjin has paid more attention to law supervision and did not emphasize personnel supervision like self-reporting appraisal as other provinces did.

These conditions make it difficult for legislatures in Tianjin to adopt self-reporting appraisal. Therefore, at least for legislatures in Tianjin, conducting self-reporting appraisals proves that they have strong "supervision consciousness" and "capabilities." The Dongli District People's Congress, for example, conducted self-reporting appraisals in the mid-1990s, but stopped using them soon after due to a lack of support from the municipal legislature and the Party.[22] For this reason, the People's

[18] "Beijingshi renda changweihui shouci dui fushizhang jinxing pingyi" (Beijing Standing Committee of People's Congress evaluated one vice-mayor for the first time)," *Zhongguo renda xinwen*, 23 June 2001, <http://zgrdxw.peopledaily.com.cn/gb/paper7/9/class00070004/hwz145263.htm>.
[19] Interview with legislative leaders and senior staff: Tianjin, April 2001.
[20] Quanguorenda, *The Supervisory System and Works of State Power Organs*, pp. 223–38.
[21] Quanguorenda, *An Exploration for the Supervisory Works of People's Congresses*, pp. 235–41.
[22] Interview with legislative leaders and senior staff: Tianjin, May 2001.

Congress of Heping District has been waiting a long time for a more opportune time to conduct the appraisals.[23]

Except for the adoption of new supervisory measures, other differences exist between legislatures in the Tianjin area with regard to daily supervision of governments. But objective and apparent criteria to measure them are not currently available. The differences are in a sense muted because the people's congresses in Tianjin are less confrontational. Since the Party in Tianjin likely wishes to hold on to its power over personnel matters and wants its legislatures to avoid public exercise of personnel authority, the legislatures would not openly wield their authority. Instead, legislatures prefer to make suggestions about the operations of governments and to resolve problems by government themselves.[24] For this reason, Tianjin does not offer the dramatic scenes found in other provinces, where legislatures have openly exercised power by means of, for example, dismissing senior officials.

Generally speaking, local legislatures in Tianjin that have conducted both forms of appraisals, such as Nankai, Hexi, and Hangu District People's Congresses, are said to be the most effective in supervising governments. Legislatures that have never adopted them, like the Xiqing and Beichen District People's Congresses, are considered to be the least effective.[25] This is an expected result, since appraisals, especially self-reporting appraisals, are among the most effective supervisory measures, as explained above. For instance, the Nankai District People's Congress has been supervising the district government more effectively since the early 1990s. In 1993, it was the first legislature in Tianjin to adopt self-reporting appraisals, and it required the district Party committee to change the director of a government bureau based on the results. In 1998, the legislature formulated a regulation that all leading officials should be appraised at least once during their five-year terms of office. And it strengthened self-reporting appraisals by introducing democratic assessments (*minzhu ceping*) in 1999, in which appraisal members put appraisals to a vote. Nankai has also conducted

[23] Feng Wuming, "Kaituo chuangxin tuidong renda gongzuo quanmian shang shuiping" (Bringing forth new ideas in a pioneering spirit, and promoting the works of people's congress to higher level), *Tianjin renda gongzuo*, No. 1 (January 2000), p. 19.
[24] Interview with legislative leaders and senior staff: Tianjin, August 2000, and March and May 2001.
[25] Interview with legislative leaders and senior staff: Tianjin, May 2001.

deputies' appraisals since 1992 and has become a role model in the Tianjin area.[26]

The people's congresses of Xiqing and Beichen Districts, however, the richest areas in Tianjin (see Table 7.1), have supervised governments ineffectively by not using these forms of appraisals. Xiqing and Beichen appear to attach great importance to cooperation with governments with an eye toward developing the regional economy. Overseeing governments by use of appraisals, in their view, is considered not to be closely related with economic development and to harm otherwise harmonious legislative-executive relations.[27] Instead, they faithfully repeat the municipal Party committee's line of considering law supervision a major oversight measure and promoting work supervision through law supervision. In fact, they only carry out examinations and review government reports on law enforcement.[28]

There are also differences among the legislatures in the Tianjin area with regard to the execution of supervision on specific areas. For example, the Dagang and Hangu District People's Congresses, which are located on the coast of the Bohai Sea, are pacesetters of law enforcement examinations in relation to environmental protection. They reportedly conducted rather thorough examinations to determine whether district governments have properly implemented environmental protection laws in the 1990s, and they have also been able to make governments reduce pollution in their respective districts.[29] As for the responsibility system of department law enforcement, the Hebei District People's Congress pioneered it in 1992, three years before the municipal legislature decided to implement it throughout Tianjin in 1995. Hebei District's experience

---

[26] Interview with legislative leaders and senior staff: Tianjin, August 2000 and March 2001; Kang Ziming (ed.), *Nankai renda ershinian 1979–99* (*Twenty Years of Nankai People's Congress, 1979–99*) (Tianjin, 1999), pp. 29–30, 592–600.

[27] Interview with legislative leaders and senior staff: Tianjin, May 2001.

[28] Chen Hong'en, "Yifa lüxing zhiquan chongfen fahui renda changweihui zuoyong" (Implementing authority in accordance with laws, fully giving the rein to the people's congress standing committee's function), in Bianweihui (ed.), *Zhongguo tupian: Jinian Tianjinshi difang renda changweihui chengli ershi zhounian zhuankan* (*China in Pictures: Special Issue on Commemorating the 20th Anniversary of People's Congress Standing Committees in Tianjin*) (Beijing: Zhongguo tupianshe, 2000), p. 31.

[29] Interview with legislative leaders and senior staff: Tianjin, May 2001; Liu Shujie and Yang Weili, "Jiada lidu zengqiang shixiao tuidong zhifa jiandu jiancha gongzuo shang shuiping" (Promoting the work of examination to higher level by adding power and strengthening effect), *Tianjin renda gongzuo*, No. 5 (May 2000), pp. 23–24; Meng Dehui, "Renzhen xingshi zhiquan tuidong jingji fazhan" (Seriously exercising power, promoting economic development), in Bianweihui, *China in Pictures*, pp. 24–25.

had become the basis on which other people's congresses in Tianjin conducted the system.[30]

FACTORS BEHIND UNEVEN LEGISLATIVE ROLE
FULFILLMENT

According to Table 7.1, the level of economic development is negatively
correlated with legislative supervision over governments. The correlation
value is −.521, which implies that higher economic development of a district (county) results in less effective legislative supervision of government, and vice versa. This is similar to the findings of Lawrence, Oi, and
Rozelle on the relationship between the dissemination of democratic villagers' committee elections and economic development. Lawrence argues
that village democracy may flourish in economically less developed areas,
and Oi and Rozelle conclude that as villagers' income increases and villages become linked to the rest of the economy, villagers' participation
in contested elections decreases.[31]

Meanwhile, the political leadership in a region is a vital factor in
bringing about the differences of legislative supervision over governments. People involved in legislatures in the Tianjin area regard the leadership of both legislatures and the Party at the same level as the most
important factor in determining whether the legislatures can conduct
effective supervision of governments. The legislative leaders, especially
the chairperson of a people's congress, should have "strong supervision consciousness" and "resolution to cope with problems" in order
for the legislature to adopt new effective supervisory measures.[32] When
a people's congress adopts a new supervisory measure, it is the legislative leaders who decide first whether the legislature will use it on the
basis of considering their own situation and other regions' experiences.
Next, they submit an implementation plan to the Party committee at the
same level for approval and support, and report to the provincial-level
people's congress for record (*beian*). Thus, without this initiative from
legislative leaders, the legislatures cannot employ new effective supervisory measures.

---

[30] Interview with legislative leaders and senior staff: Tianjin, May 2001; Tianjinshi,
Overall Annals of Tianjin, p. 488.
[31] Lawrence, "Village representative assemblies," p. 67; Oi, "Economic development,
stability," pp. 125–44; Oi and Rozelle, "Elections and power," pp. 513–39.
[32] Interview with legislative leaders and senior staff: Tianjin, August 2000 and March
2001.

Strong consciousness and resolve on the part of legislative leaders is one thing; approval and support from Party leaders at the same level is another. In a sense, the latter is more critical than the former, as legislatures cannot adopt new supervisory measures without the prior approval of Party leaders and cannot implement the measures effectively without the Party's support. In fact, when legislatures introduced appraisals, Party leaders participated to make the government accept legislative supervision. When the Hexi District People's Congress conducted its first deputies' appraisal in 1992, the Party secretary attended the mobilization meeting for the appraisal and stated publicly that the Party had given prior approval to the appraisal and strongly supported it. The secretary also requested that other state organs "closely cooperate with it [the people's congress] to accomplish its intended aims."[33] Other legislatures had similar experiences. When the Tanggu District People's Congress attempted to appraise senior government officials in 1998, Party leaders acted as members of an ad hoc appraisal group in order to lend the Party's authority to the legislature.[34]

For this reason, the most active legislatures are generally those that get the strongest support from Party committees. A case in point is the Nankai District People's Congress, which is considered to have one of the best records in Tianjin for supervising governments. It takes pride in having the Party's full support of its activities. For instance, the district Party committee convened work conferences on legislature twice to display its support for the congress in 1994 and 1999, while the municipal and most other same-level Party committees hosted the conference only once in 1994.[35] Also, the Hangu District People's Congress, which is one of the strongest legislatures in Tianjin in terms of supervision over governments, wields considerable authority over leading officials through self-reporting appraisals, because the district Party committee decided to record appraisal results on personnel files (*dang'an*). Since the results on files stay with officials for the rest of their lives and affect

[33] Zhao Mengchen (ed.), *Hexi renda ershinian* (*Twenty Years of Hexi People's Congress*) (Tianjin, 2000), pp. 584–87.

[34] Wang Kelin (ed.), *Tanggu renda ershinian huimou 1980–2000* (*Reflections on 20 Years of Tanggu People's Congress, 1980–2000*) (Tianjin, 2000), pp. 123–24.

[35] Zhonggong Nankaiqu weiyuanhui, "Guanyu guanche yifa zhiguo jiben fanglüe jin yibu fahui renda zuoyongde yijian" (Opinions on implementing the fundamental plan of government according to law and further giving the rein to the people's congress's functions), *Tianjin renda gongzuo*, No. 1 (January 2000). pp. 22–23.

their future careers, the appraisals matter significantly for cadres.[36] The Party in Tanggu District took an even more positive measure to strengthen the power of the people's congress: it decided to combine legislative appraisal of senior officials with the Party's year-end cadre assessment in 1998.[37]

Institutional constraints and the actual power relations among the Party, governments, and legislatures make the political leadership of both the Party and legislatures the most critical factor in faithfully accomplishing legislative supervision over government. Chinese legislatures suffer from severe institutional constraints and disadvantageous political conditions. First, local legislatures lacked secure legal protection when they employed new supervisory measures, and their supervision through these measures could entail political risks. In addition, legislatures had a less powerful position than governments in the political system. For example, as of 2000 in Tianjin, only two out of eighteen chairpersons of legislatures concurrently served as (vice-)secretary of Party committees.[38] Even on the critical issue of deciding whether the Party approves a legislature's request to employ new supervisory measures, most legislative leaders can only express their opinions instead of casting a vote. In contrast, government heads, such as vice-secretary and the second-in-commands in the Party hierarchy, directly influence the Party's decisions. Thus, without the support of Party leaders, legislatures cannot adopt new supervisory measures that governments object to, and cannot faithfully fulfill their duty.[39]

Meanwhile, China's pursuit of rapid economic growth has brought about changes in the incentives of political leaders with regard to political reforms. Economic growth has been regarded as the supreme political goal of China in the reform era, and all state organs, including legislatures, are required to strive to accomplish this goal. Whether or not the

---

[36] Liu Hanrui, "Guanche 'sange daibiao' sixiang jiaqiang renda gongzuo lingdao" (Strengthening the leadership of people's congress works through implementing 'Three Representatives' thought), *Tianjin renda gongzuo*, No. 8 (August 2000), pp. 22–23.

[37] Wang, *Reflections on 20 Years of Tanggu People's Congress*, p. 124.

[38] With the start of the 10th NPC in March 2003, about 74.1 percent of (deputy-) secretaries of provincial-level Party committees concurrently serve as chairpersons of provincial-level people's congresses, compared to 32.2 percent during the 9th NPC (1998–2002). This aims at raising the political status of legislatures in the Party hierarchy. Lian Yuming (ed.), *Zhongguo guoqing baogao 2003 (A Report of China's National Conditions 2003 Year)* (Beijing: Zhongguo shidai jingji chubanshe, 2003), pp. 15–16.

[39] Interview with legislative leaders and senior staff: Tianjin, August 2000 and March 2001.

economic wealth of a region increases has been a critical factor affecting the career prospects of local political leaders. Under these circumstances, if a government delivers economic development and performs well, Party leaders in the region are likely to pay less attention to the legislative supervision of government. That is because the pursuit of rapid economic growth for local political elites located in an economically developed region is a more legitimate and powerful path to promotions than any others, such as conducting radical political reforms. The Party leaders may even hinder the faithful execution of legislative supervision over governments, since it can be an obstacle to governments' efficient implementation of regional economic policies.

The negative attitude of Party leaders toward legislative supervision over governments tends to discourage legislative leaders from conducting effective supervision of governments. Furthermore, legislative leaders themselves may actually be satisfied with their status if governments help legislative work with ample budgets and acknowledge legislative authority through timely reporting of important work and faithful implementation of deputies' suggestions. Political leaders of the Party and legislatures located in the wealthiest districts in Tianjin seem to behave precisely in this manner.

Party leaders located in an economically less developed region, such as Nankai, Hedong, Hexi, Hebei, and Tanggu Districts in Tianjin, may pay more attention to legislative development. Taking the initiative in strengthening legislative functions and as a result becoming a role model in political reform can be an attractive and rational path to career promotions for local political elites, who cannot accomplish the Party's goal of rapid economic growth due to scarce material resources and poor infrastructure. The strong political support of Party leaders may encourage legislative leaders in the region to assume more risk-taking attitudes in adopting new effective oversight measures. In this fashion, the concerted efforts of the political leadership from both the Party and legislature in economically less developed locales can induce legislative development.

In this regard, the experimentations of direct election reform at township level in some regions are very suggestive. According to studies on the experimentations in Dapeng Town of Shenzhen Municipality and Buyun Township of Suining City in Sichuan Province from 1998 to 2002, political leadership like the Party secretaries was a vital factor in executing radical electoral reforms in these regions. Local political elites in Buyun, the studies argue, initiated audacious political reform for various reasons: a sense of political responsibility, pressure from the outside, and personal political entrepreneurship. Of those factors, local governments' competition to become a forerunner of "institutional innovation" and individual political leaders' pursuit of "achievements in their official career" (*zhengji*) were the most important in enabling the regions to implement radical political reform. In particular, the political leaders of economically less developed regions, who had little chance to promote themselves through economic success, pursued political reform more enthusiastically for their future careers.[40] This is one of the most important reasons Buyun, which is located in an economically less developed region, continued to experiment with the direct election of town chief in 2002 – notwithstanding the discouragement from the center – while the economically affluent Dapeng gave up the experimentation altogether.

POLITICAL IMPLICATIONS OF FINDINGS

Local people's congresses in the Tianjin area differ in their role fulfillment in terms of performing legislative supervision over government. Some legislatures conduct oversight more effectively through stronger supervisory measures, while others do not. Two factors seem to be correlated with these differences. One is the political leadership of both legislatures and the Party at the same level, and it is very important in encouraging legislatures to supervise governments more effectively. If legislative leaders are willing to take political risks and Party leaders support them, the legislatures can employ effective measures for supervision. The other is economic development, but it is negatively correlated with supervision. Legislatures located in more economically affluent areas tend to supervise governments less effectively.

---

[40] Huang Weiping and Wang Yongcheng (eds.), *Dangdai zhongguo zhengzhi yanjiu baogao II* (*A Research Report on the Contemporary Chinese Politics II*) (Beijing: Shehui kexue wenxian chubanshe, 2003), pp. 298–315; Huang Weiping and Zou Shubin (eds.), *Xiangzhenzhang xuanju fangshi gaige: Anli yanjiu* (*Case Studies on the Election Reforms of Township-Level Government Chiefs*) (Beijing: Shehui kexue wenxian chubanshe, 2003), pp. 213–36; Lianjiang Li, "The politics of introducing direct township elections in China," *China Quarterly*, No.171 (September 2002), pp. 704–23. On the various experimentations of direct election reforms, see Huang Weiping (ed.), *Zhongguo jiceng minzhu fazhande zuixin tupo* (*The Recent Breakthrough of China's Grassroots Democratic Development*) (Beijing: Shehui kexue wenxuan chubanshe, 2000); Shi Weimin, *Gongxuan yu Zhixuan* (*Open Elections and Direct Elections*) (Beijing: Zhongguo shehui kexue chubanshe, 2000).

The extant institutional constraints and the power relations between major forces make political leadership the most important factor in legislative development. Because current Chinese laws and institutions do not provide legislatures with adequate legal protection, they should thus depend upon the resolution of legislative leaders as well as the Party's support for their courageous pioneering in supervision. In addition, as legislatures have a lower political status than governments in the Chinese political system, they need the support of Party leaders to overcome the resistance of governments during supervision. The pursuit of rapid economic growth in an economically developed region, however, has discouraged Party leaders from supporting legislatures' effective supervision of governments. In other words, the execution of a more radical political reform is not an attractive path of career promotion for the political elites located in wealthier regions.

This chapter suggests an implication for China's political reform prospects. It confirms the fact that without the formation of a strong reformist political leadership, China will not carry out relatively radical political reforms, such as the overall implementation of direct elections for basic-level government heads and the independence of the judicial branch from the influence of the Party and governments. These reforms are not directly correlated with rapid economic growth. In addition, they will bring about the restructuring of major political forces' power relationships as well as stimulating ordinary people's political participation. Thus, as is true in the case of the strengthening of legislative supervision, strong reformist political leadership is necessary for the execution of these political reforms. However, against the conventional wisdom of the modernization thesis, the enormous economic development that China has achieved and is expected to achieve cannot play an important role in this regard. On the contrary, further fast economic growth, as Przeworski and Limongi point out, may delay the implementation of radical political reforms by consolidating the power base of the present Chinese authoritarian regime.[41]

On the other hand, administrative reforms, such as the restructuring of government organizations and personnel, and governance according to law, will continue to be the pacesetter of China's political reforms in the near future. These reforms are closely associated with the advancement of administrative efficiency and governments' pursuit of rapid economic growth. Furthermore, they do not need the restructuring of

---

[41] Przevorski and Limongi, "Modernization," pp. 159–60.

major political actors' power relationships and will not seriously infringe the Party's monopoly of political authority. Therefore, so long as China pursues rapid economic growth as its paramount goal and a strong reformist political leadership is not present, administrative reforms will continue to be emphasized as a key political reform.

8

Conclusion: The Development of Local Legislatures and Political Development in China

Since the 1990s, Chinese local people's congresses have emerged as a strong political force in local politics, along with the CCP and governments. Reform and opening-up policies have been the main movers behind the enhanced status and intensified roles of Chinese legislatures. The introduction of a market economy and the implementation of legalization policy (i.e., governance according to law) are especially important in determining which roles of Chinese legislatures have been strengthened. In short, the execution of both marketization and legalization policies fostered the establishment of state lawmaking and supervisory systems, and this resulted in the strengthening of Chinese legislatures' lawmaking and supervisory roles.

The implementation of marketization and legalization policies, however, has created a unique phenomenon by which the roles of Chinese people's congresses have been strengthened in a selective manner. The lawmaking power of Chinese legislatures at both central and local levels has already been recognized as the proper authority of legislatures, and their lawmaking autonomy from the Party and governments and actual lawmaking productivity have increased significantly since the 1990s. Meanwhile, Chinese local legislatures have begun to exert substantial influence in the supervision of governments and courts since the 1990s, while the NPC has not yet exercised such supervisory power. In contrast, Chinese legislatures exert only limited influence in the representation role, although the changing role fulfillment of deputies has shown the potential for Chinese legislatures to wield power in this arena. Until now, the CCP, as the sole ruling party, can claim to represent the interests of all Chinese people.

Given the peculiarity of the Chinese political system (i.e., a party-state) and the conflict between legal relations and actual power relations among the Party, legislatures, and governments, local legislatures have been forced to employ delicate development strategies. Although the Constitution states that Chinese legislatures are "state power organs" rather than just lawmaking bodies, their political status in the political system is lower than that of governments and of course the Party. In addition, they have faced disadvantageous conditions in the developmental process, such as a lack of experience and poor legal and institutional support for major legislative activities.

With a view to securing their survival and development, local legislative leaders have proven to be surprisingly adept in choosing strategies tailored to their political goals. Local legislatures have striven to get the support of, rather than to pursue autonomy from, the CCP. Meanwhile, they have tried to cooperate with governments instead of confronting them, and have employed a relatively aggressive engagement strategy regarding courts. Local legislatures have also used the strategy of public mobilization to make up for their poor organizational and personnel capabilities relative to governments, by for instance encouraging social organizations and even ordinary citizens to participate in lawmaking and supervisory activities. In the process, relations between local legislatures and social organizations have developed as a form of state-society relations that differs from those of the Party/government and social organizations.

Finally, as path dependence theory predicts, local legislatures have been strongly influenced by their earlier legislative institutions and experiences. When they began to function again around 1979, they could not escape the constraints of the past experiences and institutions, because those were their own trustworthy foundations which Chinese legislatures could consult and whose example they could follow. Accordingly, democratic centralism and legislative-executive integration were re-introduced as the organizational and operational principles of the Chinese legislative system, and Western-style legislative systems were rejected from the start except for applying lawmaking techniques chiefly concerning economic laws. In a word, local legislatures in various regions, in many cases without direction from higher-level legislatures and the NPC, have separately had to explore their own developmental path and to build their individual legislative models under the strong influence of the legacy and the constraints of the Chinese political system.

As a consequence, the development of local people's congresses has occurred in varying ways from region to region, even among legislatures in the same province. Some people's congresses in a region started to experiment with new measures of lawmaking and supervision of their own volition. Once these measures proved to be very effective and politically risk-free, other legislatures gradually followed in the wake of pioneering legislatures. Sometimes, local legislatures dispatched delegations to the pioneering legislatures in order to learn "advanced experiences" when enacting new local laws and supervising state organs in their regions. Also, provincial people's congresses, mostly with the prior approval and support of a territorial Party committee at the same level, convened experience-exchange seminars or training classes for lower-level legislatures in their jurisdiction in an attempt to proliferate new institutions. As a result, uneven development of activities of local legislatures ensued. And in the developmental process, the political leadership of both the Party and legislatures, not the level of economic development, has been the biggest contributing factor causing variation.

This fashion of legislative development in China will continue in the foreseeable future unless a radical political reform takes place. That is, under the strong restrictions of the Chinese party-state and the continued rejection of Western-style legislative systems, past legislative institutions and experiences will have an enormous influence on local legislatures, and at the same time, the political leadership will remain the most vital factor promoting legislative development to a higher level. Maybe this can be applicable to the developmental path of the whole political system in China.

LEGISLATIVE DEVELOPMENT AND POLITICAL DEVELOPMENT IN CHINA

A democratically elected and operated legislature is crucial to a modern democratic political system, and China is no exception. That is, democratization in China requires further legislative development.[1]

---

[1] On the political reforms and democratic prospects in China, see Suisheng Zhao (ed.), *China and Democracy: Reconsidering the Prospects for a Democratic China* (New York and London: Routledge, 2000); Suzanne Ogden, *Inklings of Democracy in China* (Cambridge, MA: Harvard University Asia Center, 2002); Bruce Gilley, *China's Democratic Future; How It Will Happen and Where It Will Lead* (New York: Columbia

Three attributes of legislatures are critical for democracy. First of all, legislatures differ from governments and courts insofar as they are representative bodies composed of members elected by the people. The main principle of democracy (i.e., rule by the people) is thus embodied in legislatures.[2] In addition, the main functions of legislatures are indispensable in making a political system run in a democratic way. Democracy necessitates important policies be decided in accordance with popular will and civil rights be protected from the encroachment of state power. Legislatures help realize these goals through legislation, supervision, and representation.[3] Finally, legislatures are responsive to popular will not least because legislative members face regular elections. Moreover, legislatures enact laws and supervise governments openly except in a few instances, and ordinary people can witness these activities. In contrast, governments generally make decisions behind closed doors, and small groups of high-level officials and experts lead these processes.[4]

A caveat is in order here. Despite the importance of legislatures to democracy, in reality legislatures play a less significant role even in Western democracies. In short, governments or executive branches, rather than legislatures, dominate modern administrative states. For instance, with the exception of the United States, governments ordinarily take the initiative in lawmaking by setting the policy agenda and drafting laws. So David Olson insists on a "90 percent rule": 90 percent of all drafted laws are submitted by cabinet, and 90 percent of submitted laws are passed in legislature.[5] Legislatures' supervision over governments and their participation in the decision-making process face similar problems.

University Press, 2004); Jae Ho Chung, (ed.), *Charting China's Future: Political, Social, and International Dimensions* (Lanham, MD: Rowman & Littlefield, 2006); Lowell Dittmer and Guoli Liu (eds.), *China's Deep Reform: Domestic Politics in Transition* (Lanham, MD: Rowman & Littlefield, 2006); Minxin Pei, *China's Trapped Transition: The Limits of Developmental Autocracy* (Cambridge, MA: Harvard University Press, 2006); Randall Peerenboom, *China Modernizes: Threat to the West or Model for the Rest?* (New York: Oxford University Press, 2007).

[2] David M. Olson, *Democratic Legislative Institutions: A Comparative View* (Armonk, NY: M.E. Sharpe, 1994), pp. 3–4; David Close, "Introduction: Consolidating democracy in Latin America: What role for legislatures?" in David Close (ed.), *Legislatives and the New Democracies in Latin America* (Boulder, CO: Lynne Rienner Publishers, 1995), p. 4.

[3] Jean Blondel, *Comparative Legislature* (Englewood Cliffs, NJ: Prentice Hall, 1973), p. 5.

[4] Olson, *Democratic Legislative Institutions*, p. 1.

[5] Ibid., p. 84.

For this reason, some scholars have put forward a "weak legislature" argument since the 1960s.[6]

The role of legislatures in the Third World is even more tightly circumscribed. For instance, South Korea and Taiwan are cases of successful democratic transition among developing countries. However, legislatures in both countries played only marginal roles prior to their transitions to democracy in the 1980s. It is noteworthy that both political leaders and the general populace in East Asian developmental states like South Korea and Taiwan placed higher priority on economic development than political democratization. And authoritarian political systems, geared to mobilizing the populace toward economic development, survived for more than three decades. Pilot agencies such as South Korea's Economic Planning Board had greater roles in politics than legislatures by, for instance, drafting and carrying out industrial policies.[7] It was generally after democratization that legislatures became important state organs in South Korea and Taiwan in which major state policies were decided and budgets were allocated through negotiations and compromises between legislative members, and state power was restricted by virtue of legislative oversight.

These limitations are of significance to China. Like Taiwan and South Korea before democratization, China's top priority for the past three decades has been rapid economic growth, together with the maintenance of the CCP's one-party rule, rather than political democratization. In addition, China has needed efficient bureaucratic agencies rather than representative bodies for implementing economic policies and managing social problems. In a sense, as the experience of the other East Asian states illustrates, legislatures are sometimes not suitable for swiftly implementing economic policies and effectively coping with social problems resulting from the rapid transition of social-economic structures. To reiterate, we should not overestimate the significance of legislatures in modern political systems, especially in the Third World.

Meanwhile, legislative development has different values in a country's political development depending largely on how we understand

---

[6] Blondel, *Comparative Legislature*, p. 3.

[7] Chalmers Johnson, *MITI and the Japanese Miracle: The Growth of Industrial Policy, 1925–1975* (Stanford: Stanford University Press, 1982), pp. 305, 311, 315–20; Chalmers Johnson, "The developmental state: Odyssey of a concept," in Meredith Woo-Cumings (ed.), *The Developmental State* (Ithaca, NY: Cornell University Press, 1999), pp. 32–60; Ming Xia, *The Dual Developmental State: Development Strategy and Institutional Arrangements for China's Transition* (Aldershot: Ashgate, 2000), pp. 27–30.

political development. Scholars define political development in different ways.[8] The two most common perspectives on political development are "democratization" and "institutionalization." Legislative development has limited significance if we interpret political development as democratization, but if we view political development as institutionalization, legislative development is much more important than the former understanding.

According to a minimalist or procedural definition, democracy refers to a political system where free and fair elections for major leadership positions are regularly implemented and where there are guarantees of universal political participation and citizens' political rights.[9] From a democratization perspective, the primary measure of political development is the existence of free and competitive elections. Thus, competitive elections indicate the degree to which a country is politically developed and whether the country is democratic or authoritarian. In contrast, the degree of legislative development is not a main criterion for judging a political system.

Viewed from this perspective, the introduction of competitive elections rather than legislative development is more important for China's democratization, and past legislative development has contributed to political development (i.e., democratization) to only a limited extent. China's democratization has been showcased by direct elections for government chiefs at the township level in some regions, in addition to villagers' committee elections throughout the country. These government chief elections need to be implemented in all parts of the country, and also at higher levels of government (like counties and provinces), and ultimately as high up as the presidency. Moreover, the one-party system must be replaced with a multiparty system, and political rights of all Chinese citizens must be guaranteed as a precondition for free competitive elections. Only under these conditions will Chinese legislatures function

---

[8] Samuel P. Huntington, "The goals of development," in Myron Weiner and Samuel P. Huntington (eds.), *Understanding Political Development* (Prospect Heights: Waveland Press, 1987), pp. 3–32; Samuel P. Huntington and Jorge I. Dominguez, "Political development," in Fred I. Greenstein and Nelson W. Polsby (eds.), *Handbook of Political Science: Macropolitical Theory*, Vol. 3 (Reading, MA: Addison-Wesley, 1975), pp. 1–11.

[9] Robert A. Dahl, *Polyarchy: Participation and Opposition* (New Haven, CT: Yale University Press, 1971), pp. 4–5, 7–8; Robert A. Dahl, *On Democracy* (New Haven, CT: Yale University Press, 1998), pp. 37–8, 85–6; Samuel P. Huntington, *The Third Wave: Democratization in the Late Twentieth Century* (Norman: University of Oklahoma Press, 1991), p. 7.

as true representative bodies, and only then will legislative development be significant for democratization in China.

It should be recalled, however, that China's leaders have envisioned legislative development as a means of introducing a proper legal system and precipitating the rationalization of governance, both of which are necessary to implement the Party's reform and opening-up policies. That is, the roles of Chinese legislatures have been strengthened to support the rule of the CCP by creating a division of labor between legislatures and governments, not as a measure to pursue democratization. Therefore, in this view, past legislative development is irrelevant to Chinese democracy.

In retrospect, the history of political democratization indicates that the roles legislatures perform in democratic transition are limited. Some scholars argue that legislative systems in Western countries have contributed to the development of liberal democracies by representing public opinion in policymaking and supervising executive power.[10] This is true, but only in a long-term view. Democratization in the Third World and former socialist countries since the 1970s illustrates that legislatures have played a limited role. In fact, previous studies on democratic transition have paid little attention to the role of legislatures. Most studies instead focus on the interactions between economic development and democratization, political pacts between ruling elites and opposition forces, and the development of civil society.[11]

Undeniably, democratization in the Third World and former socialist countries generally begins outside legislatures. That is, in many cases, democratic transition starts with the activated anti-government campaign of dissidents and frequent large-scale mass protests against authoritarian rule attended by students, workers, and the middle class, after a period of incubation during which various civil organizations take shape and sociopolitical problems (including abrupt economic recession and enormous unemployment, widespread political corruption, and relentless oppression of human rights) accumulate to an extent exceeding

---

[10] Close, "Introduction: Consolidating democracy in Latin America," p. 5.
[11] Seymour Martin Lipset, "Some social requisites of democracy: Economic development and political legitimacy," *American Political Science Review*, Vol. 53, No. 1 (March 1959), pp. 69–105; Doh Chull Shin, "On the third wave of democratization: A synthesis and evaluation of recent theory and research," *World Politics*, Vol. 47, No. 1 (October 1994), pp. 135–70; Adam Przeworski and Fernando, "Modernization: Theories and Facts," *World Politics*, Vol. 49, No. 2 (January 1997), pp. 155–83; Adam Przeworski, *Democracy and Market: Political and Economic Reforms in Eastern Europe and Latin America* (Cambridge: Cambridge University Press, 1991).

the limitation of popular endurance. In contrast, legislatures generally enter the scene in a later phase of democratic transition. As state organs enacting constitutions and basic rules for countries, they tend to emerge as political arenas after authoritarian systems collapse and nationwide debates about the establishment of new democratic political systems begin.[12] Legislatures can subsequently change the main battleground of political struggle from the streets to negotiating tables, allowing various political forces to offer opinions about possible new political systems.[13]

It is not yet clear whether Chinese legislatures can play even such a limited role in the democratic transition in China. The records of legislatures make for pessimistic reading. For example, neither the NPC nor local people's congresses played a meaningful role in democratic struggles such as the 1987 pro-democracy students' protests and the 1989 Tiananmen Incident. One member of the NPC Standing Committee, Hu Jiwei, attempted to convene an extraordinary meeting of the NPC Standing Committee with a view to discussing the legitimacy of the martial law announced by the State Council in the 1989 Tiananmen tragedy. However, he did this without the permission of the NPC Standing Committee, and his effort to question the martial law was in vain.

Meanwhile, legislative development has far greater implications for political development in China if political development is understood as institutionalization. For many Third World and former socialist countries, political development does not need to be limited to democratization in general and the introduction of Western-style liberal democracy in particular. Other sociopolitical objectives, such as state integration, the establishment of state authority and capacity, the guarantee of minimal civil and political rights, the maintenance of social order and law, and the equal distribution of socioeconomic values, may be more urgent than the introduction of liberal democracy.[14]

Political development, from an institutionalization perspective, refers to a political system's cultivation of capacities to execute the tasks assigned to it by society.[15] For example, Samuel Huntington defines

---

[12] Przeworski, *Democracy and Market*, pp. 51–99.
[13] David M. Olson and Philip Norton (eds.), *The New Parliaments of Central and Eastern Europe* (London: Frank Cass, 1996), pp. 241–42.
[14] Robert A. Packenham, "Legislature and political development," in Allan Kornberg and Lloy D. Musolf (eds.), *Legislatures in Developmental Perspective* (Durham, NC: Duke University Press, 1970), pp. 576–77.
[15] Kornberg and Musolf, "On legislature in developmental perspective," in Kornberg and Musolf, *Legislatures in Developmental Perspective*, p. 6.

political development as the institutionalization of political organizations and procedures. In this definition, institutions refer to stable, valuable, and repeated patterns of behavior, while institutionalization refers to the attainment of values and stability on the part of organizations and procedures.[16] In addition, this perspective put political stability above political democratization or the expansion of political participation. Modernization, according to this argument, inevitably delivers greater political participation. Disorder and instability will emerge in the absence of effective political institutions that can accommodate explosive political participation. Thus, political institutionalization should be accomplished ahead of political democratization in order to maintain political order and social stability.[17]

Legislative development, viewed from this perspective, is a necessary component of political development. Indeed, legislatures have significantly contributed to political development (i.e., institutionalization) in China in the past three decades. With the introduction of a market economy, China has quickly become a more diversified and complex society. This transformation has required the Chinese state to exercise authority in a more sophisticated and institutionalized way, and thus all state organs – including legislatures and courts as well as governments and military – have to become more specialized. Put differently, China faces a new political challenge insofar as it must shift from "bureaucratic rule" – wherein the CCP and governments dominate – to "real politics," whereby each state organ (including legislatures and courts), social organizations, and even ordinary people jointly take part in political processes in a way that contributes to the making of major state policies. Legislative development, which entails clarified jurisdiction, greatly increased organizational capacities, and the institutionalized activities of legislatures, addresses part of this new challenge. Thus, the history of legislative development over the past three decades provides evidence that China has made great progress in political development (i.e., institutionalization).

But, to reiterate, China needs more than legislative development to become a democracy. Chinese democratization calls for not only far strengthened legislatures but also free competitive elections, a multiparty system, and the guarantee of people's political rights. Only these

---

[16] Samuel P. Huntington, *Political Order in Changing Societies* (New Haven, CT: Yale University Press, 1968), pp. 12–24.
[17] Ibid., pp. 4–5; Huntington and Dominguez, "Political development," p. 14.

measures will allow Chinese legislatures to develop into truly democratic representative bodies that exercise full legislative authority, such as policymaking and budget allocation based on popular will and power, like their counterparts in liberal democracies. In this way, legislative development can become an integral part of China's democratization. Ultimately, the further development of Chinese legislatures depends on democratization in China, and not vice versa.

Selected References

Almén, Oscar. "Authoritarianism Constrained: The Role of Local People's Congresses in China." Ph.D. Dissertation, Göteborg University, 2005.

Arat, Zehra F. "Democracy and economic development: Modernization theory revisited." *Comparative Politics* 21, no. 1 (October 1988): 21–36.

Baum, Richard, and Alexei Shevchenko. "The 'state of the state'," in *The Paradox of China's Post-Mao Reforms*, ed. Merle Goldman and Roderick MacFarquhar. Cambridge, MA: Harvard University Press, 1999.

Blondel, Jean. *Comparative Legislature*. Englewood Cliffs, NJ: Prentice Hall, 1973.

Brook, Timothy, and B. Michael Frolic, eds. *Civil Society in China*. Armonk, NY: M.E. Sharpe, 1997.

Burkhart, Ross E., and Michael S. Lewis-Beck. "Comparative democracy: The economic development thesis." *American Political Science Review* 88, no. 4 (December 1994): 903–10.

Chamberlain, Health B. "Civil society with Chinese characteristics?" *China Journal*, no. 39 (January 1998): 69–81.

Chan, Anita. "Revolution or corporation? Workers and trade unions in post Mao China," in *China's Quiet Revolution: New Interactions between State and Society*, ed. David S.G. Goodman and Beverley Hooper. New York: St. Martin's Press, 1994.

Chang, Ta-kuang. "The making of the Chinese bankruptcy law: A study in the Chinese legislative process." *Harvard International Law Journal* 28, no. 2 (Spring 1987): 333–72.

Chao, Chien-min. "The procedure for local legislation in mainland China and legislation in national autonomous area." *Issues & Studies* 30, no. 9 (September 1994): 95–116.

Cheek, Timothy. "From market to democracy in China: Gaps in the civil society model," in *Market Economics and Political Change: Comparing China and Mexico*, ed. Juan D. Lindau and Timothy Cheek. Lanham: Rowman & Littlefield, 1998.

Chen, An. *Restructuring Political Power in China: Alliance and Opposition, 1978–98*. Boulder, CO: Lynne Rienner Publishers, 1999.

Chen, Feng. "Legal mobilization by trade unions: The case of Shanghai." *China Journal*, no. 52 (July 2004): 27–45.

Cheung, Peter T. Y. "Guangzhou and Tianjin: The struggle for development in two Chinese cities," in *Cities in China: Recipes for Economic Development in the Reform Era*, ed. Jae Ho Chung. London: Routledge, 1998.

Chung, Jae Ho, ed. *Charting China's Future: Political, Social, and International Dimensions*. Lanham, MD: Rowman & Littlefield, 2006.

Clarke, Donald C. "The execution of civil judgments in China." *China Quarterly*, no. 141 (March 1995): 65–81.

Close, David. "Introduction: Consolidating democracy in Latin America," in *Legislatives and the New Democracies*, ed. David Close. Boulder, CO: Lynne Rienner Publishers, 1995.

Dahl, Robert A. *On Democracy*. New Haven, CT: Yale University Press, 1998.
    Polyarchy: Participation and Opposition. New Haven, CT: Yale University Press, 1971.

Diamant, Neil J., Stanley B. Lubman, and Kevin J. O'Brien, eds. *Engaging the Law in China: State, Society, and Possibilities for Justice*. Stanford: Stanford University Press, 2005.

Dicks, Anthony. "The Chinese legal system: Reforms in the balance." *China Quarterly*, no. 119 (September 1989): 540–75.

Dickson, Bruce J. *Red Capitalists in China: The Party, Private Entrepreneurs, and Prospects for Political Change*. Cambridge: Cambridge University Press, 2003.
    "Do good businessmen make good citizens? An emerging collective identity among China's private entrepreneurs," in *Changing Meanings of Citizenship in Modern China*, ed. Merle Goldman and Elizabeth J. Perry. Cambridge, MA: Harvard University Press, 2002.

Ding, Yijiang. *Chinese Democracy after Tiananmen*. New York: Columbia University Press, 2001.

Dittmer, Lowell, and Guoli Liu, eds. *China's Deep Reform: Domestic Politics in Transition*. Lanham, MD: Rowman & Littlefield, 2006.

Dowdle, Michael William. "Constructing citizenship: The NPC as catalyst for political participation," in *Changing Meanings of Citizenship in Modern China*, ed. Merle Goldman and Elizabeth J. Perry. Cambridge, MA: Harvard University Press, 2002.

Duckett, Jane. *The Entrepreneurial State in China: Real Estate and Commerce Department in Reform Era Tianjin*. London: Routledge, 1998.

Epstein, Edward J. "Law and litigation in post-Mao China," in *Domestic Law Reforms in Post-Mao China*, ed. Putman B. Potter. Armonk, NY: M.E. Sharpe, 1994.

Foster, Kenneth W. "Embedded within state agencies: Business associations in Yantai." *China Journal*, no. 47 (January 2002): 41–65.
    "Associations in the embrace of an authoritarian state: state domination of society?" *Studies in Comparative International Development* 35, no. 4 (Winter 2001): 84–109.

Frolic, B. Michael. "State-led civil society," in *Civil Society in China*, ed. Timothy Brook and B. Michael Frolic. Armonk, NY: M.E. Sharpe, 1997.

Gallagher, Mary E. *Contagious Capitalism: Globalization and the Politics of Labor in China*. Princeton, NJ: Princeton University Press, 2005.

"China: The limits of civil society in a late Leninist state," in *Civil Society and Political Change in Asia: Expanding and Contracting Democratic Space*, ed. Muthiah Alagappa. Stanford: Stanford University Press, 2004.

Gilley, Bruce. *China's Democratic Future; How It Will Happen and Where It Will Lead*. New York: Columbia University Press, 2004.

Gries, Peter Hays, and Stanley Rosen. "Introduction: Popular protest and state legitimation in 21st-century China," in *State and Society in 21st-century China*, ed. Peter Hays Gries and Stanley Rosen. London: Routledge Curzon, 2004.

Gu, Edward. "State corporatism and the politics of the state-profession relationship in China: A case study of three professional communities." *American Asian Review* 19, no. 4 (Winter 2001): 163–99.

He, Baogang. *The Democratic Implications of Civil Society in China*. London: Macmillan Press, 1997.

Hendrischke, Hans. "Tianjin – Quiet achiever?" in *The Political Economy of China's Provinces: Comparative and Competitive Advantage*, ed. Hans Hendrischke and Feng Chongyi. London: Routledge, 1999.

Hook, Brian, ed. *Beijing and Tianjin: Toward a Millennial Megalopolis*. Hong Kong: Oxford University Press, 1998.

Howell, Jude. "New directions in civil society: Organizing around marginalized interests," in *Governance in China*, ed. Jude Howell. Lanham, MD: Rowman & Littlefield, 2004.

Huntington, Samuel P. *The Third Wave: Democratization in the Late Twentieth Century*. Norman: University of Oklahoma Press, 1991.

"The goals of development," in *Understanding Political Development*, ed. Myron Weiner and Samuel P. Huntington. Prospect Heights: Waveland Press, 1987.

Political Order in Changing Societies. New Haven, CT: Yale University Press, 1968.

Huntington, Samuel P., and Jorge I. Dominguez. "Political development," in *Handbook of Political Science: Macropolitical Theory*, ed. Fred I. Greenstein and Nelson W. Polsby, Vol. 3. Reading, MA: Addison-Wesley Publishing, 1975.

Johnson, Chalmers. "The developmental state: Odyssey of a concept," in *The Developmental State*, ed. Meredith Woo-Cumings. Ithaca, NY: Cornell University Press, 1999.

MITI and the Japanese Miracle: The Growth of Industrial Policy, 1925–1975. Stanford: Stanford University Press, 1982.

Kennedy, Scott. *The Business of Lobbying in China*. Cambridge, MA: Harvard University Press, 2005.

Kornberg, Allan, and Lloy D. Musolf. "On legislature in developmental perspective," in *Legislatures in Developmental Perspective*, ed. Allan Kornberg and Lloy D. Musolf. Durham, NC: Duke University Press, 1970.

Lawrence, Susan. "Village representative assemblies: Democracy, Chinese style." *Australian Journal of Chinese Affairs* no. 32 (July 1994): 61–68.

Li, Lianjiang. "The politics of introducing direct township elections in China." *China Quarterly*, no.171 (September 2002): 704–23.

Li, Lianjiang, and Kevin O'Brien. "The struggle over village elections," in *The Paradox of China's Post-Mao Reforms*, ed. Merle Goldman and Roderick MacFarquhar. Cambridge, MA: Harvard University Press, 1999.

Lin, Sen. "A new pattern of democratization in China: The increase of provincial powers in economic legislation." *China Information* 7, no. 3 (winter 1992–93): 27–38.

Lipset, Seymour Martin. "Some social requisites of democracy: Economic development and political legitimacy." *American Political Science Review* 53, no. 1 (March 1959): 69–105.

Lubman, Stanley B. *Bird in a Cage: Legal Reform in China after Mao*. Stanford: Stanford University Press, 1999.

"Introduction: The future of Chinese law." *China Quarterly*, no. 141 (March 1995): 1–21.

MacFarquhar, Roderick. "Reports from the field: Provincial People's Congresses." *China Quarterly*, no. 155 (September 1998): 656–67.

McCormick, Barrett L. "China's Leninist parliament and public sphere: A comparative analysis," in *China after Socialism: In the Footsteps of Eastern Europe or East Asia?* ed. Barrett L. McCormick and Jonathan Unger. Armonk, NY: M. E. Sharpe, 1996.

McCormick, Barrett L., Su Shaozhi, and Xiao Xiaoming, "The 1989 democracy movement: A review of the prospects for civil society in China." *Pacific Affairs* 65, no. 2 (Summer 1992): 182–202.

Mezey, Michael L. "The functions of legislatures in the Third World," in *Handbook of Legislative Research*, ed. Gerhard Loewenberg. Cambridge, MA: Harvard University Press, 1983.

Comparative Legislatures. Durham, NC: Duke University Press, 1979.

Migdal, Joel S., Atul Kohli, and Vivienne Shue. "Introduction: Developing a State-in-society Perspective," in *State Power and Social Forces: Domination and Transformation in the Third World*, ed. Joel S. Migdal, Atul Kohli, and Vivienne Shue. Cambridge: Cambridge University Press, 1994.

Needler, Martin C. "Conclusion: The legislature in a democratic Latin America," in *Legislatures and the New Democracies in Latin America*, ed. David Close. Boulder, CO: Lynne Rienner Publishers, 1995.

Nelson, Daniel N. "Editor's introduction: Communist legislatures and communist politics." *Legislative Studies Quarterly* 5, no. 2 (May 1980): 161–73.

Nevitt, Christopher Earle. "Private business associations in China: Evidence of civil society or local state power?" *China Journal*, no. 36 (July 1996): 25–43.

North, Douglass C. "Institutions," *Journal of Economic Perspectives* 5, no. 1 (Winter 1991): 97–112.

Institutional Changes and Economic Performance. Cambridge: Cambridge University Press, 1990.

O'Brien, Kevin. "Neither transgressive nor contained: Boundary-spanning contention in China," in *State and Society in 21st-century China*, ed. Peter Hays Gries and Stanley Rosen. London: Routledge Curzon, 2004.

"Hunting for political change." *China Journal*, no. 41 (1999): 159–69.

"Chinese People's Congresses and legislative embeddedness: Understanding early organizational development." *Comparative Political Studies* 27, no. 1 (April 1994): 80–109.

"Agents and remonstrators: Role accumulation by Chinese People's Congress deputies." *China Quarterly*, no. 138 (June 1994): 359–80.

"Implementing political reform in China's villages." *Australian Journal of Chinese Affairs*, no. 32 (July 1994): 33–60.

Reform without Liberalization: China's National People's Congress and the Politics of Institutional Change. Cambridge: Cambridge University Press, 1990.

O'Brien, Kevin, and Laura M. Luehrmann, "Institutionalizing Chinese legislatures: Trade-offs between autonomy and capacity." *Legislative Studies Quarterly* 23, no. 1 (February 1998): 91–108.

O'Donnell, Guillermo, and Philippe C. Schmitter. *Transitions from Authoritarian Rule: Tentative Conclusions about Uncertain Democracies*. Baltimore, MD: Johns Hopkins University Press, 1986a.

O'Donnell, Guillermo, Philippe C. Schmitter, and Laurence Whitehead, eds. *Transition from Authoritarian Rule: Comparative Perspectives*. Baltimore, MD: Johns Hopkins University Press, 1986b.

Ogden, Suzanne. *Inklings of Democracy in China*. Cambridge, MA: Harvard University Asia Center, 2002.

Oi, Jean C. "Economic development, stability and democratic village self-governance," in *China Review 1996*, ed. Maurice Brosseau, Suzanne Pepper, and Tang Shu-ki. Hong Kong: Chinese University Press, 1996.

Oi, Jean C., and Scott Rozelle. "Elections and power: The locus of decision-making in Chinese villages." *China Quarterly* no. 162 (June 2000): 513–39.

Oksenberg, Michel. "China's political system: Challenges of the twenty first century." *China Journal*, no. 45 (2001): 21–35.

Olson, David M. *Democratic Legislative Institutions: A Comparative View*. Armonk, NY: M.E. Sharpe, 1994.

Olson, David M., and Michael Mezey, "Parliament and public policy," in *Legislatures in the Policy Process: The Dilemmas of Economic Policy*, ed. Olson and Mezey. Cambridge: Cambridge University Press, 1991.

Olson, David M., and Philip Norton, eds. *The New Parliaments of Central and Eastern Europe*. London: Frank Cass, 1996.

"Legislatures in democratic transition," in *The New Parliament of Central and Eastern Europe*, ed. David M. Olson and Philip Norton. London: Frank Cass, 1996.

Packenham, Robert A. "Legislatures and political development," in *Legislatures in Developmental Perspective*, ed. Allen Kornberg and Lloyd D. Musolf. Durham, NC: Duke University Press, 1970.

Paler, Laura. "China's Legislation Law and the making of a more orderly and representative legislative system." *China Quarterly* 182 (June 2005): 301–18.

Parris, Kristen. "Private entrepreneurs as citizens: From Leninism to corporatism." *China Information* 10, no. 3/4 (Winter/Spring, 1996): 1–28.

Pearson, Margaret M. *China's New Business Elite: The Political Consequences of Economic Reform.* Berkeley: University of California Press, 1997.

Peerenboom, Randall. *China Modernizes: Threat to the West or Model for the Rest?* New York: Oxford University Press, 2007.

Pei, Minxin. *China's Trapped Transition: The Limits of Developmental Autocracy.* Cambridge, MA: Harvard University Press, 2006.

"Chinese civic associations: An empirical analysis." *Modern China* 24, no. 3 (July 1998): 285–318.

Perry, Elizabeth J. "Trends in the study of Chinese politics: State-society relations." *China Quarterly*, no. 139 (September 1994): 704–13.

Polsby, Nelson W. "Legislatures," in *Handbook of Political Science*, Vol. 5. ed. Fred I. Grenstein and Nelson W. Polsby. Reading, MA: Addison-Wesley Publishing, 1975.

Potter, Pitman B. *From Leninist Discipline to Socialist Legalism.* Stanford: Stanford University Press, 2003.

The Chinese Legal System: Globalization and Local Legal Culture. London and New York: Routledge, 2001.

"The Chinese legal system: Continuing commitment to the primacy of state power." *China Quarterly*, no. 159 (September 1999): 673–83.

"Curbing the party: Peng Zhen and Chinese legal culture." *Problems of Post-Communism* 45, no. 3 (May/June 1998): 17–28.

Przeworski, Adam. *Democracy and Market: Political and Economic Reforms in Eastern Europe and Latin America.* Cambridge: Cambridge University Press, 1991.

Przeworski, Adam, and Fernando Limongi. "Modernization: Theories and Facts." *World Politics* 49, no. 2 (January 1997): 155–83.

Rieselbach, Leroy N. *Congressional Politics: The Evolving Legislative System.* Boulder, CO: Westview Press, 1995.

Saich, Tony. "Negotiating the state: The development of social organizations in China." *China Quarterly*, no. 161 (March 2000): 124–41.

Seidman, Ann, Robert B. Seidman, and Janice Payne eds. *Legislative Drafting for Market Reform: Some Lessons from China.* London: Macmillan, 1997.

Shi, Tianjian. "Economic development and villagers' elections in rural China." *Journal of Contemporary China* 8, no. 22 (1999): 425–42.

"Mass political behavior in Beijing," in *The Paradox of China's Post-Mao Reforms*, ed. Merle Goldman and Roderick MacFarquhar. Cambridge, MA: Harvard University Press, 1999.

"Village committee elections in China: Institutionalist tactics for democracy." *World Politics* 51, no. 3 (April 1999): 385–412.

Shin, Doh Chull. "On the third wave of democratization: A synthesis and evaluation of recent theory and research." *World Politics* 47, no. 1 (October 1994): 135–70.

Tanner, Murray Scot. *The Politics of Lawmaking in China: Institutions, Processes, and Democratic Prospects.* New York: Oxford University Press, 1999.

"The National People's Congress," in *The Paradox of China's Post-Mao Reforms*, ed. Merle Goldman and Roderick MacFarquhar. Cambridge, MA: Harvard University Press, 1999.

"Organization and politics in China's post-Mao lawmaking system," in *Domestic Law Reforms in Post-Mao China*, ed. Putman B. Potter. Armonk, NY: M.E. Sharpe, 1994.

"The erosion of Communist Party control over law-making in China." *China Quarterly*, no. 138 (June 1994): 381–403.

Tsai, Kellee S. *Capitalism without Democracy: The Private Sector in Contemporary China.* Ithaca, NY and London: Cornell University Press, 2007.

Unger, Jonathan. "'Bridges': Private business, the Chinese government and the rise of new associations." *China Quarterly*, no. 147 (September 1996): 795–819.

Unger, Jonathan, and Anita Chan. "Corporatism in China: A developmental state in an East Asian context," in *China After Socialism: In the Footsteps of Eastern Europe or East Asia?* ed. Barrett L. McCormick and Jonathan Unger. Armonk, NY: M.E. Sharpe, 1996.

Vanneman, Peter. *The Supreme Soviet: Politics and the Legislative Process in the Soviet Political System.* Durham, NC: Duke University Press, 1977.

Walder, Andrew G., and Gong Xiaoxia. "Workers in the Tiananmen protests: The politics of the Beijing Workers' Autonomous Federation." *Australian Journal of Chinese Affairs*, no. 29 (1993): 1–29.

Wank, David L. *Commodifying Communism: Business, Trust, and Politics in a Chinese City.* Cambridge: Cambridge University Press, 1999.

"Private business, bureaucracy, and political alliance in a Chinese city." *Australian Journal of Chinese Affairs*, no. 33 (January 1995): 55–71.

Weinbaum, Marvin G. "Classification and change in legislative system: With particular application to Iran, Turkey, and Afghanistan," in *Legislative Systems in Developing Countries*, ed. G. R. Boynton and Chong Lim Kim. Durham, NC: Duke University Press, 1975.

Welsh, William A. "The status of research on representative institutions in eastern Europe." *Legislative Studies Quarterly* 15, no. 2 (May 1980): 275–308.

White, Gordon, Jude Howell, and Xiaoyuan Shang, *In Search of Civil Society: Market Reform and Social Change in Contemporary China.* Oxford: Clarendon Press, 1996.

Whyte, Martin K. "Urban China: A civil society in the making," in *State and Society in China: The Consequences of Reform*, ed. Arthur Lewis Rosebaum. Boulder, CO: Westview Press, 1992.

Woo, Margaret Y. K. "Law and discretion in contemporary Chinese courts," in *The Limits of the Rule of Law in China*, ed. Karen G. Turner, James V. Feinerman, and R. Kent Guy. Seattle and London: University of Washington Press, 2000.

Xia, Ming. *The Dual Developmental State: Development Strategy and Institutional Arrangements for China's Transition.* Aldershot: Ashgate, 2000.

"Political contestation and the emergence of the provincial People's Congresses as power in Chinese politics: A network explanation." *Journal of Contemporary China* 9, no. 24 (2000): 185–214.

"Informational efficiency, organizational development and the institutional linkages of the provincial people's congresses in China." *Journal of Legislative Studies* 3, no. 3 (Autumn 1997): 10–38.

Yang, Dali L. *Remaking the Chinese Leviathan: Market Transition and the Politics of Governance in China.* Stanford: Stanford University Press, 2004.

Yep, Ray. "The limitations of corporatism for understanding reforming China: An empirical analysis in a rural county." *Journal of Contemporary China* 9, no. 25 (November 2000): 547–66.

Zhang, Xin, and Richard Baum. "Civil society and the anatomy of a rural NGO." *China Journal*, no. 52 (July 2004): 97–107.

Zhang, Yunqiu. "From state corporatism to social representation: Local trade unions in the reform years," in *Civil Society in China*, ed. Timothy Brook and B. Michael Frolic. Armonk, NY: M.E. Sharpe, 1997.

Zhao, Suisheng, ed. *China and Democracy: Reconsidering the Prospects for a Democratic China.* New York and London: Routledge, 2000.

Bai, Guangquan, ed. *Kaichuang chengshi quji renda gongzuode xinjumian* (Pioneering New Situation of Big City District People's Congresses). Beijing: Zhongguo minzhu fazhi chubanshe, 1997.

Bianzhuan weiyuanhui, ed. *Shanghai gonghui nianjian 1998* (Shanghai Trade Unions Yearbook 1998). Shanghai: Wenhui chubanshe, 1998.

ed. *Shanghai gonghui nianjian 1999* (Shanghai Trade Unions Yearbook 1999). Shanghai: Wenhui chubanshe, 1999.

Bianzhuan xiaozu, ed. *Banli renda daibiao jianyi zhengxie weiyuan ti'an gongzuo ziliao huibian* (Collections on the Working Materials of Implementing People's Congress Deputies' Proposals and CPPCC Members' Motions). Beijing: Zhongguo zhanwang chubanshe, 1989.

Bianweihui, ed. *Zhongguo tupian: Jinian Tianjinshi difang renda changweihui chengli ershi zhounian zhuankan* (China in Pictures: Special Issue on Commemorating the 20th Anniversary of People's Congress Standing Committees in Tianjin). Beijing: Zhongguo tupianshe, 2000.

Cai, Bingwen, ed. *Shanghai renmin daibiao dahui zhi* (Annals of Shanghai People's Congresses). Shanghai: Shanghai shehui kexueyuan chubanshe, 1998.

Cai, Dingjian, and Chenguang Wang, eds. *Renmin daibiao dahui ershinian fazhan yu gaige* (Twenty-Years' Development and Reform of People's Congresses). Beijing: Zhongguo jiancha chubanshe, 2001.

Cai, Dingjian. *Zhongguo renda zhidu* (People's Congress System in China). Beijing: Shehui kexue wenxian chubanshe, 1993.

Cao, Siyuan. *Pochan fengyun* (A Stormy Situation of Bankruptcy). Beijing: Zhongyang bianyi chubanshe, 1996.

Chen, Yaoliang, ed. *Ruiyi jinqude xianji renda gongzuo* (Resolute Progress of the Works of County-level People's Congresses). Beijing: Zhongguo minzhu fazhi chubanshe, 1997.

Chuanzhoushi Lichengqu rendazhi biancan weiyuanhui, ed. *Chuanzhoushi Lichengqu rendazhi* (Gazette of Licheng District People's Congress in Chuanzhou City). Beijing: Zhongguo minzhu fazhi chubanshe, 1994.

Constitution of the People's Republic of China. Beijing: Foreign Languages Press, 1999.

Dong, Shouan, ed. *Minzhu fazhi jianshede zuyin* (The Footprints of Democracy and Legal System Construction). Beijing: Zhongguo minzhu fazhi chubanshe, 2000.

Guangdongsheng rendazhidu yanjiuhui, ed. *Yifa zhishengde tantao* (An Inquiry into the Governance of Province According to Law). Beijing: Zhongguo minzhu fazhi chubanshe, 1997.

Hangzhoushi renda, ed. *Zhongxin chengshi renda gongzuode xinjinzhan* (New Developments in the Works of Core City People's Congresses). Beijing: Zhongguo minzhu fazhi chubanshe, 1997.

Hu, Xiabing, and Feng Renqiang, eds. *Sifa gongzheng yu sifa gaige yanjiu zongshu* (Summary on the Researches of Judicial Justice and Reform). Beijing: Tsinghua daxue chubanshe, 2001.

Huang, Jiren. *Yige Quanguorenda daibiaode riji* (A Diary of an NPC Deputy). Chongqing: Chongqing chubanshe, 1997.

Huang, Sha, and Yankun Meng, eds. *Shanghai funüzhi* (Annals of Shanghai Women). Shanghai: Shanghai shehui kexue chubanshe, 2000.

Huang, Weiping, and Shubin Zou, eds. *Xiangzhenzhang xuanju fangshi gaige: Anli yanjiu* (Case Studies on the Election Reforms of Township-Level Government Chiefs). Bejing: Shehui kexue wenxian chubanshe, 2003.

Huang, Weiping, and Yongcheng Wang, eds. *Dangdai Zhongguo zhengzhi yanjiu baogao IV* (A Research Report on Contemporary Chinese Politics IV). Beijing: Shehui kexue wenxian chubanshe, 2004.

——— eds. *Dangdai zhongguo zhengzhi yanjiu baogao II* (A Research Report on the Contemporary Chinese Politics II). Beijing: Shehui kexue wenxian chubanshe, 2003.

Huang, Weiping, ed. *Zhongguo jiceng minzhu fazhande zuixin tupo* (The Recent Breakthrough of China's Grassroots Democratic Development). Beijing: Shehui kexue wenxuan chubanshe, 2000.

Hubeisheng Wuxueshi renda changweihui, ed. *Xianxiang renda gongzuo yanjiu* (A Study on the Works of County- and Township-level People's Congresses). Beijing: Zhongguo minzhu fazhi chubanshe, 1994.

Jinniuqu rendazhi bianzhuan weiyuanhui, ed. *Chengdushi Jinniuqu rendazhi* (Gazette of Jinniu District People's Congress in Chengdu City). Chengdu: Sichuan renmin chubanshe, 1995.

Kang, Ziming, ed. *Nankai renda ershinian 1979–99* (Twenty Years of Nankai People's Congress, 1979–99). Tianjin: 1999.

Lian, Yuming, ed. *Zhongguo guoqing baogao 2003* (A Report of China's National Conditions 2003 Year). Beijing: Zhongguo shidai jingji chubanshe, 2003.

Liu, Hainian, Lin Li and Guangxing Zhang, eds. *Yifa zhiguo yu lianzheng jianshe* (Governance According to Law and Building of Honest and Clean Government). Beijing: Zhongguo fazhi chubanshe, 1999.

Liu, Lixian, and Zhihui Zhang, eds. *Sifa gaige redian wenti* (Hot Issues on Judicial Reform). Beijing: Zhongguo renmin gong'an daxue chubanshe, 2000.

Liu, Zheng, and Xiangqing Cheng. *Renmin daibiao dahui zhidude lilun he shijian* (Theory and Practice of People's Congress System). Beijing: Zhongguo minzhu fazhi chubanshe, 2003.

Liu, Zheng, Youmin Yu, and Xiangqing Cheng, eds. *Renmin daibiao dahui gongzuo quanshu* (Overall Book on the Works of People's Congresses). Beijing: Zhongguo fazhi chubanshe, 1999.

Lu, Xueyi, ed. *Dangdai Zhongguo shehui jieceng yanjiu baogao* (A Research Report on Contemporary Chinese Social Classes). Beijing: Shehui kexue wenxian chubanshe, 2002.

———. ed. *Dangdai Zhongguo shehui liudong* (Social Mobility in Contemporary China). Beijing: Shehui kexue wenxian chubanshe, 2004.

Niao, Jie, ed. *Zhongguo zhengfu yu jigou gaige* (Ahang) (Chinese Government and Structural Reform) (Vol. 1). Beijing: Guojia xingzheng xueyuan chubanshe, 1998.

Peng, Chong. *Minzhu fazhi lunji* (Collections on Democracy and Rule of Law). Beijing: Zhongguo minzhu fazhi chubanshe, 1993.

Peng, Zhen. *Lun xinshiqide shehui zhuyi minzhu yu fazhi jianshe* (A Discussion on Socialist Democracy and Construction of Rule of Law in the New Era). Beijing: Zhongyang wenxian chubanshe, 1989.

Qiao, Xiaoyang, ed. *Lifafa jianghua* (An Introduction to the Legislation Law). Beijing: Zhongguo minzhu fazhi chubanshe, 2000.

Qichao bangongshi, ed. *'Shanghai qingshaonian baohu tiaoli' lifa jishi* (Lawmaking Record on the Shanghai Juvenile Protection Regulation). Shanghai: Shanghai shehuikexue chubanshe, 1987.

Quanguorenda changweihui bangongting lianluoju, ed. *Wo zenyang dang renda daibiao* (How to Act as a Deputy to People's Congresses). Beijing: Zhongguo minzhu fazhi chubanshe, 2000.

Quanguorenda changweihui bangongting yanjiushi, ed. *Difang renda 20nian* (Twenty Years of Local People's Congresses). Beijing: Zhongguo minzhu fazhi chubanshe, 2000.

———. ed. *Difang renda jiandu gongzuo tansuo* (An Exploration for the Supervisory Works of Local People's Congresses). Beijing: Zhongguo minzhu fazhi chubanshe, 1997.

———. ed. *Woguo dangqian falü shishide wenti he duice* (Problems and Countermeasures in Law Enforcement in China). Beijing: Zhongguo minzhu fazhi chubanshe, 1997.

———. ed. *Difang renda xingshi zhiquan shilie xuanbian* (Selected Cases on Local People's Congresses Exercising Their Power). Beijing: Zhongguo minzhu fazhi chubanshe, 1996.

———. ed. *Difang renda shi zenyang xingshi zhiquande* (How Local People's Congresses Exercise Their Power). Beijing: Zhongguo minzhu fazhi chubanshe, 1992.

———. ed. *Renmin daibiao dahui wenxian huibian* (Selections on the Documents of People's Congresses). Beijing: Zhongguo minzhu fazhi chubanshe, 1992.

ed. *Zhonghua renmin gongheguo renmin daibiao dahui wenxian ziliao huibian 1949–90* (Collections on the Documents of PRC People's Congresses 1949–90). Beijing: Zhongguo minzhu fazhi chubanshe, 1990.

Quanguorenda neiwu sifa weiyuanhui sifashi, ed. *Shehui zhuyi minzhu fazhi jianshede youyi tansuo* (A Beneficial Exploration of Socialist Democratic and Legal System Construction). Beijing: Zhongguo minzhu fazhi chubanshe, 1993.

Shanghai gongyun bianzhuan weiyuanhui, ed. *Shanghai gongyunzhi* (Annals of Labor Movement in Shanghai). Shanghai: Shanghai shehui kexue chubanshe, 1997.

Shanghaishi renda changweihui fagongwei, ed. '*Shanghaishi xiaofeizhe quanyi baohu tiaoli' shiyi* (An Interpretation on the Shanghai Consumers' Rights Protection Regulation). Shanghai: Shanghai renmin chubanshe, 2003.

ed. '*Shanghaishi laodong hetong tiaoli' shiyi* (An Interpretation on the Shanghai Labor Contract Regulation). Shanghai: Shanghai renmin chubanshe, 2002.

Shanghai renda changweihui yanjiushi, ed. *Shijian yu tansuo* (Practice and Exploration) (Vol. 4) Shanghai: Fudan daxue chubanshe, 2003.

Shi, Weimin. *Gongxuan yu Zhixuan* (Open Elections and Direct Elections). Beijing: Zhongguo shehui kexue chubanshe, 2000.

Sun, Weiben, ed. *Renda gongzuo shouce* (Handbook for the Works of People's Congresses). Beijing: Zhongguo minzhu fazhi chubanshe, 1997.

Tan, Shigui, ed. Zhongguo sifa gaige yanjiu (A Study on Judicial Reform in China). Beijing: Falü chubanshe, 2000.

Tang, Juan, and Shulin Zou, eds. *2003nian Shenzhen jingxuan shilu* (A Document of 2003 Competitive Elections in Shenzhen). Xian: Xibei daxue chubanshe, 2003.

Tianjinshi difangzhi bianxiu weiyuanhui, ed. *Tianjin tongzhi: zhengquan zhi renmin daibiao dahui juan* (Overall Annals of Tianjin: Regime Annals People's Congress Volume). Tianjin: Tianjin shehui kexueyuan chubanshe, 1997.

Wang, Jianying, ed. *Zhongguo gongchandang zuzhishi ziliao huibian* (The Compilation of Documents of the CCP Organizational History). Beijing: Zhonggong zhongyang dangxiao chubanshe, 1994.

Wang, Kelin, ed. *Tanggu renda ershinian huimou 1980–2000* (Reflections on 20 Years of Tanggu People's Congress, 1980–2000). Tianjin: 2000.

Wang, Liming. *Sifa gaige yanjiu* (Research on Judicial Reform) (Revised edition). Beijing: Falü chubanshe, 2001.

Wang, Min. *Guojia quanli jiguande guomin jingji jihua he yusuan jiandu jizhi* (The Supervisory System of State Power Organ over National Economic Plans and Budges). Beijing: Zhongguo minzhu fazhi chubanshe, 1993.

Wang, Ming. *Minjian zuzhi tonglun* (General Discussion on Civil Organizations). Beijing: Shishi chubanshe, 2004.

Wu, Bo. *Xian jieduan Zhongguo shehui jieji jieceng fenxi* (An Analysis on Classes in Contemporary Chinese Society). Beijing: Tsinghua daxue chubanshe, 2004.

Xin, Chunying, and Lin Li, eds. *Yifa zhiguo yu sifa gaige* (Governance According to Law and Judicial Reform). Beijing: Zhongguo fazhi chubanshe, 1999.

Xu, Xianghua, ed. *Xin shiqi Zhongguo lifa fansi* (A Reflection on Chinese Lawmaking in New Era). Shanghai: Xuelin chubanshe, 2004.

   ed. *Xin shiqi Zhongguo lifa sixiang* (Chinese Lawmaking Thoughts in New Era). Shanghai: Xuelin chubanshe, 2004.

Xu, Yijun. *Zoujin renda* (Entering People's Congress). Beijing: Zhongguo minzhu fazhi chubanshe, 2001.

Xu, Zuxiong, and Yanwen Zhu, eds. *Minzhu fazhi yu renda zhidu* (Democratic Legal System and People's Congress System). Shanghai: Fudan daxue chubanshe, 1999.

Yang, Fengchun, ed. *Zai shengji renda gongzuo gangwei shang* (On the Posts of Provincial People's Congresses). Beijing: Zhongguo minzhu fazhi chubanshe, 1996.

Yuan, Ruiliang. *Renmin daibiao dahui zhidu xingcheng fazhanshi* (A History of Formation and Development of People's Congress System). Beijing: Renmin chubanshe, 1994.

Yun, Shihong, and Kaiyang Zhu, ed. *Renmin daibiao dahui zhidu fazhanshi* (A History on the Development of People's Congress System). Nanchang: Jiangxi renmin chubanshe, 2002.

Zhang, Geng, ed. *Zhongguo lüshi zhidu fazhande lichengbei: 'Zhonghua renmin gongheguo lüshifa' lifa guocheng huigu* (A Milestone in the Development of China's Lawyers Institution: A Retrospect on the Lawmaking Process of the Law of PRC on Lawyers). Beijing: Falü chubanshe, 1997.

Zhang, Wei. *Renda jiandu zhineng yanjiu* (A Study on the Supervisory Function of People's Congresses). Beijing: Zhongguo falü chubanshe, 1996.

Zhao, Baoxu, ed. *Minzhu zhengzhi yu difang renda* (Democratic Politics and Local People's Congresses). Xian: Shaanxi renmin chubanshe, 1990.

Zhao, Mengchen, ed. *Hexi renda ershinian* (Twenty Years' of Hexi District People's Congress). Tianjin: 2000.

Zhi, Liu, Weimin Shi, Xiaodong Zhou, and Yunhao Wu. *Shuju xuanju: Renda daibiao xuanju tongji yanjiu* (Data Elections: Studies on the Statistics of People's Congress Deputy Elections). Beijing: Zhongguo shehui kexue chubanshe, 2001.

Zhonggong zhongyang zuzhibu ketizu, ed. *Zhongguo diaocha baogao 2000–2001: Xin xingshi xia renmin neibu maodun yanjiu* (A Research Report on China 2000–2001: Studies on Contradictions among the People in New Situations). Beijing: Zhongyang bianyi chubanshe, 2001.

Zhonghua quanguo zonggonghui, ed. *Zhonghua renmin gongheguo gonghuifa jianghua* (An Explanation on the Law of PRC on Trade Unions). Beijing: Zhongguo gongren chubanshe, 2001.

   ed. *Zhonghua quanguo zonggonghui qishinian* (Seventy Years of the All-China Federation of Trade Unions). Beijing: Zhongguo gongren chubanshe, 1995.

Zhou, Wenxian, ed. *Difang renda gongzuo lilun yu shiwu* (Theory and Practice of the Works of Local People's Congresses). Beijing: Zhongguo minzhu fazhi chubanshe, 2000.

Zhu, Guanglei. *Dangdai Zhongguo zhengfu guocheng* (Contemporary Chinese Government Process). Tianjin: Tianjin renmin chubanshe, 1997.

Zhuzhoushi rendazhi bianzhuan weiyuanhui, ed. *Zhuzhoushi rendazhi* (Gazette of Zhuzhou City People's Congress). Changsha: Hunan chubanshe, 1991.

Zou, Shulin, ed. *2003nian Beijingshi quxian renda daibiao jingxuan shilu* (A Document of 2003 Competitive Elections of Deputies to District and County People's Congresses in Beijing). Xian: Xibei daxue chubanshe, 2004.

Zuigao renmin fayuan yanjiushi, ed. *Renmin fayuan wunian gaige gangyao* (An Outline of the Five-Year Reforms of People's Courts). Beijing: Renmin fayuan chubanshe, 2000.

Index

1989 Tiananmen Incident
and Hu Jiwei, 170

agencies of Chinese local
people's congresses
education, science, culture
& health committee
(*jiaokewenweihui*), 39
financial & economic affairs
committee (*caijingwei*), 32
interior and judicial affairs
committee (*neisiwei*), 71
legislative Affairs Work Committee
(*fagongwei*), 26
legislative committee (*fazhi
weiyuanhui*), 26
work committees (*gongzuo
weiyuanhui*), 49
appraisal of government bureaus
and officials (*pingyi*), 58
focuses of, 59
history of, 59
problems of, 61–62
procedures (steps) of, 59
supervisory effect of, 60–61
types of, 59
approaches for Chinese
legislative studies
checks and balances
perspective, 8

decision-making model, 7
integrated historical-structural
approach, 7
network approach, 8
structural-functional
approach, 6

changed legal-political conditions
for deputies, 87
Deputy Law, 87
legislative work conference, 47,
88, 157
party center's policy, 88
public expectation, 89
China's lawmaking system, 18
Chinese people's congresses
Local people's congresses
(LPCs), 13
National People's Congress
(NPC), 2
civil society theory, 115, 140, 141
argument of, 115
limits of, 115–16
Consumers' Rights Protection
Regulation in Shanghai
Consumers' Rights Protection Law,
37, 135
recall (*zhaohui*) system, 38
Shanghai Consumer Association
(SCA), 37, 131

Deliberation of draft laws,
    26, 29, 30, 35
  two-step-deliberation and three-
      reading *(liangshen sandu)*, 29
  unified investigation and
      deliberation *(tongyi shenyi)*,
      29–30
differentiation of deputies'
    role fulfillment
  cadres, 105–8
  composition of deputies, 101
  intellectuals, 104–5
  private entrepreneurs *(siying
      qiyezhu)*, 108–11
  theory of legislator-constituent
      relationship, 101
  workers and peasants, 102–4

East Asian developmental model, 167
economic development, 156
  and legislative development, 156
  and villagers' committees, 156
election experiments, 159
  in Buyun Township of Suining City
      in Sichuan, 159
  in Dapeng Town of Shenzhen, 159
Enterprise Bankruptcy Law, 18
examination of law enforcement
    (zhifa jiancha), 55
  history of, 55
  problems of, 57–58
  procedures (steps) of, 56
  supervisory effect of, 56–57
extension of state perspective, 120
  horizontal disaggregation, 121
  vertical disaggregation, 120–21

governance according to law
    (yifa zhiguo), 15, 18
Guangdong Phenomena, 2

individual case supervision
    (gean jiandu), 69
  history of, 70
  objection from judicial officials of,
      74–75
  procedures (steps) of, 71

institutionalization prior to
    liberalization, 42

judicial problems, 67, 74, 79
  "local protectionism", 78–79
  difficulty in enforcing court
      decisions *(zhixingnan)*, 80
  judicial corruption *(sifa fubai)*, 69
  judicial fairness
      (sifa gongzheng), 65
  judicial independence
      (sifa duli), 65

Labor Contract Regulation in
    Shanghai, 32, 33, 131
  "10+3 provision", 34
  Federation of Industry and
      Commerce, 32, 33, 34,
      123, 131
  Labor Law, 32, 33, 36, 108, 135,
      136, 138
  Provision of Shanghai on Labor
      Contract, 32
  Shanghai General Trade Union
      (SGTU), 33
  trade associations
      (hangye xiehui), 32
lawmaking guidelines, 26, 40
  "experience-based legislation"
      (jingyan lifa), 27
  "legislation in advance"
      (chaoqian lifa), 27–28
legalization perspective
    (fazhihua), 119
  institutionalization, 17, 26, 42,
      119, 168, 170, 171
  necessity of, 119–20
legislative development strategy
  "embeddedness" strategy, 43
  cooperation with government,
      48–51
  gaining support of the party, 45–48
legislative supervision over courts, 66
  "legislative corruption"
      (renda fubai), 75
  backgound of, 66–69
  judicial response, 74

supervisory measures, 69
switch of legislative supervision
  from government to court, 69
legislative-executive relations,
  11, 25, 40, 48, 51, 155
"90 percent rule", 25
administration regulation, 25
department protectionism
  (bumen zhuyi), 23–24
financial problems of
  legislatures, 50
legislative-judiciary-party relations
  connecting legislative supervision
    with public opinion
    supervision, 78
  coordination of the party's
    political-legal committee
    (xietiao ban'an zhidu), 77
  legislatures' united operation
    of higher and lower level
    (shangxia liandong), 76
  system of a court of "second
    instance being of last instance"
    (liangshen zhongshenzhi), 76
  system of request for instructions
    on cases (anjian qingshi
    zhidu), 76
legislative-party relations, 20
  "request and report system"
    (qingshi huibao zhidu), 46
  legislative autonomy, 48
  party group (dangzu), 46
  principle of party leadership, 45
legislative-social organization
    relations, 121
  authorizing government agency
    (dengji guanli jiguan), 122
  institutional mechanism of, 123–24
  joint conferences (lianxi huiyi),
    124–25
  needing of the support and
    cooperation of social
    organizations, 122
  professional business units (yewu
    zhuguan danwei), 122
  status of social organizations in
    party hierarchy, 123–24

supervisory relations
  (jiandu guanxi), 122
  two-tier registration system, 122
legislatures' role in
  democratization, 171–83
letters and visits (xinfang), 66, 67, 89
limits of legislative supervisory
  measures, 52–53
local people's congresses in Tianjin
  Beichen District, 154, 155
  Dagang District, 92, 149, 155
  Dongli District, 153
  Hangu District, 154, 155, 157
  Hebei District, 155
  Heping District, 154
  Hexi District, 149, 154, 157, 159
  Nankai District, 92, 147, 149,
    154, 157
  Tanggu District, 149, 157,
    158, 159
  Xiqing District, 149

new supervisory measures, 16, 44,
  53, 92, 146, 149, 154, 157, 158
  "bandwagoner", 53
  "inactive", 53
  "pioneer", 53
  appraisal of government bureaus
    and officials (pingyi), 44
  examination of law enforcement
    (zhifa jiancha), 44
  individual case supervision
    (gean jiandu), 53, 69
  law supervision paper
    (falü jiandushu), 53
  responsibility system of department
    law enforcement (bumen zhifa
    zerenzhi), 53
new trend in elections of deputies
  Beijing Phenomena (Beijing
    xianxiang), 84
  Shenzhen Phenomena, 84

O'Brien, Kevin
  approach, 7
  deputies to Chinese people's
    congress, 5

O'Brien, Kevin (cont.)
  legislative development strategy
    (embeddedness), 11
  villagers' committee, 5, 107, 143
opening-up legislation, 26, 30
  legislation hearings
    (lifa tingzhenghui), 31
  soliciting public opinions, 31–32
Organic Law of Villagers'
  Committees., 144

pattern of development of
  new organizations, 81
people's congress system
  (renda zhidu)
  democratic centralism (minzhu
    jizhong), 12–13
  legislative-executive integration
    (yixing heyi), 12, 13
personnel files (dang'an), 60, 157
policy-providers, 97
  examples of deputy bills, 99
  limits of decision-making by
    Chinese legislatures, 97
  meaning of, 98
political development, 168
  as democratization, 168–70
  as institutionalization, 171
  in the Third World and socialist
    countries, 169
political leadership, 156
  and legislative development, 159
  and villagers' committees, 157
propaganda and exemplary roles, 100
  meaning of, 100
  role models (mofan), 100
public reflectors (reflection)
  "deputy hotline" (zhitong
    kuaiche), 96
  bills (yian) and proposals
    (jianyi), 96
  bridge-building (qiaoliang), 95
  meaning of, 95
  types of activities, 95–96
public supervisors (supervision), 91
  deputy small groups
    (daibiao xiaozu), 92

focus of, 92
implementation rate (luoshilü), 94
individual supervision, 93
ordinary activities of, 92
policy of, 91

Shanghai Municipal
  People's Congress
  Civil Defense Regulation, 21
  Conscription Work Regulation, 21
  Firework Security Regulation, 21
  legislative planning, 20–21
  Trade Unions Regulation, 21, 129
Shenyang Incident, 1
Shenyang People's Congress, 52, 73
social organizations
  (shehui tuanti), 113
  increasing number of, 113
  non-governmental organizations
    (NGOs), 117
  people's organizations
    (renmin tuanti), 121
social organizations' participation
  in lawmaking, 126
  background of, 126–28
  drafting small group
    (qichao xiaozu), 128
  Implementing Regulation on
    Women's Rights Protection
    Law in Guangdong, 130
  Implementing Regulation on
    Women's Rights Protection
    Law in Shanghai, 130
  lawmaking participatory small
    group (lifa canyu xiaozu), 128
  Lawyers Law, 130
  lobbying by social organizations,
    131–33
  protection of rights and interests
    through participation from
    the origin (yuantou canyu
    weiquan), 127
  Regulation on Juvenile Protection
    in Shanghai, 130
  Regulation on Promoting the
    Development of Trade
    Associations in Shanghai, 133

Regulation on Trade Unions in Chinese-Foreign Joint Companies, 129
Shanghai Communist Youth League (SCYL), 130
Shanghai Women's Federation (SWF), 130
social organizations' participation in legislative supervision, 134
background of, 135–37
joint supervision with party and government, 136
labor supervisors of trade unions *(gonghui laodong jiandu weiyuan)*, 136
participatory methods of, 137–39
supervisory effect of, 139
trade unions' supervisory committees on labor-related laws *(gonghui laodong falü jiandu weiyuanhui)*, 136
state corporatism, 114, 115, 116, 117, 118, 121, 140
argument of, 116–17
clientelism, 117
criticism of, 117–18
Schmitter, Philippe C. 116, 144
State-owned Industrial Enterprise Law, 18
system of investigating the responsibility for misjudged cases *(cuoan zeren zhuijiuzhi)*, 72–73

Tanner, Murray S. 7, 18
Three perspectives of this research
actual power relations, 8, 10–12

marketization and legalization, 8, 9–10
path dependence, 8, 12–13
Tianjian Shi, 62, 67, 89, 144, 145
Tianjin, 145
appraisal of law enforcement *(zhifa pingyi)* in, 152
general background of, 148
Higher People's Court, 152
legislative supervision over government in, 149–56
legislative work conferences in, 152
Municipal People's Congress, 149
total number of people's congress deputies at various levels, 86
traditional legislative supervisory measures
inspection *(shicha)*, 51
questions and interpellation *(zhixun)*, 51
review of draft budget, 51
review of government work report, 51
review of socio-economic development plan, 51
special investigative commissions, 51, 54
Supervisory Law, 52
types of role fulfillment by deputies
opinion reflectors (reflection), 16, 84
policy-providers, 84, 91, 103, 104, 111
public supervisors (supervision), 84
regime agents, 16, 83, 84, 85, 100
remonstrators, 3, 16, 83, 84, 95, 107, 110

Lightning Source UK Ltd.
Milton Keynes UK
UKOW04f1659170717

305394UK00010B/80/P